Stable Weight

A Memoir of Hunger, Horses, and Hope

Smitty ready and willing for a halter and Christmas Camp in 2014 © Lisa Whalen

Stable Weight

A Memoir of Hunger, Horses, and Hope

Lisa Whalen

Hopewell Publications

Published by Hopewell
Publications, LLC
PO Box 11, Titusville, NJ
08560-0011
(609) 818-1049

info@HopePubs.com
www.HopePubs.com

International Standard Book Number: 9781933435558

Library of Congress Control Number: 2020942493

First Edition

Printed in the United States of America

For Jim, Pat, and James Whalen, and for Julie Dettinger, who
will always be one half of the Sisters Whalen

––––––––––

"Consciousness works by telling a story,
one that is whole, continuous, and stable.
When that story breaks, consciousness rewrites it.
Each revised draft claims to be the original.
And so, when disease or accident interrupts us,
we're often the last to know."

–*The Echo Maker* by Richard Power

––––––––––

Visit https://lisawhalen.wixsite.com/lisawhalen,
or follow @LisaIrishWhalen on Facebook,
Twitter, Instagram, and Pinterest.

Table of Contents

Acknowledgments

I am fortunate to have gained hope from many who encouraged me to take up space and bring this book into the world.

Sara Engbloom, for her compassion, wisdom, and skill in treating eating disorders.

The Emily Program, for providing a path to health and guidance as I traveled it.

The Spiral Writers, for convincing me I had something to say.

Leanne Zainer, for mentorship, friendship, and more concise sentences.

Matt Ryan, for believing in me, giving my book a chance, and editing with such skill and kindness.

Christopher Klim and Hopewell Publications for producing books that enrich our world and considering mine worthy of joining them.

Gail Folkins, for advice and mentorship through AWP's Writer to Writer program.

Marnie Freedman, for keen insights about turning a jumble of ideas into a book.

Tom and Liz McCadden, for the gift of learning to ride horses.

Seventh Farm's horses, for leading me back to myself.

Chad Kochmann, for being strong and silly as spouse extraordinaire.

Grandma Mary Galvin, for being a model of feminism long before I knew that word.

Grandpa Howard Whalen, for his generous support of my education.

My family—Jim, Pat, and James Whalen, and Julie Dettinger, for everything.

Author's Note

This book reflects my recollections of experiences over time. It has been edited for narrative consistency; some events have been compressed, and some dialogue has been recreated. To protect privacy, I have changed names and identifying details of some individuals, but the essence of the story is unchanged.

Buck watches riders prepare for lessons from the paddock in early fall 2015 © Lisa Whalen

Prologue

Every rider knows she'll fall; she just doesn't know when. I thought accepting falls as inevitable would make rising from them easier.

It didn't.

I'd had a few close calls by the time I began my sixth year of English horseback riding lessons at age 42, but I had never fallen. I was proud of my stickiness in the saddle. I chalked it up to strength and balance I'd gained competing on my high school gymnastics team before my life plunged into a depression I called "A.C."

Asked to predict my fall from a horse, I wouldn't have picked a leaden March morning in 2017. The fluttery stomach I sometimes felt before a fence-jumping lesson didn't stir when I crossed the St. Croix River on I-94 and glimpsed green interstate signs announcing exits for Hudson, Wisconsin. The Carmichael Road exit marked a turning point in the drive from my home in St. Paul, Minnesota, to the school in rural Wisconsin, and in my self-image: from confident professor to insecure student.

Since advancing to Seventh Farm riding school's top fence-jumping class, I'd felt like a D student among valedictorians—an uncomfortable sensation for an educator. My classmates, a few of whom were two decades younger than me, learned with youth's spongy brains and lithe bodies, but they had always been kind and supportive as they outrode me, so I'd settled self-consciously into my role as class straggler.

Winter straggled, too. Beyond my SUV's window, ice veiled the St. Croix River. I missed the water's startling sapphire sparkle. My breath often caught when it appeared as if from a fairy tale the second my tires thunked onto the bridge. The river's clarity made it a different species from the muddy Mississippi I crossed commuting in the opposite direction to the college where I taught. The Mississippi also hibernated beneath ice late into spring, storing energy for its swirling summer current, but summer felt as far off as the horizon now hidden behind the steep incline that led to Hudson.

Gravel popped beneath my Isuzu Amigo's treads to signal my arrival at Seventh Farm. I pulled to a stop beneath a row of pines and studied the other salt-spattered vehicles, noting which riders had arrived.

I pushed open the barn's creaky wood door and stepped onto its concrete aisle just as the furnace's roar subsided. In the quiet, horses chomped on breakfast, occasionally knocking a metal shoe against a stall wall as they scrounged for errant oats. While my eyes adjusted to dim light from bulbs screwed into the peak overhead, I breathed in Seventh Farm's perfume: a blend of dry lumber, fresh hay, oiled leather, sweat-soaked saddle pads, and pine shavings that covered stall floors. Nothing in the air or atmosphere forecast my fall.

I set my keys, water bottle, phone, and helmet on the tack room's table and saw that Liz, one of Seventh Farm's owners, had listed which horse each rider should groom and tack for lessons. Beside my name, her loopy print declared "Smitty."

Yes! I hadn't ridden Smitty for a long time.

Nothing seemed amiss as the barn's garage door rumbled open and I walked to the paddock. True to his affable nature, Smitty didn't tense as I tiptoed around cairns of manure dotting the frozen ground. Nothing about pulling a leather halter over his ears or securing its buckle near his cheek hinted that a fall stalked me.

I clipped Smitty's halter into the aisle's crossties and surveyed his hide while warming my hands in my jacket's pockets. Smitty's winter coat, as dark and dull as coffee grounds, looked clean. I smiled at his resemblance to Bullwinkle. His front legs looked like cue sticks jointed with billiard balls and stood wider than shoulder width. His ears rested at 45 degrees, suggesting antlers. His snub-nose muzzle and tendency to stick out his tongue gave the impression he'd just delivered a hokey punchline.

Under saddle, however, Smitty moved with a panther's grace and a hummingbird's precision. His cue sticks could churn like pistons and launch like rockets. He made such a willing partner that Liz had ridden him, rather than her pedigreed mare, in competition the previous summer. If I didn't know better, it would be impossible to match the moose-horse dozing beside me with the Thoroughbred photographed soaring over a fence like a dancer mid-leap.

I should have considered the power Smitty could exert to clear fences like the one pictured, but I didn't.

I didn't have consequences in mind when I saddled Smitty and led him to the indoor arena, where standards held a pole 16" inches above the sand. I'd jumped that height countless times on other horses, so I wasn't worried.

I beamed as Smitty's canter rocked me like a boat on ocean swells. The rubber bit in his mouth telegraphed his footfalls through braided reins clasped against my palms. Our pace was rhythmic, our approach smooth, but Smitty went long, leaving the ground further from the fence than was ideal.

I bobbled. My calves swung away from Smitty's flanks. I pitched forward and saw nothing but black mane as my nose threatened to part it. Then I lay on the ground.

Sand disturbed by my left arm coming to rest like a spoon behind my right arced into the air. Grains tumbled in slow motion, triggering memories from a different kind of fall when I was 17, when I pitched forward and saw nothing but colored plastic arcing toward the windshield as my car crashed in A.C.'s aftermath.

Now, I lay in fetal position

What's broken? How's my head? Can I teach tomorrow? Headlines linking NFL concussions to dementia and suicide flicked through my mind followed by images of similar injuries associated with riding. The most dramatic I'd witnessed had happened to my friend, Becky.

A year after we started riding together at Seventh Farm, she flew from the saddle, landed flat on her back, and conked her head—not once, but twice. She got back in the saddle both times, but the falls unearthed damage that old concussions had buried like fossils in her brain. She suffered headaches. She struggled to concentrate and make decisions. She burst into tears without warning. She forgot details. All were potentially career-ending flaws for a paralegal.

Becky had been adamant that she wouldn't stop riding; she just needed a break to recover. I urged her not to rush getting healthy, reminded her that riding would be there whenever she felt ready to return. She never did. I didn't see or hear from her again. A few months later, the same thing happened to a lawyer I'd ridden with.

Until Becky fell, I'd worried less about my head than my body. I wore a helmet, so I'd figured my head would be fine. I'd feared broken bones that would interfere with teaching or with exercise I depended on to manage my eating disorder—another outcome of A.C.

Becky's fall highlighted how heavily I depended on intellect to be a safe space. When an eating disorder had held my body captive and depression had sapped my energy in A.C.'s wake, intellect's cool embrace had quelled my psyche's fevers enough that I could function.

Awareness of how falling could impact my intellect made worries about broken bones seem foolish. Bones could mend, but head injuries rewired neurons. Ended careers. Damaged relationships. Stole memories. Altered identities.

Time snapped back from my slow-motion dive from the saddle. The sand settled. In my head, I saw the body I had starved, whittled with surgery, hidden with loose clothing, and was still working to accept, cartwheel from Smitty's back to land in a heap. Embarrassment heated my cheeks. A voice at the back of my head scolded, "Clumsy. Ungainly. Bulky. Ugly."

Anxious to wipe the image from my mind and Liz's, I leapt to my feet and brushed sand from my shirtsleeves. I ran a palm across my butt and felt sand gush from my breeches' waistband.

"Are you OK?" Liz asked.

I was grateful she didn't move from where she stood in the arena's center; a fuss would intensify my embarrassment.

She studied me with measured calm, looking like she'd stepped from an equestrian catalogue in black riding boots and vest, white shirtsleeves, and lavender scarf. The only flaw—saddle stains on her tan breeches—made her authentic.

I smiled. "Yeah, I'm fine."

Was I? Reassure first, question later: That had been my people-pleasing impulse since childhood. Eating disorder treatment had helped me recognize the straight line that ran from pleasing others to starving myself to landing in a hospital psych ward. I'd since learned to harness my people-pleasing compulsion, but when stressed, exhausted, or caught by surprise, the reflex to reassure fired, no more under my control than my knee when struck by a doctor's rubber mallet.

I dashed to where Smitty stood and grabbed the reins, fearful he'd take off running, though the arena offered nowhere to go. He gazed at me with blue-black eyes, looking thoughtful. When he blinked and sighed, I sighed with relief, too: My sudden dismount hadn't fazed him.

"Take a second to catch your breath," Liz suggested. She adjusted the mic pack clipped to her waist and said at a louder volume, "Walk Smitty around while we talk about what went wrong."

I took inventory as I plodded through the sand. *Nothing hurt, thank God.* But how could I know for sure? My body liked to betray me. It and I were still negotiating the terms of our relationship. Would a joint swell under cover of night and attack at first light? Would my brain misfire?

"So, what do you think happened?" Liz asked.

I must have answered, but I don't remember what I said. I didn't know what had happened. That's what scared me.

Falling had felt nothing like close calls, where I'd sensed something off before my balance wavered. This time, I hadn't sensed anything. Everything about our ride had been fine and then... not.

Though I don't remember how I answered Liz's question, I know my voice shook. My throat constricted. Pressure built behind my eyes.

No. I will NOT cry. I'm unhurt, for God's sake! I swallowed hard to wrangle my voice, which often spooked when I needed it most.

Liz explained what she'd seen and what I could do to prevent it from happening again. My breathing normalized, my feet planted and lifted reliably, but my emotions jangled like wind chimes in a squall.

Liz glanced at me from the corner of her eye. What she saw must have reassured her. She nodded at the mounting block in the corner and said, "Let's try that again."

I knew the adage: "Get right back in the saddle after a fall." I felt its truth like metal in my marrow. I needed to jump that fence again, or fear would root in my gut and grow, but I didn't care. Just thinking about it ignited flashbacks: The lurch of my body coming unseated, taking with it everything I knew about riding and the bubble of safety in which my privileged life unfolded. The impact of that bubble bursting mimicked the impact of my post-A.C. car accident. But I was supposed to be different now. I had learned A.C.'s lessons and moved on. Hadn't I? Goosebumps rose on my forearms, dislodging sand stuck inside my sleeves.

I don't want to jump that fence.

Liz wouldn't force me, but deciding whether to jump felt bigger than a riding lesson. It felt like a culmination, a drawing together of elements in my life's story.

Riding had pulled my self's shards together and reset them. It continued healing me every day. Would I throw it away due to landing embarrassed but unhurt? Because that's what would happen if I didn't jump. I had let perfectionism drive my life's plot long enough to know how the coming months would play out. I'd find reasons to feel disillusioned. *I'm not improving fast enough. I'll never be as good as I want to be. I can't keep dumping time and money into something I don't do well.* I'd skip a lesson to sleep in. I'd skip another to avoid driving to Hudson in bad weather or road construction or heavy traffic. Skipping two lessons would lead to three and then six. Finally, I'd quit because I only did things perfectly or not at all. Once eating disorder treatment had revealed perfectionism's role in my ill health, I'd recognized it in every thought and deed since childhood: One fall ruined riding. One betrayal shattered a relationship. One bite ensured a binge. One setback derailed a journey.

Later, I'd look back at that moment and understand that my choice whether to jump was shaped by more than fear of injury. The word "choice" alone triggered my most painful memories of falling, of grasping for and losing control, of landing on a psych ward's carpet.

St. Paul, Minnesota, January 2004

On my second night in Regions Hospital's psych ward, I reached behind my neck to tie strings on the gown a nurse had given me. Despite the circumstances, it bothered me that the gown's blue diamond pattern didn't match the cotton pants' gray polka-dots. Then I swallowed two antidepressants the ward psychiatrist prescribed and lay down, restless until I discovered that the fetal position kept the mattress's lumps from digging into my ribs.

My stomach's churning woke me at 1:00 a.m. I gagged. I didn't want to vomit in bed but wasn't sure I could make it down the hall to the dorm-style bathroom in time.

I rose shakily to my feet. My head whirled. Sweat gathered in my lower back. In the mirror opposite my bed, my ash-brown hair hung in clumps. Moonlight revealed glazed, dilated pupils nearly hiding irises that had faded from blue to pewter. I had become one of the zombies whose medicated stares and blank smiles had scared me during my orientation to the ward 24 hours earlier.

I stepped toward my room's door. Black spots hovered in my vision. I stilled, closed my eyelids, and breathed deeply until the spots vanished.

I lurched down the hall with a smoldering gut.

A woman in the nurses' station spotted me and did a double-take. "Are you OK? You're awfully pale."

"I... I think I might pass out." I sagged against the hallway wall.

An aide vaulted the station's half-wall and caught my arm just in time to slow my descent.

The nurse rushed to my side and wrapped a blood pressure cuff around my arm.

I watched from above as a voice I didn't recognize spoke from my mouth. "Can I lie down?"

My body didn't wait for an answer, just flattened to orange carpet worn in the center by decades of footfalls. *Gross,* I thought. Then, *who cares?* It felt so good not to care.

"My stomach's on fire," my mouth reported. It moaned. My eyes squeezed shut.

The cuff tightened around my arm. The nurse's face became a pale pink haze. Then everything went black.

The nurse sighed with relief when I came to. "Your pressure dropped, but it's rising. Do you feel better?"

"A little."

Though I had eaten since breakfast, I tasted its scrambled eggs on my tongue, smelled them on my breath. *Gross,* I thought again.

"I'll carry her back to her room," the aide told the pink haze.

I shook my head. "N-o-o-o-o." My bathroom scale's numbers flashed red in my mind's eye: 145. I pictured the aide staggering beneath my weight. *Too much. There's too much of me.* I tried to sit up.

"Whoa! Relax. Lay back," he said. "Why don't you want me to carry you?"

"I—" I grappled for words that ducked out of reach.

"What? You don't think I can?" He winked. "I bet I can. I won't drop you; I promise."

"No..." *You can't know I take up more space than I'm allowed.* I wanted to explain, but my brain wouldn't work. I imagined smacking my head with my palm the way I'd once seen teenage boys smack pinball machines. I tried to stand.

"OK, OK." He put his hands out to stop me. "I won't carry you. We don't have a wheelchair handy. What if I wheel you to your room on an office chair?"

I nodded.

He helped me rise, shoved a padded chair beneath my butt, and rolled me back to bed.

The same resistance to being carried clutched my chest as I considered Liz's suggestion that I jump the fence that had thrown me. I'd lost 15 pounds since being hospitalized, but maybe I'd fallen because there was still too much of me for Smitty to carry.

I don't want to jump that fence.

I glimpsed the mounting block's peeling brown paint. To land safely, I had to figure out what had gone wrong. My brain understood Liz's explanation; my body didn't. Part of it remained curled on its side in the sand, where its imprint was still visible. I needed to go back to that spot and collect my missing pieces. I needed to retrace every footfall until I discovered where I had first begun falling.

To move forward, I had to go backward.

PART I: FALLING
Chapter 1 - Smitty: Identify Your Exposition

Seventh Farm Riding School, December 2014

At the start of Seventh Farm's three-day Christmas Camp, Liz interrupted my attempts to pick ice from Smitty's hooves. "If he's too much for you, I'll put you on a different horse tomorrow, OK?"

I nodded, but my chest filled with muddied emotions: resentment that Liz assumed I wasn't up to the challenge, worry she might be right, determination to prove her wrong, and excitement about riding Smitty for the first time.

I'd registered for Christmas Camp in an attempt to reclaim affection for the holiday. I'd once loved its crisp cold and pine-needle scent, colored lights and strangers' smiles. I'd even liked its 90-minute midnight Mass because candlelight transformed winter's dark hush from oppressive to reverent. And I would never forget the magic of my fifth-grade teacher letting us join the other class to watch Masterpiece Theater's *Tale of Two Cities* on the last day before Christmas break. Huddled around the TV with friends I only saw during lunch, I finally felt like I belonged at the school I had joined halfway through third grade.

Christmas was complicated by my best holiday at 16 (B.C.), and my worst at 17 (A.C.). Neither the season nor I had been the same since. I hoped, as I ran a brush over the thin white scar on Smitty's rear leg, that spending December 22-24 with horses would change my attitude. Riding Smitty would help. It was hard not to smile in his presence. Like Bullwinkle's, his origin story held comedic appeal.

Liz and Tom had gotten Smitty for free when his owner couldn't find a buyer. His gangly build made him clumsy, and his history as an "only child" made him awkward. He didn't know herd rules, so he bungled overtures to his new Seventh Farm family. The herd's lowest-ranking members shunned him; its highest-ranking members roughed him up.

Then Penny, a small mare who didn't like anyone, took a shine to Smitty. We riders laughed when she neighed like a giggling school girl every time he passed. Penny's big crush and small size belied her fierceness. No one crossed her, as evident from her hide's lack of bite and kick marks. Her infatuation worked like a Mafioso's vouching for a new pledge to la familia. By the time her unrequited love ran its course, Smitty had slotted himself into the herd. Then he'd surprised everyone with his talent for jumping.

We didn't jump during that first day of Christmas Camp, but Liz pointed at me with a gloved hand and warned, "You have your work cut out for you."

I knew what she meant. Each horse and rider brings to their pairing a unique Nature-Nurture combination: leg length and work ethic, height and training, aptitude and experience. A rider must know her horse well enough to account for his Nature-Nurture mix and how it will interact with her own. I inherited a build not suited to riding: a long torso, short legs, round thighs, and tight hamstrings. Smitty inherited a thick neck and big head, which gave him a downhill bent. If a rider didn't keep him collected, that bent would lead to lameness.

I gathered the reins and held in mind the image Liz used to explain collection: keeping the horse uphill. I needed to feel Smitty's haunches push his body up and forward like a rear-wheel drive car instead of reaching and pulling with his front legs. That inclined position would minimize wear on front legs nature hadn't intended to carry a rider's weight.

Keeping a horse uphill is all about lines, I remembered, checking to see that the one stretching from my elbows, through the reins, to the bit in Smitty's mouth was straight. I pulled my heels back so they lined up with my hips and shoulders. I visualized a straight path from my current location to the next imaginary fence. If I held those lines, I'd set Smitty up to jump in an arc instead of a peak.

The effort required to keep Smitty uphill became clear when we practiced a sitting trot, staying still in the saddle instead of rising and falling with the horse's motion. I pressed down and forward against the saddle, but Smitty's lumbering gait still made me bounce. My butt's *whap, whap* against the leather embarrassed me.

"Fun, isn't he?" Liz asked wryly.

I nodded and laughed, but I was sincere. Smitty *was* fun.

By the lesson's end, my legs burned with fatigue, but I relished the soreness.

I secured Smitty in the crossties just as Liz clomped up behind me in her winter boots. She watched me tug on a leather billet to release the saddle girth from Smitty's belly. "You did better than I thought you would on him. I didn't expect you to do that well."

"Thanks!" I beamed before I caught the unintended insult in her comment. I shrugged as she walked away, deciding to toss the insult and pocket the compliment.

I wished Sara, my eating disorder therapist, could see my reaction to Liz's comment. It was a stark contrast to the reaction I'd described when I sat in her office as a new client at age 28 and said of A.C., "I broke. My breastbone cracked when I got the news. I don't mean like a 'broken heart.' It felt physical, like a fracture. Every time I inhaled, the halves' jagged edges grated. The pain dulled after a while, but I've been misaligned ever since."

Sara was new to The Emily Program that afternoon in April 2002, too, so recently hired by the eating disorder clinic tucked into St. Paul's Mac-Groveland neighborhood that she hadn't unpacked. The bare ivory walls and gray carpet didn't prevent the office from feeling cozy. Her presence rounded the corners and softened the light.

She was as unadorned as her office. I'd liked that about her immediately because it suggested authenticity. Blonde and fair, she appeared fresh-faced rather than wan without makeup. Her only concession to decoration was a gold wedding band. Otherwise, she covered an enviably thin body with pantsuits and loafers in conservative colors. I studied her stylish black jacket while I waited for her reply to what I'd said. She didn't seem inclined to comment, so I forged ahead.

"I know saying I broke sounds like teenage melodrama, and it probably is, but that's what happened. Ever since, I've felt like I'm falling, reeling in space with nothing to grasp and nowhere to land."

I picked at my cuticles—a nervous habit. Fingers on both hands bore rips in various stages of healing. The jagged line I tore on my thumb wept clear fluid. Its pink pulp throbbed. The physical pain comforted because it was clearer, sharper, and more localized than the dysfunction I struggled to describe.

"When I was a kid, I felt like I had antennae. They picked up on currents beneath the surface, like what someone meant versus what they said, how someone felt versus how they acted. But my antennae stopped working when I broke, and my mind got scratched, like a record. I keep catching on what happened and replaying it to see how I became..." I gestured vaguely at my body. "This. I'm a different person than I used to be. Back then I was pure. Now I'm... polluted."

I inhaled and held my breath, braced for skepticism I'd come to expect when I mentioned betrayals 12 years in the past. "Get over it," people said. As if I hadn't tried. As if I weren't more exasperated than anyone by my inability to move on.

I suspected my eating disorder and depression were rooted in those betrayals, but I didn't know how or why. Neither did anyone else. Other therapists had been stumped. Sara seemed like the first willing to consider how jumbled pieces fit together in a life story whose plot I was desperate to gain control of so it would stop wreaking havoc.

"If I'm asked to remember when something happened—like my first car accident or the Berlin Wall coming down—a timeline of my life pops up in my head. A thick, black mark bisects it where I broke. Left of that mark is B.C.—you know, like historians refer to events that happened 'Before Christ'? Right of that mark is A.C. I date everything according to where it falls in relation to that mark."

I risked a glance up from my cuticle to gauge Sara's reaction. "What you're describing sounds like PTSD."

Post-Traumatic Stress Disorder? I knew what it was, but I had never considered it might apply to me.

"But PTSD is what soldiers get from combat, or rape victims—people who have experienced trauma. My... thing was nothing like that." My voice sharpened with resentment when I added, "as people like to point out."

Sara shook her head. "Everyone processes things differently. Among soldiers who return from the same combat situation, some transition to civilian life easily, while others break down. PTSD is diagnosed by symptoms, not precipitating events. What matters is an event's *impact*—how it disrupts a person's life. The more sensitive someone is, the less it takes to create trauma."

Sara flicked a glance at the clock above her blond wood desk. "I have another client coming, so we're out of time, but I want to give you something."

She opened a box labeled "office" in black Sharpie and dug through it. "Since I know you like to read..." She smiled shyly, pulled two paperbacks from the box, and handed them to me.

I studied the creased covers: *The Drama of the Gifted Child* by Alice Miller[1] and *The Highly Sensitive Person: How to Thrive When the World Overwhelms You* by Elaine Aron[2].

"I think you'll relate to what these authors say. They explain the links between sensitivity, trauma, and depression."

I returned Sara's smile, grateful to have an ally as familiar and trustworthy as books.

The books' contents mingled with a lesson I taught the following week. On the classroom whiteboard, I drew and labeled a model of traditional narrative structure. "This is Freytag's Pyramid," I told 35 students whose expressions ranged from intrigued to comatose. "It existed long before the Greeks described it in 350 B.C.E. It still shapes nearly every book, play, movie, and TV show. In fact, it's so integral to human experience, it shapes how we think about our lives."

I pointed to the model's color-coded parts as I defined them.

"Exposition: This horizontal line establishes the setting and introduces the protagonist (hero).

1. Alice Miller, *The Drama of the Gifted Child and the Search for the True Self* (New York: BasicBooks, 1981).
2. Elaine Aron, *The Highly Sensitive Person: How to Thrive When the World Overwhelms You* (New York: Broadway Books, 1997).

"Inciting Incident: This event creates conflict. Something jolts the protagonist from her static state.

"Rising Action: This incline shows how the conflict sends the protagonist on a journey of discovery, where she encounters obstacles, like villains, natural disasters, disease, fate, or her own flaws. Each obstacle forces her to decide whether she'll continue her journey.

"Climax: This peak is the protagonist's make-or-break moment. She'll either succeed or fail in fulfilling her journey's purpose.

"Resolution: This short decline relieves the story's tension because the conflict is resolved—happily or unhappily."

Students rustled notebook pages and zipped backpacks. A glance at the clock confirmed class was almost over. I gave a parting reminder. "We'll discuss character archetypes next week. Look for Freytag's pyramid as you read the assigned story."

Students' commotion peaked as they gathered their belongings, then fell away as they filed from the room. I began erasing the model but stopped mid-swipe when I saw what remained: Freytag's Pyramid without the Resolution. *That's me.* Or, me with PTSD: stuck at the summit of an unresolved climax. I could hardly wait to tell Sara about my discovery.

Days later, I waited in an alcove outside Sara's office and stared out the window at trees ready to bud. Their branches looked spindly against spring's blue sky and weak sun. They reminded me of antennae. I had been stunned to see that word, along with an inner world I'd never mentioned to anyone, in *The Highly Sensitive Person.* The book claimed that approximately 10% of people are more sensitive than average and use invisible antennae to detect emotional disruptions in their surroundings.

"Aron says constant crying during infancy is a sign of high sensitivity," I blurted as soon as I sat across from Sara. I couldn't hide my excitement at the way Aron's logical explanations lined up with my experiences[3]. "That matches the story my parents always tell about when I was a baby."

She raised her eyebrows. "Oh? What's the story?"

The scene took shape in my head the way it always did: with me as an external narrator. *The Drama of the Gifted Child* explained that phenomenon, too. A highly sensitive person needs external calm to feel internal calm, so when she identifies others' needs as sources of atmospheric disturbance, she tries to fill them. Soothing others earns their approval, which reinforces her inclination to please. To please more effectively, she observes herself from an outsider's point of view and modifies her behavior according to external cues until they supersede internal cues. Paired with perfectionism, her external focus invites an eating disorder.

When I began telling Sara my infancy story, I left my body to float above my parents, Jim and Pat Whalen, in February 1975, as they indulged in their first restaurant meal since they'd married more than a year ago.

As soon as they placed their order, Baby Lisa began fussing. Within seconds, she was a tempest of wet cheeks and body-shaking gasps. The other diners glared and shifted in their seats. The new parents squirmed. They tried a rattle, bottle, and keys, but nothing calmed their daughter.

Just as Jim rose to cancel their order, the waiter brought their entrees. They couldn't afford to pay without eating, couldn't eat while the baby screamed.

---

3. Elaine Aron, *The Highly Sensitive Person: How to Thrive When the World Overwhelms You* (New York: Broadway Books, 1997).

Jim gathered his daughter in his arms and headed for the bathroom, where he paced the tile and sang lullabies while Pat ate spaghetti at a table for two. When she finished, the parents traded places.

On the drive home, Pat sighed with gratitude for the elixir of car rides, the only tonic that soothed the infant's angst. The vibration of tires on pavement and thrum of a 1971 Dodge Demon's engine lulled the baby when nothing else could.

They parked in front of an apartment building on Larpenteur Avenue across from the University of Minnesota's St. Paul campus. Streetlights cast shadows on boulevard snowdrifts. Jim grasped Pat's elbow to steady her as she carried their daughter up the icy front walk. Salt crackled beneath Pat's boots.

Entryway heat came as a welcome relief, though it dried eyes grainy with fatigue. Even Jim's empty arms felt heavy. He glanced at the bundle cradled against his wife's chest. The baby's eyelids spasmed from a dream. The couple shared a rueful smirk, then ascended the stairs.

The following morning, sun pierced icicles dangling from the gutters and cast rainbows on the kitchen wall. Fortified by coffee, the couple wound scarves around their necks, tucked them into down jackets, and stepped into the hallway.

The neighbor's door groaned open as Jim locked their own. A woman in a pink bathrobe and slippers grabbed the newspaper on her mat. She spotted the couple and exclaimed, "Oh, look! The baby's not crying for once! It's a miracle!" Before they could reply, the neighbor ducked back into her den. The parents traded embarrassed glances and crept down the hall, hoping to make it through Mass without similar exchanges.

"My pediatrician said I had colic and switched me to soy formula. It didn't help much. My parents claim I didn't stop crying for more than a few hours at a time until I started walking."

I thought again of the passage in Aron's book I'd photocopied so I could keep it[4]. The passage explained that a highly sensitive person has higher levels of cortisol, the stress hormone, from birth. Cortisol piques her fight-or-flight response, making her attuned to the slightest disturbances, like noises, temperature shifts, or tense social exchanges, because they represent potential threats. Defenseless, she's programed to alert her protectors by crying.

Crying throughout infancy may have been the first sign I showed of susceptibility to eating disorders, but Nature had buried the seeds of my post-A.C. fall much earlier in my story's exposition.

As if foreshadowing, my exposition opens with trauma caused by hunger. All four great-great-grandparents fled Ireland's potato famine, which destroyed everything they'd known and loved. They arrived in America's Midwest to face a new threat. Proprietors displayed signs proclaiming, "No Irish, blacks, dogs." Employers advertised that "Irish need not apply."

A flood of destitute immigrants during the 1860s pushed America's anti-Catholic sentiment to its summit. My ancestors began with two strikes against them in a country that declared, "Three strikes and you're out." To survive, they had to please the people throwing pitches and counting swings. That meant they had to be perfect: stay cleaner, work harder, act friendlier, sacrifice more.

My paternal grandpa was raised on stories of hardship "back home," then faced a new but achingly familiar threat: The Great

---

4. Elaine Aron, *The Highly Sensitive Person: How to Thrive When the World Overwhelms You* (New York: Broadway Books, 1997).

Depression. The stock market's plunging red line, along with the culture of deprivation and hoarding it fostered, watermarked Grandpa's DNA. That mark appeared on every page in his story and its sequels, but it's most visible in his marriage to a woman named Julia in 1940. Though he could afford not to, he moved Julia into the two-bedroom house he shared with his parents. I know little of my great-grandparents except that relatives' described Grandpa's mother as "domineering." Julia's behavior suggests the living arrangements were less than ideal. When she fell ill with kidney disease, she chose to convalesce at her parents' house instead of in the one where she'd lived with her husband and six-year-old son (my dad). Dad remembers only a few short visits with Julia before she died.

In his grief, Grandpa clung to what his ancestors had claimed was the means to a happy ending: religion. He and Dad attended daily 6:00 am Mass, then returned to a house girded by mourning and mortared by iconography. When my siblings and I visited decades later, Grandpa's 19th century Denver dwelling remained a house of worship. We dipped our fingers in holy water in a font affixed to the front entryway before making the Sign of the Cross. We examined prayer cards ringing mirrors, dried palms tucked behind crucifixes, rosaries glittering on nightstands and end tables. But Grandpa had made his greatest show of devotion long before we entered the story. Irish custom dictated that each family produce a priest or nun, so when Dad turned 14, Grandpa sent his only child to seminary school in Missouri.

I only know Reverend Jim Whalen as a character in tales from a distant time, the subject of photographs that show his wavy brown hair shining beneath altar spotlights in a Minnesota church. Green and gold vestments slide down his freckled arms as he holds up a bowl and chalice. He chants phrases I'll know by heart from a tender age: *Take this bread and eat it. Take this wine and drink it. Do this in memory of me.*

I enter the story after Jim has left the priesthood and married Pat, a former nun working as a secretary in Minnesota, where she, too, had been raised to fulfill Irish custom. The couple is joined a year later by a daughter who won't stop crying. Perhaps her antennae detected turmoil in letters and cassettes addressed to Grandpa that returned unopened, calls placed to his black Bakelite phone that went unanswered. Dad's rejection of Irish custom tore a rift in his relationship with Grandpa that he didn't know how to mend. Desperate, he appeared unannounced on Grandpa's doorstep and held up the first grandchild like an offering.

I thought of that moment where my life story could have branched in either direction—back toward or forever bent away from Grandpa—as I stared at the mounting block in Seventh Farm's arena 40 years later, sand clinging to my skin, Smitty's reins resting in my hand. I had to decide which way my story would go: back toward or bent away from riding. I wished for an offering I could hold up to an equine god. Or better yet, an oracle. Custom dictated that a rider get back in the saddle after she fell, but custom hadn't worked out as intended for my parents. If they hadn't bucked what Irish tradition had demanded, I wouldn't exist.

Maybe their story's U-turn was a sign indicating which branch I should follow.

Without an oracle, I could only look to my past and revisit wisdom proffered by a sage named Buck.

Chapter 2 - Buck: Stop Trying to Be Perfect

Seventh Farm Riding School, August 2011

"Pick up a posting trot," Liz shouted from the outdoor arena's gazebo. *Oh, God.* My heart launched fireworks that burst in my bloodstream and set my muscles twitching.

Ordinarily, Liz's command wouldn't faze me. I'd learned to post—to rise and fall with the horse's stride—during my earliest riding lessons months ago. But her words took on new significance that steamy Sunday in August 2011 because they signaled the start of competition.

I didn't want to compete. I'd chosen Seventh Farm for lessons because it was one of the only schools that didn't require competing. Though surprised, I wasn't worried when Liz announced that Seventh Farm would host a show because participation was optional. Showing would probe my most sensitive vulnerabilities, the same ones that had sent me plunging to a psych ward's carpet after A.C. Eating disorder treatment had helped me mute internal judges so harsh I grew sick at the suggestion I might be observed, but I wouldn't risk relapsing into anorexia. Besides, I liked that riding got me out of my head and made me feel strong. *Why ruin that by adding unnecessary pressure?* I managed to hide the fact that I hadn't registered for the show until friends cornered me in the tack room just before the deadline.

"It'll be low-pressure," Becky said. "I learned *a ton* riding in a small show a while ago. You'll regret not doing it."

"Probably, but I'm not ready. I get too nervous," I replied.

"Pffft! Everyone's nervous," said the lawyer who, like Becky, eventually quit riding after a fall. She gestured toward the outdoor arena with her helmet. "You'll get over the nerves once you're out there."

"I've never even seen a show," I said. "I'll just watch so I know what to expect."

I stuffed my helmet into its cloth bag and scrubbed my scalp with my fingertips before pulling my shoulder-length mop into a bun.

"I can tell you what to expect. C'mon, the show won't be fun without you," Becky said.

I should have known I didn't stand a chance against a lawyer and a paralegal. They batted down every objection like I was opposing counsel. Finally, Becky grabbed a registration form from the table and held it out.

I'll call in sick, I decided as I clopped across the parking lot in unzipped paddock boots. Forfeiting the fee would be worth avoiding the stress. I'd think of the money as a donation to the horses' care. Resolved and relieved, I tossed my riding bag onto the Amigo's gray passenger floor mat and climbed behind the wheel.

My conscience wouldn't let me off the hook despite anxiety that disturbed my sleep. The morning of the show, I woke at 4:00 a.m. My stomach refused breakfast, so I tossed a protein bar in my bag and paced the kitchen floor. Reverting to a childhood game, I stepped from one beige tile to another without touching the taupe grout. With every glance at my microwave's clock, I swung from praying time would stop so I wouldn't have to compete to hurrying time forward so I could end the anticipation.

Get a grip! You're being ridiculous.

It didn't dawn on me until I passed downtown St. Paul, headed into the sun on I-94 with my stomach roiling and limbs tingling, that my apprehension about showing mirrored my apprehension about teaching observations. Both meant that an older male in a position of authority applied subjective criteria to evaluating how well I got an unpredictable partner to perform. No matter how carefully I prepared, a college class could derail quickly if a student arrived high, hungover, homesick, heartbroken, or having refused to read assigned pages. Horses' moods and motivations could be as mysterious as students', and I had less mastery of riding than teaching.

An hour later, however, I sat atop Buck, whom I hadn't ridden for months, and waited to enter the arena as one of four riders in the show's first division.

"Sorry," I whispered to Buck when he craned his neck to glare at me. I tested the stirrup length one last time, rested my butt in the saddle's leather valley as gently as I could, and vowed to stop fidgeting. To reinforce my apology, I scratched Buck's favorite spot, where the hair on his neck switched from hickory brown to birch white.

It wasn't quite 10:00 a.m., but heat shimmered like an apparition haunting the asphalt that separated Seventh Farm from a residential neighborhood. Weeks without rain had crisped lawns and shriveled shrubs. Sun pummeled my shoulders and ricocheted off arena sand that functioned like a million microscopic mirrors. My black t-shirt intensified the heat. I'd known it would, but black was the most effective color at camouflaging the side effect my antidepressant's label called "excessive sweating." Damp rings already circled my underarms. Beads trickled from my lower back to soak my breeches' waistband. By the time I finished riding, my clothes and I would be as limp as leaves dangling morosely from a maple just beyond the arena rail.

To distract myself from fear and sweat, I ran my fingers through Buck's coarse, black mane and reminded myself that he was an old hand at 26, rarely ruffled by anything. I took comfort knowing Buck's pinto coat would make it easier to see whether I'd asked him to lead with the correct leg as we trotted or cantered. *Left leg white, right leg brown.* "That will also make it easier for everyone to see when you get it wrong," carped a voice in my head. *Great.*

Speaking of the judge... Tom, Liz's husband and co-owner of Seventh Farm, shuffled past me and into the arena with a blue ribbon that read "Judge" pinned to his breast pocket. His boots and frayed denim hems sent dust rising from the sand and sticking to the sunscreen on my arms. Liz followed him to the gazebo then shouted those infamous words, "Pick up a posting trot!"

I squeezed Buck's sides with my heels and sat for a few strides to time his steps. When the moment felt right, I let my hips follow his upward momentum. I played on a loop in my head everything I could remember about posting: *Your hips should mimic windshield wipers. Don't force the motion; let the horse's movement toss you up. Pause at the top of your rise like a swing at its peak. Touch down softly in the saddle, like you're sitting on a bird's nest.* I held my back rigid to counter my shoulders' natural slump. "Smile with your collarbones," I remembered my first instructor saying repeatedly.

The longer I followed Liz's directions, the more I forgot about the audience watching from beyond the rail. My concentration narrowed to what I felt in my seat and hands. Each time Buck slowed or shifted toward "downhill" movement, I pressed with my calves to drive him forward and upward. Except for a few glimpses of other riders struggling to canter or turn-and-reverse, I focused on my connection with Buck to the exclusion of everything else.

By the time Liz ended our division, I felt better about my ride than I could have hoped. Buck's canter strike offs had been clean and on the correct lead. His turn-and-reverses had traced perfect teardrops in the sand.

"You did great!" Becky stage-whispered when I walked Buck past the arena's entrance. "You're the only one who got the correct leads. I'm sure you're in first place."

The lawyer, who stood beside Becky, gave me a thumbs-up.

I grinned with pride and relief. I felt buoyant as I lined Buck up beside my competitors' horses.

Tom stepped from the gazebo wearing a straw fedora that matched his hair color. He studied notes jotted on clipboard pages, squinted up at us, and said, "Fourth place out of four goes to... Lisa Whalen."

My innards seized. Heat rushed to my face in a blaze. A smattering of polite applause rippled from the knoll, where spectators hunched beneath umbrellas. My competitors offered me smiles meant to be supportive but that didn't hide pity and relief. *This is why I didn't want to show!*

I worried that this moment, like the one that had divided my life's timeline into B.C. and A.C., would scratch my memory's vinyl. My mind would catch on it and replay the preceding ride until I heard every discordant mistake at ear-splitting volume. I wanted to bury my face in Buck's mane, but I pushed my mouth's corners into a smile I hoped appeared gracious. *At least I can go home now.* I couldn't wait to dunk my head beneath a shower's icy spray.

I had just slipped my right boot from the stirrup and prepared to swing my leg over Buck's back when Liz told us to walk our horses toward the rail for round two.

What?

My competitors and I traded uneasy looks.

"C'mon, let's go!" Liz chided, clapping her hands. "There are three rounds before the next division. If you don't get moving, we'll be here until tomorrow."

I have to do that three more times? My stomach recoiled like a spiked football. I imagined three more tremulous rides, three more announcements of fourth place, three more flutters of sympathetic applause. *Should I fake an injury? Can I simply opt out?*

Quitting would be childish. I didn't want to be a sore loser, but I also didn't want to spend another 45 minutes staving off panic in addition to heatstroke.

My desire to avoid drawing attention won out. I handed the white ribbon Liz had given me to a student working as the show gopher, slotted the reins between my fingers, and steered Buck away from the gazebo.

"Hey, c'mere," Tom yelled, waving to me with his clipboard.

He walked toward me, then grabbed the reins beneath Buck's chin and led us away from the other riders.

"Look, everyone did well on the basics, so I had to apply more advanced criteria. You didn't maintain a rhythm. Buck's pace at the walk and trot was all over the place."

"Oh." I cleared my throat, which felt clogged with dust.

"Next time, establish a rhythm in each gait and maintain it."

I nodded. Sweat trickled down my temple. I swiped at it and dried my fingertips on my breeches, leaving ovals that looked like fingerprints.

"You look tight, like you're really nervous or something." Tom toed the sand with his boot, sending more dust into the air.

"I *am* really nervous," I said, unable to suppress a defensive edge.

"Don't be."

Ha! If only it was that easy.

"There's no reason to be nervous. It will just make everything harder."

"OK," I said, unconvinced.

Tom grabbed my boot and shook it. The metal stirrup encircling it glinted in the sun. "Look at this. See how tense you are? Relax!" He repeated the word, drawing it out for effect. "Relaaaaaaax."

I exhaled and softened in the saddle.

"That's not enough." Tom shook my heel more forcefully. "Loosen up!" He poked my thigh with his index finger. "See that?"

I looked where he was pointing and saw a raised U above my kneecap: My quadriceps were flexed. *Let go. Let it go.*

"That's better. I want you to ride *that* relaxed."

My reply barely rose above a whisper. "OK."

Tom let go of my boot and headed for the gazebo.

I tried to swallow past the lump in my throat, but my tongue stuck to the roof of my mouth.

"Hey."

I looked up to find Tom staring at me over his shoulder. "Just ride. Have fun. Stop trying to be perfect." When he stepped forward, the gazebo's shadow swallowed his fedora.

Ah, there it is. Tom had uttered the magic words: "Stop trying to be perfect." Sara had said the same thing in a million gentle ways as she'd helped me understand how perfectionism distorted my perception. Within my internal world, perfectionism fueled an eating disorder the way water vapor fueled a hurricane. The heat of observation was all it took to set my brain spinning. Unless cooled, my mind channeled anxiety until intensifying rotation prevented me from separating cause from effect, perception from reality.

My first inkling that riding could help me battle perfectionism had appeared on a similarly scorching summer morning months earlier. The barn had offered some relief then, its aisle funneling any breeze the trees managed to wheeze. I'd arrived to find stall doors gaping open and the tack room deserted. I savored the cool quiet while I struggled to zip new half-chaps around my calves. Their leather would protect my skin from chafing against the saddle and stabilize my lower leg as I learned to post.

They're supposed to be tight, I reminded myself, feeling fat when the zippers resisted.

I'd grown less squeamish about wearing clothes that clung, but I would never feel comfortable in anything tight. The tan breeches I wore for the first time that morning were case in point. Their stretch-cotton fabric spotlighted every bulge and dimple. Pulling them on at home, I'd caught myself reverting to old habits: resting my hands on my hips to gauge my torso's thickness, laying a palm against my belly to check its flatness, pushing against the floor with my toes when I sat to prevent my thighs from spreading. Uneasy, I'd chosen a navy t-shirt long enough to cover my butt, which I considered too big for my 130-pound figure.

Half-chaps zipped, I left the tack room to check my reflection in the bathroom mirror. My midsection looked floppy despite the loose shirt, but I couldn't do anything about it. I shrugged and tucked a wayward curl into the ponytail secured at my nape. I sighed, donned my helmet, and snapped off the light.

Once in the saddle, I forgot to suck in my stomach and gauge my thighs' spread—one of many reasons riding had felt therapeutic from the moment I sat on a horse. Another reason was that it taught me to listen to my body.

"If you can learn to post on Buck," Jeneen, my Introduction to Riding instructor, said, "posting on any other horse will be a cinch."

I made excuses the first two times Buck refused to halt. *The heat must be getting to him, too.* No wonder. The metal building felt like a kiln. I glanced at hayloft doors thrown open to admit a breeze that never materialized. Beyond them, miniature pines edged the property before giving way to green and yellow scrub that extended to County Road F and then up a rock face that concealed the horizon. Nothing stirred beneath a hazy sky the color of dingy laundry.

I finally got Buck to halt. When we were supposed to keep trotting, however, he slumped into a lazy walk every time he felt my balance shift.

"Don't get frustrated," Jeneen cautioned when she caught me clenching my teeth. "You'll be grateful for Buck's sensitivity to your balance when you learn to canter."

Maybe. Right then, it was pissing me off. I knew what seemed like obstinance on Buck's part resulted from unclear signals on mine, but it felt designed to provoke. I was trying *so hard* to get everything right, and I was failing.

Jeneen called me over to where she stood in the arena's center.

"I'm not frustrated with him; I'm frustrated with myself," I blurted. "You know that, but Buck doesn't. You're a perfectionist, aren't you?" Jeneen laughed when my mouth fell open in surprise.

"I can tell." Her smile softened. "You're trying to be perfect. Don't. Perfection doesn't exist. Horses aren't perfect, and their imperfection lets you off the hook.

"Ah, see?" Jeneen pointed at my shoulders, which had relaxed as soon as she'd declared me off the hook. "Now, look at your knees. See how tight they are? They're pressing against the saddle when you post. What does squeezing with your knees tell the horse?"

"To halt," I replied, sheepishly.

"That's why Buck keeps stopping."

"Got it."

"Good. Stop trying to be perfect; just keep moving forward." Jeneen patted Buck's shoulder and then motioned toward the rail. "Off you go..."

I repeated Jeneen's advice in my head as I worked to post without tensing: *Stop trying to be perfect; just keep moving forward.* I imagined the phrase on a sticker affixed to the Amigo's bumper. *Forget a sticker, I need a tattoo.*

Instead of ink, I invested in riding, where Buck helped me practice imperfection. His irritation with my pre-show jitters was a clue I'd missed until Tom's fedora faded into shadow. The sight reminded me of two fedoras that had faded in and out of my mind's shadows during childhood.

"That's what you get, Dummy," the first fedora-clad figure said when pain flared in my four-year-old finger.

"Heh, heh, heh," the second figure chuckled.

I studied my finger. It pulsed purple where I had pressed the tip into tar that snaked the gap between my home's driveway and Glen Rose Avenue's curve. Strips like the one I'd poked slithered across roads all over my hometown of North Platte, Nebraska. Sometimes I pretended they were balance beams and walked heel-toe until I wobbled and fell off. I liked the way my sandals' soles waffled their tacky surface. I had wanted to see if they could preserve my fingerprint the same way they did my shoes' designs. I hadn't realized that tar hot enough to waffle was hot enough to burn.

I glanced at the house to see if my parents had seen me flinch and jerk my hand from the pavement, proving I was as dumb as the fedora figures thought. I didn't see anyone peering past the front porch from our living room window, so I let out the breath I'd been holding.

The fedora figures had known the tar would burn but told me to touch it anyway. I was glad no one could hear their laughter. I was the only one who could ever hear them because I was the only one who knew they existed. I called these imaginary friends The Trench Coat Guys because, along with fedoras, they wore London Fog coats buttoned and belted over dress shirts and ties, like the *Sesame Street* puppets who stole the "Golden –an" and put it in the tan van for Dan and Fran. Their favorite pastime was getting me in trouble, so they materialized every time I faced decisions or heightened stakes.

Although The Trench Coat Guys were bullies, I didn't tell anyone about them because I didn't want them to disappear. Overhearing their predictions of all the ways I'd screw up was like having a periscope that allowed me to scan the horizon for danger before I surfaced. Whatever they suggested was usually Bad, which oriented my needle toward Good. Nothing tasted sweeter than outsmarting them to foil their evil plans. Sometimes they got the best of me, though, like when I'd touched the tar. They'd really gotten the best of me the first time they'd appeared.

Then, they'd sat beside me on the red and black upholstery in my parents' Dodge Demon. I'd peeped through the back window when the car came to a stop at Cody Park. A crowd had gathered. My stomach quivered. Hair rose on my legs, which

Lisa Whalen

were bare between my white ankle socks and my pink dress's frilly hem.

I stuck close to Mom and Dad as we neared a knoll where kids ran in every direction. I wondered if I'd have to play with them. Excitement in my parents' voices hinted that I would like what was to come, but the chaos made my heart pound.

Dad squatted beside me and explained that I should find eggs hidden all over the park and put them in my basket. I looked from his long sideburns to my pink bucket's interior and nodded.

At the word "go" I scrambled onto the knoll. I plucked one egg and then another from the grass, astonished they lay in plain sight. *I don't even need to hunt!* Some eggs bore stickers I could redeem for candy. When an older boy snatched one from my hand, I wanted to protest, but I didn't know if that would be Bad. Before I decided, Trench Coat Guy #1 hissed, "Get moving! Everyone else is doing better than you."

"Yeah, they're better than you," Trench Coat Guy #2 echoed.

I ran faster.

When a P.A. announcement ended the hunt, I looked in my basket. Seven eggs lay at the bottom, three marked with stickers. *Is that enough? Is that Good?*

I heard my name and looked up to see Mom waving me toward her. Just before I reached her, a toddler in a white dress and pigtails wandered into my path. She stopped, stared into her empty basket, raised her face to the sky, and howled. I took in the tears glistening on her cheeks and snot running from her nose. They made me sad. The girl reminded me of the little sister I had recently gained. Then I remembered that a big sister's job was to care for younger kids. I plucked a yellow egg from my basket and held it out. "You can have this one."

The toddler quieted. She looked at me and blinked. She took the egg and put it in her basket, where it settled with a thunk. Her dad appeared and knelt beside her. "Thank you!" he said. He smiled at me and asked the toddler, "What do you say, honey?"

"Thank you," she parroted.

"You're welcome," I said, shyly. Embarrassed by the attention, I turned and skipped to where Mom and Dad waited.

"I saw you give that girl an egg," Mom said. "That was really nice. I'm proud of you."

Dad tousled my hair. "Good going, honey!"

"Pfft!" Trench Coat Guy #1 huffed. He rolled beady black eyes that glittered on his Kermit-green face. "You gave her an egg without a sticker. Now she won't get any candy. That's selfish."

"Yeah, selfish," #2 repeated. He shook his baby-blue head in disgust.

My shoulders sank. The Guys were right. I had given the girl an unmarked egg because I wanted candy. And I knew better. I'd learned in Catholic catechism class that being good meant being like Jesus. He and his followers gave away everything they owned to people who had nothing. *That* was Good. Selfishness was Bad.

I stared at my white, patent leather shoes, now grass-stained along their toes.

Guy #1 tsked. "You ruined your new shoes. How wasteful!"

Guy #2 shook his head. "Wasteful!"

Wasting was Bad, too.

Shame twisted my stomach as I collected candy for my marked eggs and walked to the car between Mom and Dad.

The Guys piled into the backseat beside me, crossed their arms, smirked, and gloated all the way home.

Seeing Tom's fedora fade into shadow had reminded me of The Trench Coat Guys' existence, but I didn't realize until months later that The Guys were modeled after more than just *Sesame Street* puppets. Their real-life counterparts, like any characters, were shaped by my story's setting. And it, too, had been birthed by hunger.

North Platte would have remained a frontier fort where the Platte River branched into North and South if not for Buffalo Bill Cody. Cody rose to prominence in the 1860s by hunting bison and selling the meat to workers who had no other sustenance to fuel their labor on the Kansas Pacific Railway. When the railway was complete, Cody created Buffalo Bill's Wild West, a show that featured Annie Oakley and toured internationally. Then he retired on a 4,000-acre ranch beside the North Platte River.

The same rails that built Cody's fortune led my family to North Platte in 1977. By then, the Kansas Pacific Railway had become the Union Pacific Railroad (UPRR). UPRR hired Dad as a substance abuse counselor for workers at its hub, Bailey Yard.

Bailey was the world's largest rail yard and swelled North Platte's population to 20,000, but it couldn't shrink Cody's influence. His name appeared on streets, parks, schools, athletic complexes, and a model trading post that featured his 30-foot likeness. His Wild West imprint permeated the town's culture.

I didn't care much for Cody or the Wild West, but I found Bailey Yard fascinating. The crash that resulted when linemen rolled one car down an incline called a hump into another car and forced the coupling mechanism to link made my ribs rattle, but I liked how each impact traveled down the line of cars. The rhythmic noise and motion soothed me, let me believe I could find order in a chaotic world. On summer nights, I fell asleep lulled by that distant thunder.

My preference for Bailey Yard over Fort Cody reflected my parents' discomfort with life in North Platte. Absent the vocabulary to articulate clashing lifestyles and values as the source of their discomfort, I boiled it down to sound and clothing. Yard workers wore overalls, cussed without shame, and laughed readily with a smoker's crackly lungs. Dad had quit smoking before I was born, concocted eccentric substitutes for profanity, and left our house on weekday mornings wearing a London Fog trench coat buttoned and belted over his shirt and tie. He returned in the evenings disgruntled with clients' Wild West resentment of employer and law enforcement interference in their recreation, even when it affected their handling of 150-ton engines to tragic ends.

Dad called the town's wildest citizens "North Platte Yahoos," rarely uttering the phrase without disdain. The Yahoos drank hard and often, on the job and off, at the bar and behind the wheel. They drove pickups with souped-up engines, oversized tires, undersized mufflers, and shotguns in the rear window. They roared down residential roads at all hours, taking potshots at speed limit signs and turning corners on two wheels so their tires squealed. Country music blared from their radios; beer bottles flew from their windows. Between spitting brown saliva from chew tucked in their lips, they shouted "Ya-hooooo!" or "Yeeeeeeee-haw!" and hit on every female who dared make herself visible.

Dad warned my little sister, Julie, and me to stay away from the Yahoos, which wasn't hard because most lived beyond the viaduct, where UPRR tracks sprawled like an octopus. We church-going families stuck to our territory, and the Yahoos stuck to theirs—except when Nebraskaland Days punctured the boundary.

For one week in June, residents turned out for the event's carnivals, rodeos, and parades. The year I turned five, my dance teacher announced that my class would appear on a Nebraskaland Days parade float. I couldn't wait! I already loved everything about dance: purple leotards and tights. Tap shoes' metallic clack. Batons that glinted when twirled. The image of birds weighing down my middle fingers when I held out my arms. Most of all, I loved the chartreuse tutu and sequined tiara I'd wear on the float. Unfortunately, I needed an accessory my classmates didn't, one that put me in the Yahoos' crosshairs.

Two days before the parade, I hung upside down from my knees on our swingset's trapeze. I planned to do a penny drop, but my legs slipped before I was ready. I landed face-first in the grass.

Air whooshed from my lungs. My nose burned. My vision blurred. Sunlight grew a tail that stretched across the yard. I raised my head and wiped my hand across my lip. It came back covered in blood. My breath returned with a gasp to wrench a scream from my throat.

Mom examined my face and determined nothing was broken. She led me to the recliner, gave me a bag of frozen peas, and convinced me to lie still. She let me stay awake past bedtime so she could watch for a concussion that never emerged.

The next morning, purple flares ringed my eyes. My face swelled to the point that our neighbor saw me in our yard and asked if I was visiting from out of town. The Trench Coat Guys bore smug smiles.

My face didn't improve much before the parade. My Dorothy Hamill haircut couldn't hide the damage. Mom assured me no one would notice, but I insisted on wearing adult sunglasses that Julie and I used for playing dress-up. When gray clouds hovered over the parade loading zone, the world looked shrouded in shadow, but I wouldn't leave the glasses behind.

My teacher lifted me onto the float, handed me a Styrofoam lollipop that was part of our costume, and signaled to the driver that we were ready.

A stalled vehicle near the front of the parade stranded our float on the viaduct's peak. Yahoos lined the pedestrian path on either side wearing frayed Wrangler jeans, Stetson hats, and boots with toes pointier than Mom's church shoes. Muscles bulged beneath shirts unsnapped to chest-level. Beer sloshed from red plastic cups they raised overhead. The float put me at eye level, inches from their outstretched arms.

Their rowdiness grew with their impatience at the parade's standstill. They mimed twirling lassos to catch and reel us in. My sunglasses drew their attention. They pointed at me, laughed, and begged me to take the glasses off. "Let's see those eyes, baby!"

They gestured to my swollen face and howled, "Look at those pudgy cheeks! I'm gonna climb up there and pinch 'em!"

Another Yahoo added, "You've been sucking on that lollipop, haven't you, roly-poly? You can suck on my lollipop, too." His buddies slapped him on the back as they doubled over with laughter.

I sat stone-faced and pretended not to hear, but tears collected on my lower lids. The Trench Coat Guys delighted in my pathetic attempt to hide behind sunglasses. They tallied each deficit the Yahoos pointed out: *clumsy, chubby, shy, dumb.* I absorbed these into my identity as readily as my body absorbed nutrients and stored fat.

Though the Yahoos were probably harmless, their slurred voices marked them as unpredictable. Their behavior seemed unconstrained by rules I thought universal. I didn't understand lust but recognized its mocking cousin in their comments. Fear, like the sunglasses, tinted my vision, convincing me that malice glowed in their glazed eyes. They seemed like animals teetering on the blade-thin edge of bloodlust. I longed to disappear, but flesh rolling over my leotard's sequined bust confirmed that there was too much of me to conceal. *If I were smaller, they wouldn't see me.*

As if that idea gave our float the push it needed to get over the viaduct's hump, our wheels began rolling. From the summit, I watched vehicles ahead of ours stutter forward and willed them to keep going. They must have because that's where my parade memory crashes into memories linked to it by theme rather than chronology.

I sensed a shift in adult conversation and looked up from competing with Julie and Beth to see who could cross the cobblestone street without stepping on any cracks. Three Yahoos had stopped Beth's mom, Joan, in the middle of an empty downtown road while we ran errands. They commented on her t-shirt and sneakers, then cited a Nebraskaland Days' rule: Anyone caught not wearing Western clothes could be thrown in the dunk tank.

Yahoo One gestured over his shoulder at a metal cattle trough hauled into the town square and filled to the brim.

Joan played along, laughing even as the Yahoos reached for her. When Yahoo One grabbed her arm, she realized they weren't kidding.

"Guys, these little girls are with me. I'll give you a raincheck, OK?"

Yahoo One ran his eyes over our threesome as if assessing how far he could chuck us. "The girls ain't dressed right either."

I sucked in a breath but said nothing.

Yahoo Two grasped Joan's other arm. Yahoo Three bent to grab her ankles. "We'll just carry ya over there," Yahoo One explained. Something about his smile reminded me of spiders wriggling from a nest.

"Hey, c'mon. Not right now." Joan pulled her arms free. Her purse swung wildly from her elbow. Her face had paled since I'd first looked up.

"Leave my mom alone!" Beth wailed. Tears rolled down her cheeks.

"I don't wanna go in the tank!" Julie howled.

I went mute. My voice had vanished, and I wished I could, too.

"Aw, shit," Yahoo One griped.

Julie cried harder, assuming bad words meant bad guys with bad intentions.

The Yahoos took in Julie's blue eyes, wide with fear, and her halo of white-blonde hair. They watched Beth shudder trying to draw breath.

"Don't cry!" Yahoo Two said. "We're just teasing. See?" He held up his hands like a bank robber caught in the act.

"Great! Now look what you've done." Joan laughed, but her voice shook. "Thanks a lot!"

"We're just havin' fun," Yahoo One replied. He let go of Joan's arm. "You gals have a nice day."

The Yahoos disappeared as quickly as if Joan had waved a wand.

Joan dug Kleenexes from her purse and doled them out. "It's OK. They're gone. No one's going in the tank." She looked us over, noting cheeks reddened by tears and sun. "Tell you what," she said. "Let's get some ice cream."

I didn't know, as Joan protected and comforted us that afternoon, that my family would soon return the favor.

"He has a gun!" Joan yelled when she burst through our home's back door.

Dad slammed and locked the door behind her, then rushed from the family room.

What is Joan doing here? Why is she so scared? I'd never imagined the woman who was so brave when facing down Yahoos, so funny when letting us eat potato chips as an after-school snack, so gentle when giving me my first perm, could look as wild as she did that afternoon. I hunted for clues as to why Mom had called Julie and me in from the backyard so early, but I couldn't find any. Nothing about the scene made sense to my six-year-old brain.

"What's—"

"Shhh. Not now," Mom told me. She checked the lock on the patio's sliding glass door and pulled the blinds. "I'll explain later. Don't go near any windows."

Dad returned carrying a BB gun—a hand-me-down from Grandpa and the only weapon my parents ever owned. He stood at the door Joan had come through, peering out at the street through its half-moon window.

"Stay back," Dad said. He held out his arm to herd me away from the door.

I gathered from the adults' whispered comments that the situation had something to do with Beth's dad, Cal. He definitely scared me, but I hadn't realized he could scare adults. When I crossed Glenn Rose Avenue to visit Beth on summer afternoons,

Cal was often dozing on the couch or entombed in the master bedroom with its shades drawn. Some days he sat at the kitchen table drinking beer and chain smoking with a buddy. Words I'd never heard but knew enough not to repeat exploded like landmines in their conversation. I prayed they wouldn't notice when I tiptoed down the hall to the bathroom or, worse, when Beth and I walked past the kitchen going from her room to the rec room.

I hadn't been so lucky one afternoon the year before.

"Hey, c'mere," Cal commanded when he saw us.

I took two steps past the line where the living room carpet met the kitchen linoleum.

"Closer." Smoke curled from Cal's nose. He tapped his cigarette in a metal ashtray, then let it dangle from two fingers and gestured with it as he spoke. "Let me see your wrist."

I held out my freckled arm, surprised it didn't tremble.

"Nice bracelet."

"Uh, thank you." I swallowed hard.

Cal's buddy slouched, arms crossed, on the opposite side of the table. He peered at me from beneath a ball cap's brim and smirked like he anticipated a punchline.

"That's Beth's bracelet. Did you steal it?" Cal's black eyes bore through the distance and nailed my feet to the linoleum.

"N-No! She s-s-said I could wear it."

I sensed Beth nodding behind me.

Cal pointed at me with his cigarette, wielding it like a weapon. "Are you gonna give it back?"

I nodded.

"You better. 'Cause if you don't..."

My eyes must have bulged. Cal knocked my shoulder with the back of his hand and cracked a grin.

"I'm just kidding." He winked.

I flashed a wobbly smile. He took a long drag, squinted, tugged the cigarette from his lips and blew smoke toward the ceiling. He nodded toward the hallway. "Go on, get outta here."

Beth and I ran for the rec room.

I don't remember mentioning that encounter, but not long after, Dad announced that Julie and I could only play at Beth's house when Cal wasn't home. If he arrived while we were there, we were to leave immediately. And we were never, under any circumstances, to get in a vehicle he was driving. I worried about being rude and how Cal might react if I left suddenly, so I learned to check for his dark gray pickup in the driveway before visiting Beth.

A few weeks after he questioned me about the bracelet, Beth and I peddled our bikes in lazy circles around a neighboring cul-de-sac, daring each other to pop a wheelie or ride with no hands. Her dad paused before turning his truck into their driveway and pulled up beside me instead. I rested my foot on the center median's curb, then realized I was trapped between it and the truck. I clenched my handlebars' rubber grips so tightly my fingers ached.

Cal's words elude me, but his message was clear: What happened at his house was none of Dad's business.

"Your Dad better watch his back. You tell him I said so."

I nodded.

Cal gave a sarcastic, two-finger salute and hit the gas so the truck's engine roared. He whipped around the median and pulled from the cul-de-sac with screeching tires.

I didn't know then that Cal also worked for UPRR but on the opposite side of a picket line from Dad. Cal was union labor; Dad was management. Cal was an alcoholic; Dad was an addiction counselor. When the union went on strike, Dad had to fill in as a scab or lose his job. When an employee was suspended for violating the company's sobriety policy, Dad determined if and when that employee returned to work. I just happened to stand in the crossfire.

My memory of what happened after Joan burst through our door is hazy. From the adult's comments, I pictured Cal's truck cruising past our house, its bed weaving with the sway of a tail through water, its headlights eyeing prey, its chrome glinting like teeth. At least once he braked at the end of our driveway and stared through his open window to size up our redbrick cube and white garage. He spotted Dad's blue eyes peering through the half-moon glass, calm but steely with resolve, and decided not to strike.

A sheriff picked Joan up from our house and accompanied her home, where she packed suitcases and moved to a motel. I never saw Beth again.

Cal, the Yahoos, and The Trench Coat Guys had buried themselves in my memory by the time I began my first semester as a college professor in fall 2003, but eating disorder treatment revealed that their impression was indelible. I would recognize its imprint in my fear of being seen, in the standard of perfection I set for myself and assumed others held, and in my apprehension toward men in positions of authority. Unfortunately, keeping my new job hinged on my first teaching observation by the male Dean of my division within the college. What I didn't know was that the experience would set a stone on the scale tipping precariously toward my January 2004 commitment to Regions' psych ward.

The day my observation was scheduled, my Master's degree was barely five months old, my teaching career only two months long. I had no track record from which I could draw wisdom or confidence.

Perfectionism led me to overprepare, so I appeared robotic. Failure to trust my instincts prompted me to fill silences before I gave students time to think. But my worst mistake was not eating enough. Anorexic tendencies that had been building since high school were becoming all-consuming. Constant hunger and the occasional binges it triggered disrupted every part of my life, from sleep to social skills. My glucose-starved brain shorted out while the dean observed. I hesitated at the wrong times. I grappled for words. My hands trembled when I wrote on the whiteboard. Still, I didn't think it had been a complete disaster.

The Dean corrected that impression during my performance review two weeks later.

"Three students came in late." He paused to stare at me from beneath a gray crewcut and shaggy eyebrows. "One walked the entire perimeter of the room and crossed in front of you *while you were speaking.* He practically climbed over other students to get a front-row-center seat. That's unacceptable! You need to nip that behavior in the bud. You should have put a stop to it on Day One. Lock the door once class starts if you have to."

I gritted my teeth to prevent them from chattering, as happened when I was nervous, angry, or exhausted. All three applied.

I'd wanted to throttle the student who'd walked in front of me. I'd told my class the day before that the dean would be visiting. When they'd asked: "So, we should be on our best behavior?" I'd laughed along, relieved that they understood the visit's significance and would have my back.

I didn't bother explaining that along with presenting a logistical nightmare, locking the door could cause irreparable harm. The class he'd observed included a lot of at-risk students. One impediment, like a locked door, was all the reason they needed to drop the class or quit college.

The dean was right, though. The student in question had been a troublemaker from the start. He was a bombast who rarely let me finish a sentence in one-on-one conversations, so I'd avoided confronting him. I simply didn't have the energy. Standing before a roomful of eyes while internal battles raged took every molecule of energy I could dredge up. Most weekday evenings I could do little more than lie catatonic in front of the TV.

"And your voice doesn't carry," the dean added. "You need to project. Walk around the room instead of writing on the board."

"OK."

He seemed ready to dismiss me, so I thanked him for his suggestions.

"Don't thank me. If you don't exude authority, students won't respect you. And they won't learn from someone they don't respect. I expect to see improvement when I observe you in the spring."

"I understand." I shook his hand and headed to my office.

I was shattered. I longed to go home and crash, but I had another class to teach. Panic swelled in my chest. My pulse beat in my temple, accompanied by a phrase that goose-stepped through my mind: *I can't. I can't. I can't.*

I'd known my first semester teaching would be challenging, but I hadn't anticipated how much propping up and pushing students required—or how much that would drain me. I'd barely slept for two months. No matter how exhausted my body felt at night, my nerve endings jangled loudest when I lay still.

Sitting behind my desk, I fantasized about donuts iced with chocolate, caramel stretching from Snickers bars—foods strictly against The Rules. I couldn't remember if there were vending machines on campus. I'd lived according to The Rules for so long that I'd developed junk food blinders, but when I felt depleted, breaking The Rules was all I could think about. I switched to imagining a red, plastic spoon ferrying mouthfuls of Dairy Queen Blizzard to melt on my tongue.

Get it together. I tried to picture students in my upcoming class I knew would participate without coercion, but fear was a riptide. It kept pulling my mind toward worst-case scenarios, drowning me in cravings for chocolate. *I can't. I can't. I can't.*

Minutes later, I hung up the phone, already second-guessing the message I'd left. Contacting Sara outside of the weekly sessions I paid for seemed like stealing. Still, I wondered how often she checked messages and hoped she'd call before my class.

I jumped at the phone's burr.

"I'm sorry to bug you," I said when The Emily Program appeared on caller ID and I picked up the receiver.

"No, no. It's OK. I'm glad you called. You can always call."

I couldn't keep my voice from quivering as I described my panic and fatigue. "I don't know how I'll make it through class."

"OK. Boil down your day to what you absolutely have to do so you won't get fired. What's the minimum you can do this afternoon?"

I ticked through a mental list, already calmer for having something other than panic to think about. "I could have students do a writing exercise and then leave campus as soon as class ends."

"Good. Do that. Nothing has to be perfect. Just get through the day. No judgment; go easy on yourself. Then, go home and relax. If you feel anxious, ask yourself, 'What's the minimum I have to do?' and then do only that."

"OK."

"I'll see you tomorrow, right?"

I nodded, then remembered she couldn't see me. "Yes. Thank you. That helps a lot. I'm sorry I bothered you. Thanks so much for calling back."

"Call again if you need to."

"I will."

I wouldn't, though. Once seemed like enough imposition.

I spent the 24 hours until my next appointment beating myself up for failing to function like a normal person.

Though seven years had passed, Sara's words quelled my panic about finishing Seventh Farm's 2011 show. *What's the minimum I have to do to get through this?* The question snapped me out of the paralysis I'd battled all week. *This is a tiny competition for my recreational hobby; what in God's name am I so worried about?* I laughed when I heard Dad's inflection in the question. He had often been the one who talked me down from mental ledges in my teens and 20s. He knew from personal experience what it felt like to teeter on that edge.

Shake it off. Big deal.

I turned the blinders I'd once developed for junk food on the judge and audience. I treated the following rounds as a chance to experiment and learn. *After all, I have nothing to lose.* I couldn't fall any further in the rankings than last place.

Afterward, Tom said he noticed the change in my riding immediately.

"You seemed more relaxed with each round. You ride well when you're not freaking out."

I couldn't help laughing as I lifted sweaty saddle pads from Buck's back. "Thanks," I replied, a wry twist in my voice.

I collected my ribbons: one white for fourth place, two red for second, one blue for first. I didn't care about them and gave them to my nieces to play with, but I was proud of having defeated perfectionism. (Well, mostly.)

Ultimately, riding in the show boosted my confidence. I'd gotten the desired responses from Buck while under pressure, which meant I was more skilled than I'd thought. I'd proven that one shortfall didn't negate my worth. One bite didn't guarantee a binge. One setback didn't derail a journey. But I had a lot more to learn about riding, about falling, rising, and feeling comfortable in my skin. And I'd have to learn quickly because one week later, I'd face down a fiery Thoroughbred named Angie.

Lisa displays her ribbons from Seventh Farm's show in August 2011 © Julie Dettinger

Chapter 3 - Angie: Take Up Space

Seventh Farm Riding School, August 2011

A crack split the air. It ricocheted off the arena's metal rafters and bounced between pine-paneled walls until absorbed by the sand beneath our boots. I startled. I'd been lulled into a daze by cicadas' droning and August's humidity, wondering how much lesson time remained. Jeneen's explanation of groundwork was interesting, but I didn't want to spend the only time I could devote to horses standing beside them; I wanted to *ride.*

My impatience to get off the ground was heightened by my pairing with Angie, a Thoroughbred I'd yearned to ride since my first lesson. I liked Buck, but Angie's trot was the fastest of the beginner horses, and she fulfilled a childhood fantasy by looking like Black Beauty. She'd been Liz's horse until she'd aged out of competing and transitioned into lessons. I'd heard that she was high-strung and hot, but she struck me as impatient rather than crazy—a smart, Type-A personality made anxious by any being who didn't know what they were doing as well as she did. I liked her confidence even more than I liked her black polka-dots; they were sprinkled across a white half-moon on her right rear foot, as if she'd requested a feminine detail to set her apart from her literary counterpart.

Angie startled at the crack, too. I didn't understand why Jeneen had smacked her boot with a riding crop to create such an ominous sound, especially given what she'd explained while we'd groomed our horses minutes earlier.

"Your ride begins long before you get in the saddle," she'd said, opening a bottle of root beer—her traditional post-ride drink. "It begins as soon as the horse sees you."

She'd leaned an elbow on the crosstie post beside me, sweat beading along graceful collar bones her green tank top exposed. "Horses bond by grooming each other. When you brush them, you're mimicking that behavior. The way you groom and tack your horse sets a tone that affects your ride."

I'd nodded, then broken eye contact to trade a brush with stiff orange bristles for one with finer green bristles, happy to move on to my favorite part of grooming. Dust the first brush had brought to the surface had flown from Angie's coat with every stroke. Soon, her hair had glimmered like onyx.

"You generate emotional energy with every thought, and horses can sense it. They're extremely sensitive to energy. It's like they're covered with antennae."

I'd perked up at the reference to antennae but slumped when Jeneen added, "If you're uncertain, the horse knows it. Horses are less likely to test you if you're confident and relaxed."

Easier said than done. Thanks to a week of horse camp when I was 12, horses didn't scare me the way they did some people, but I'd forgotten how intimidating their large heads and hooved feet could be, how unpredictable any animal appeared when unfamiliar. I had been sure Angie sensed my insecurity. She could hardly have missed that my brushstrokes paused when she twitched a flank or that I stepped back reflexively when she stomped to rid her leg of a fly.

"Horses only seem spooky until you understand that their status as prey animals shapes their every thought. Humans are predators, as are all animals whose eyes are in the front, rather than on the sides, of their head. Horses have no natural defense but to flee, so they interpret anyone—or anything, for that matter—unfamiliar as a threat."

Instead of tacking up, we'd hooked lead ropes to the horses' halters and followed Jeneen into the arena. Then we'd stood in a semi-circle and sweltered while Jeneen explained why we were learning groundwork.

"Horses communicate with their bodies. They establish relationships by giving and taking personal space. It's like a game of chicken. If Buck gets Angie to move, he's the leader. Bill can make Buck move, so Bill is higher than Buck in the hierarchy. The pony is at the bottom."

"Is the bigger horse always the leader?" a classmate had asked.

"No. Take Penny, for example."

We'd turned to look at the dirt paddock, just visible through the arena's garage door. Penny, a petite bay mare I'd heard Jeneen call a Morgan, had approached the trough, where a Thoroughbred's neck pulsed as gulps of water traveled its length. The Thoroughbred tensed. When Penny pinned her ears, the Thoroughbred backed away, water dripping from his lips.

"Penny is barely bigger than the pony," Jeneen had said to reclaim our attention, "but she's the second-highest female in the herd because she's fierce, while Charlie's near the bottom."

We'd looked at Charlie, a Thoroughbred whose cinnamon-colored coat I'd learned was called "chestnut" in horse lingo. He stood beside my classmate with his eyelids at half-mast. Although he was Angie's size and had galloped across the countryside leaping hedges and creeks before coming to Seventh Farm, he was the sweetest horse I'd met. I could see how that would make him a patsy in a culture whose currency was dominance. It also explained why his hide bore so many scars.

"A clear hierarchy keeps the herd safe. There's no time to decide who's in charge or which way to run when a predator appears. If everyone follows the leader, the group flees as a unit. Predators get confused by all that movement and struggle to pick off individuals.

"That kind of coordination requires close relationships. It can look like herdmates read each other's minds, but they're sensing emotional energy and reading body language."

Angie had heaved a sigh and shifted her weight from one back foot to the other. I'd imagined her annoyed at Jeneen's spilling of herd secrets and bitten my lip to keep from laughing.

"When you ride a horse, you're taking her away from the herd, so she feels vulnerable. You have to stand in as herd leader. Believe me, you don't want to ride a horse who doesn't trust you or thinks she outranks you. Convince the horse you're the leader before you get in the saddle and you'll have a better ride. I'm going to remind Angie that I'm the leader by getting her to move using nothing but energy."

Jeneen had unhooked Angie's lead rope and walked toward the mare's chest. Angie backed up. When Jeneen stopped, Angie halted.

Jeneen had dug a line in the sand with her heel. "I don't want Angie to cross this line because she'll enter my personal space. I'll keep her behind it while I show you something called 'disengaging the hindquarters.'"

"Horses pay more attention to our core, which is this area between your hipbones, than anywhere else. I'll send energy from my core toward the part of Angie's body I want to move and step in the direction I want her to go."

Jeneen had walked toward Angie's right hip, and Angie had swung her backend left, crossing one back hoof over the other.

"Disengaging the hindquarters is a great way to clarify your relationship. It also calms a horse if she's scared because it grounds her in her body. She has to concentrate on which foot to move where and when, so she forgets that she's freaking out.

"Angie's really good at groundwork, as you can see."

Jeneen had led Angie forward, backward, and sideways without any physical contact. She and Angie had appeared to waltz. I'd been entranced. I had started scripting how I'd describe the magic to my sister when Jeneen had smacked the crop against her boot to create that ominous *crack!*

Angie's ears sprang to attention. Her eyes widened.

Jeneen marched forward as if she intended to plow through a wall. Angie leapt backward. Then they waltzed again. Their dance had new subtlety.

"See that? *That's* what you want. Angie can do groundwork in her sleep, and she's been demonstrating in classes all week, so she was on autopilot. She wasn't truly paying attention. Now, she's keyed in on me and waiting for my cue. If I go over here, her eyes follow."

Jeneen walked to the far wall. Angie watched her every move, ears pricked, eyes focused, weight on her toes.

"Increasing your energy's intensity is like turning up your voice's volume. You don't start by yelling, but if someone doesn't hear you, you talk louder, right?"

We nodded.

"Now Angie's matching my energy. That's how your horse should be when you ride. A checked-out horse may not respond the way you need her to, and that can be dangerous."

The two waltzed again, morphing from teenagers at the Prom to Fred and Ginger in *Cheek to Cheek*.

"Ah, yes! See how Angie's licking her lips? She's happy because she feels connected to me. She knows I'm a strong leader who will keep her safe. It might seem counterintuitive, but the more sternly you remain in charge, the happier your horse will be."

Jeneen spun to face us, smiled, and raised her eyebrows. "Now it's your turn."

Oh.

I looked at Angie's 1100-pound body: her muscled chest, brawny neck, powerful haunches, and metal shoes. One kick could end me. Getting her to move without physical contact seemed like using The Force, but I'd had no Jedi training. I could barely take charge of humans in the classroom, where I could rely on language and a professional title. Now, I'd have to do it using my personal kryptonite: my body.

Jeneen stared at me expectantly, her auburn ponytail tidy despite having been inside a helmet 30 minutes ago. "Go on, just like I showed you."

Angie blinked. I sensed awareness behind her eyes, but I couldn't decipher what she thought or how she felt. That left me disoriented. I'd volunteered at a St. Paul animal shelter long enough that I could intuit messages from dogs, cats, and rabbits like we belonged to the same herd. Horses spoke an alien language. My stomach lurched. Who was I to make Angie move? Why would she? Why *should* she?

I'm the mov-ee, never the mov-er.

The thought came out of nowhere, as if spoken by an external voice. It triggered a memory. Just as falling from Smitty's back would later recall my first car accident, doubting I could make Angie move recalled my body being steered by a meaty hand on my back, a voice snarling in my ear, "Get out of the way!"

I don't remember when that phrase became a refrain, but in my memory, it was coupled to my brother's birth, which had felt like the jolt of a new freight car shoving me down the line.

The summer before I turned six, I woke to sunlight streaming through pink gingham fluttering in the window above my bed. Julie rolled to face me in an identical bed four feet away. Something felt different. The house stood still, silent. Mom hadn't come in singing "Rise and shine!"

I reached beneath the covers for Blankie and found him, a handful of fraying yarn flattened by my body overnight. I lifted him in the air and smiled at Julie. She giggled and held up her matching blankie.

From down the hall, I heard a chair scoot across the kitchen linoleum. I hopped from bed to investigate. Julie followed. We trailed our fingers along the textured hallway wall, ankles peeking from our identical nightgowns' scalloped hems. I peered around the corner and saw Dad reading a newspaper. Steam rose from a Union Pacific mug beside the paper.

Julie looked at me, her eyes wide. *Where's Mom? Why is Dad home on a weekday?*

I shrugged.

As if he could read our thoughts, Dad turned in his chair. His face shone from a fresh shave. His hair was parted, still too wet from the shower for its natural wave to rise. He wore a golf shirt, not a dress shirt and tie. No suitcoat hung on the front closet's doorknob. No briefcase and trench coat lay across the piano bench. *What's going on?*

Dad beckoned us forward. "Girls, do you know what happened overnight?"

I recognized the voice, but it didn't belong to the bedtime enforcing, lawnmower pushing, fishhook baiting, Dad I knew. It sounded like Winnie the Pooh when he discovered a jar of honey.

Dad's smile broadened to reveal a rare glimpse of small, square teeth. The air around him felt thick, smelled sweetly of grape jelly and aftershave.

"Do you know what Mom did last night?" Dad asked.

We shook our heads.

"She had a baby!"

Julie and I gasped. We hopped up and down, then danced on our tiptoes.

"And it's a *boy!*" Dad's smile increased in wattage; his aura pulsed. Something about his joy and its connection to the word 'boy' made my stomach flop like a fish out of water.

We dressed, and Dad drove us to visit Mom. Children couldn't go past the lobby, so I swung my feet from a waiting room chair and watched my Mary Janes blur. It seemed like ages before Mom emerged from the elevator cradling a blue bundle.

"Meet your new brother," said the nurse pushing Mom's wheelchair. "His name is James Patrick, just like your Dad's!" She stopped the chair and locked its wheels.

Mom smiled at us. Her brown irises looked bigger and brighter without her glasses.

The nurse said, "Your daddy was so happy to have a boy that he cried tears of joy." She glanced at Dad. "Nine pounds, nine ounces: He'll be a star linebacker!" She and Dad laughed. Then she winked at me. I wanted to stick out my tongue, but that would be Bad. I smoothed my blue dress over my thighs instead.

Throughout the following weeks, adults we saw at all the usual places, like church and the grocery store, proclaimed how exciting it was that we had a boy. They predicted playing catch, driving to Lincoln for Cornhusker football games, rebuilding Dad's Lionel train set, and earning athletic scholarships for college. They brought the baby gifts for being born and then for being circumcised. They reminded us that the baby would save our last name from extinction—a threat daughters posed when they followed two paternal generations of only children.

James did all that just by being a boy. I seethed. Then I fretted. How could I compete?

I didn't consciously connect that question to my claims as we grew that James and I mixed like lions and hyenas. I didn't have it in mind when I chose to attend an all-women's college or keep my name as a married woman. But an impulse deep in my reptilian brain linked James's arrival with what I interpreted as my fall from Dad's grace.

I also associated James' arrival with Dad's development of a temper, though that was likely a coincidence because I don't remember much of Dad or anyone else from before I turned five.

Dad's temper was a geyser like those we'd see on a family vacation to Yellowstone National Park. I often wished it took after Old Faithful because then I could predict when he would erupt. Instead, it resembled Grand or Great Fountain geyser: ever-present but rarely predictable. He presented as perpetually jovial, but pressure built beneath the surface until something set him off: a bad day at the office, a leaky toilet in the bathroom, a Cornhuskers' fumble on the 20-yard line, a daughter's spilled juice at the dinner table. Dad was never abusive, but he yelled with such volume and vitriol—and over such minor infractions—that I thought my skin would blister.

I didn't understand until adulthood that geysers don't form overnight; in some cases, their origins can be traced to the earth's formation. That was the case with Dad's anger. Its temperature began rising when his mom, Julia, became ill and moved to her parents' house. Pressure built when Julia died, leaving Dad to be raised by a grieving father and domineering grandmother. Steam formed in seminary school when Dad became an adult at age 14.

Eight hundred miles from home, Dad lived in a dorm room called a "cell" and followed a daily schedule that consisted of Mass, school, prayer, study, more prayer, and, occasionally, sports. Rituals designed to impart humility included self-flagellation, meals eaten in silence, and turns lying across the dining hall threshold so classmates stepped over (or, more often, on) their peers while going to dinner.

Graduation from the seminary offered only a fraction more freedom, as priests served when, where, and how their bishop dictated.

Civilian life reduced former sources of pressure but added new ones. Dad's North Platte job set him between a rock and a hard place, as Cal's animosity attested. Some nights he complained about his day from the second he stripped off his trench coat to the moment he granted my request to be excused from the dinner table. On those nights, I did my best to stay out of sight because nothing set him off like bad behavior.

The first and most frightening eruption that I remember happened not long before Joan burst through our back door shouting that Cal had a gun. I stood shin deep in our plastic wading pool as frigid water spilled from a hose to fill it. When my feet grew numb, I leapt from the pool and ran a lap around the yard, per the rules of a game Julie, Beth, and I had invented. I should have sensed seismic tremors in Dad's grumbling about grass blades sticking to our feet and ending up in the pool, but I didn't read the signs.

An older girl I recognized from school called to me from the sidewalk as I ran my lap. We met on opposite sides of the fence. She whispered through the chain link, "Tell Beth to get her ass out of your yard."

High on sun and fun, I ran toward the pool, spraying the phrase across the yard.

Mom sat up in her lawn chair, jostling James, who slept in her arms beneath the patio roof. "Wha-a-a-a-t?"

Dad leapt from the picnic table. "What did you just say?" He yelled. "Get over here!"

I froze mid-step. Fear rusted my joints. I wanted to rewind time the way I rewound my Olivia Newton John cassette when I missed my favorite song.

Dad stormed into the yard, grabbed me by the arm, and yanked me into the family room. I shivered in its absence of sun.

Dad seemed to vibrate. He pulled me through the house by the arm. I stumbled, uncertain where we were headed and unable to keep pace with his longer legs. He hauled me into the bathroom, cranked on the shower, and ordered me in. I registered something about never saying "ass" again. Was that what I'd done wrong?

Two smacks echoed off the tile. Their sound sickened me, disturbed me more than the sting on my butt. I stepped beneath the spray and sputtered when my shuddering lungs inhaled water. Then I sobbed.

I spent the afternoon in bed, confused and bored. At one point, I stood on the bed and talked to my sister through the window but lay down quickly after a reprimand. Shrieks and giggles filtered through the screen. Tears leaked from my eyes, tickled my ears, and dripped onto my pillow.

From that point on, I preferred to stay silent as well as invisible, and I thought twice before I spoke. But I couldn't prevent every mishap. Muddy shoes, toys left on the floor, my shyness when introduced to an adult: I never knew which transgression would turn Dad's face purple with rage. Sometimes, I infuriated him by doing nothing, like the times my

Barbie's adventures were interrupted by a voice that growled louder than the lawn mower, "Lisa, move these swings so I can mow beneath them. Now!"

I'd have been a nervous child in school regardless of parenting, but Dad's temper didn't help. I recognized my experiences in *Wasted: A Memoir of Anorexia and Bulimia*, where Marya Hornbacher wrote that trying to be perfect enough to please everyone gave her a "borderline hysterical anxiety level about school"[5].

She and I suffered crippling, self-imposed pressure every weekday morning. My skin prickled with what felt like beetles crawling on it while I dressed. Angst made it difficult to swallow the fruit and hardboiled egg Mom set out for breakfast. By the time I grabbed my Holly Hobbie lunchbox, my hands trembled.

Stepping across the classroom's threshold was like setting foot in a country whose culture I had only glimpsed through a window. I couldn't figure out why some peers bullied kids who seemed nice, if shy or awkward. Our teacher snapped at the whole class when a few kids misbehaved. I took her comments personally, strove to do better, and grew rattled when my efforts didn't staunch her irritation. I wished to be invisible, figuring that if school worked like home, the less notice I drew, the less trouble I'd attract.

Mornings generally passed without incident, but after lunch, the walls closed in. Open windows didn't help; they merely let in flies that buzzed overhead, excited by the scent of sweaty bodies and leftover food rotting in lunchboxes. My teacher's gray hair frizzed into tighter and tighter coils, as did her temper.

Some afternoons, I felt so trapped I couldn't slow my breathing. I ducked my head to hide tears that splashed onto my

5. Marya Hornbacher, *Wasted: A Memoir of Anorexia and Bulimia,* (New York: HarperPernnial, 2009), 28.

jeans because crying angered my teacher. She always caught me anyway. Eventually, she sent me to the principal. He didn't know what to do with me either, so he set up a meeting with Mom. They agreed I could walk home for lunch three days a week if I stopped crying. I relished having a break from all those eyes looking at me in the classroom, on the playground, and in the cafeteria. The peacefulness of eating lunch at home with Mom and Julie, serenaded by cicadas who left me beautifully delicate, translucent shells hooked to backyard poplars like gifts, calmed me enough that I could ride out the afternoon.

My desire to remain invisible intensified as I drew more of Dad's ire by doing nothing. In public, my presence alone was enough to anger him.

"Lisa! Get out of that guy's way!" Dad snarled, referring to someone standing motionless four feet from where I stood. He turned to the guy, shook his head, and said, as deferentially as a servant, "Sorry about that."

Whether we picked up nails at the hardware store or threaded crowds at the county fair, Dad grabbed my shirt's shoulder seam and pulled me aside before it was clear someone might need to get past.

Sometimes, Dad merely volleyed the phrase, "Watch yourself," in my direction.

That lighthearted variation burned in my gut like a briquette. I hated its seeming banality, its appearance of being nothing more than a caring parent's attempt to raise a considerate child. That's probably what it was, but it came across as a warning wrapped in colored paper. *Watch myself... what? I'm not doing anything.*

Dad ensured I wouldn't get in others' way on Sunday mornings by placing a palm on my lower back and using it like a rudder to steer me in wide arcs around adults gathered in the foyer before Mass. As if, shy as I was, I had any intention of going near them.

Getting out of the way became even more confusing when I attempted anything athletic.

"I'll do it," Dad replied to the referee's request for a sideline judge at one of my soccer games in third grade. My teammates' parents chatted and laughed while setting up lawn chairs on the sidelines, but Dad leaned in at the edge of our huddle, hands stuffed in his Dockers' pockets. His windbreaker rippled in synch with my nylon shorts as wind whipped across the plain. My teammates and I turned our backs to gales that blew hair in our eyes and set red corner flags flapping. Goosebumps rose on my forearms.

My coach didn't object to Dad's offer, but he cringed. I toed the grass with my cleat, dread building in my chest. The referee handed Dad a red flag he was to raise when the ball went out of bounds.

"Let's have a good game, girls," the referee said.

We took our positions, and the whistle sounded.

Our opponent's center-forward reached the ball first. She dribbled toward my position at halfback. I waited for her to come near so I could steal the ball, but she faked right and swerved left, catching me off-balance and zipping past.

"Come on, Lisa! Pay attention! Don't just stand there!" Dad yelled.

Am I supposed to get in her way?

I looked to the sideline for confirmation. Dad stood even with the ball, having followed it down the field, his feet an inch from the sideline. I wished he'd sit down and relax like the other parents, who sipped cocoa from travel mugs while they cheered or gossiped.

"Get moving!" Dad yelled. He tucked the red flag beneath one arm and waved me down the field with both hands.

I jogged toward the opponent dribbling the ball. Our fullback reached her before I did and booted the ball down the middle of the field.

"Pass it! *Pass* the ball! Don't just kick it down the field!" Dad shrieked.

When an opponent got around me once more, Dad griped, "Goll *Darn*-it, Lisa! What're you doing?! Play defense!"

"Goll darn-it?" an opponent sneered to her teammate.

The teammate snickered. "I know! If he's gonna yell like a psycho, he might as well cuss."

They laughed.

I hung my head.

I wanted to do the right thing, but the longer I played, the less certain I became of what that was.

The first half carried on as it had begun. Between shouting at my team to stop bunching up around the ball and play our positions, Dad ran along the sideline in a frenzy. His face turned crimson from exertion. Sweat poured down his temples. Each time the ball crossed our sideline, he launched the red flag so forcibly its nylon crackled.

During the second half, Dad abandoned yelling at the team for singling out individuals. Hearing him criticize my teammates felt like being roasted on a spit. I'd have to face some of them at school the next morning. Finally, a teammate's dad leaned forward in his chair and shouted, "Hey, Whalen! Don't yell at my daughter!" I wished a hole would open in the grass and swallow me.

The referee blew the whistle and ran to the sideline. He spoke quietly, but the wind carried his voice so that everyone heard him threaten to kick Dad off the field if he didn't settle down.

That wasn't Dad's first or last warning. I couldn't decide if I wanted him banned. Games were more fun when he wasn't there, but wanting him to go away seemed disloyal, shameful. Resenting him had to be a sin if the Sixth Commandment said I should honor my mother and father. I loved him and felt compelled to shield him from derision, but his behavior defied explanation. *What's the big deal? It's just a game.*

I quit soccer after a few seasons. So did my siblings. We quit softball and baseball, too, when Dad wasn't any calmer sitting behind a backstop.

With hindsight, I understood that Dad's ferocity about athletics was a holdover from seminary school. Sports had been the only outlet for young men steeped in hormones but expected to deny bodily urges, competitive but expected to put others ahead of themselves, rebellious but expected to embody humility. Combined with his early childhood and distance from home, where the seminary didn't allow students to visit for any reason, those pressures built up. Sports provided the only release valve.

Despite Dad's 5'7" height and husky build, he was spry into his late 60s. Buddies he saw at seminary reunions referred to him as a jock and recounted his clutch layups. No wonder remembering their pickup basketball games always made his blue eyes twinkle. No wonder he took his kids' athletic performance so seriously.

The message I interpreted was that physical exertion was less about fun or taking pleasure in my body than about striving, perfecting, enduring, and winning or losing. A person only earned approval by performing perfectly. That theme would pervade my approach to relationships as well as athletics, especially as the buildup to A.C. shifted into high gear shortly before I turned 16.

By my 15th summer, I'd quit sports. My friends worked jobs that I'd been rejected for because I'd be gone for a two-week vacation in July. My sister, Julie, spent June in Montana with her friend's family. The sophomore guy I'd dated that spring had stopped returning my calls. The notion that I'd been dumped was slowly dawning. Alone and lonely, I moped at home, feeling sorry for myself.

To combat boredom, I practiced my flute, plowed through novels from the library, and challenged my brother to Nintendo contests. I also snacked. Pretzels occupied my hands while James dominated at Super Mario Brothers. Popcorn accompanied movies. Banana bread topped with ice cream settled me for sleep. Bagels slathered in strawberry cream cheese filled the empty hours after Sunday Mass. The hand-to-mouth repetition of eating had a hypnotic effect. Rhythmic chewing distracted from unpleasant thoughts about my boyfriend's disinterest. Taste and texture muted worries about taking a sophomore honors English class in the fall.

I didn't think I was honors material. I feared the classroom would become one more arena where I embarrassed myself. Discovering Mr. Kolterman would be my honors English teacher had intensified my anxiety.

I'd known Mr. Kolterman by reputation before I'd started high school, where he became my homeroom teacher. I liked him. Everyone did. His boisterous warmth melted the chips on even the coolest senior boys' shoulders. He'd won me over permanently when he scoffed at forcing us to participate in the homeroom scooterball tournament. The thought of putting my butt on a tiny rolling platform and zinging around the gym with teams that included junior and senior guys had made my gut ache. Grateful I didn't have to endure that, I continued skulking through homeroom every morning like a ghost, hiding in carrels with my face buried in a book, struck mute by sharing an open forum with cheerleaders and upperclassmen. I'd been half-surprised Mr. Kolterman knew my name, when he'd called it to hand over my sophomore class schedule that spring. He'd distributed schedules with drama befitting his weekend community theater performances.

"Master Anderson," he'd begun in a sonorous bass voice. Then, like an oracle, he'd bestowed the junior jock's carbon copy like the fate it represented in our teenage minds. I waited an eternity as he worked his way through the alphabetical stack. When he reached the bottom, he spun in his chair to face me. He narrowed his eyes and flashed a ghoulish smile. Then he'd held out my copy and adopted Dracula's accent to boom, "Wellll-commme!" and cackle like the unhinged voice that ended Michael Jackson's "Thriller." I'd scanned my sheet. There it was: sophomore honors English with Mr. Kolterman, the toughest teacher in the district.

The only thing that made me gulp harder was upcoming auditions for Westside's Warrior Concert Band. I'd been the only ninth-grade flutist accepted, which placed a target on my back for the upcoming year.

When I ate, those worries fell away. That was part of the reason I took a break from videogames with my brother to make a late lunch one June afternoon. Not long after, I licked grease from my lips, a remnant of the grilled cheese sandwich I'd just eaten, and stood over the stove again, enjoying the icy breeze blowing from a vent near my bare feet. I adjusted the burner's heat and hummed Super Mario Brothers' theme song.

Mom walked past with a laundry basket but then stopped, backed up, and turned to face me. "Two sandwiches?"

I looked down at buttered bread browning in the skillet. Sliced cheese lay in its plastic wrapper on the counter, ready to melt and ooze from between toasted crusts. My mouth watered. "Yeah. What? I'll clean up when I'm done."

"But two sandwiches...?"

My face burned. I felt a little sick. Why *was* I making a second sandwich? I hadn't been that hungry for the first. It had tasted good, so I'd thought, *Why not have another?* Now, that seemed gluttonous.

"I didn't mean anything. I'm just surprised. You don't usually eat that much."

Don't I? I wasn't sure. I'd never thought about it.

Weight had never crossed my mind. Once I'd lost the baby fat that had caught the Yahoos' attention, I'd always eaten what I wanted and still needed tucks sewn into waistbands so my jeans wouldn't fall down. I'd expected that would remain the same, even when my fifth-grade health teacher told us, "People who don't worry about weight as kids end up overweight as adults because they don't change their habits." Though I recognized myself in the first part, I dismissed the second. *That won't happen to me.*

"But I don't have to worry about what I eat, right?"

Mom's eyebrows shot up. She tilted her head and blew out, puckering her lips like a fish. "Well, don't fill up; we'll eat an early dinner." She carried the laundry down the hall.

As I considered Mom's comment, a photo from our recent family vacation (the one that prevented me from getting a job) flashed before my eyes. Something about it had rankled; I looked different but couldn't identify why. Julie and I stood on a sidewalk in blue soccer shorts, white t-shirts, tennis shoes, and mirrored sunglasses. Hairspray girded our architectural bangs, mine dull brown, Julie's sand-dollar white. Our smiles glinted with metal railroad tracks.

Suddenly, I knew what had bothered me. Flesh padded my chin and dimpled my thighs. My shirt bloused over a rounded belly. My calves looked like fence posts. The transformation had been slow, so I'd missed it. *I've gotten fat!* I was becoming the adult my health teacher had warned about. *That's why my boyfriend stopped calling!*

I snapped off the burner, threw out the toast, and returned the cheese to the refrigerator. Then I changed clothes and headed for a track near our house, determined to run two miles.

I'd shown promise as a distance runner before I quit the track team in middle school, so jogging two miles shouldn't have taxed me.

It did.

I fought to draw moisture-laden air into my lungs with every step. Every breath smelled of grass clippings spit by mowers whose roar rose and fell with my progress around the track. At the half-mile mark, I got a stitch in my side but ignored it.

When I finished the two miles, I thought again of my fence-post calves and ran sprints up the hill beside the track. My legs shook. My muscles turned to rubber. But once spent, I felt good. Really good. Like I'd shed some of the pollutants that made me too much, that made me Bad.

After showering, I weighed myself: 143 pounds at 5' 4" tall with a small frame. *Ugh.* Not even close to the pixie my elementary school classmates had fussed over, treating me like Tinkerbell because I'd been so much smaller and thinner than everyone else. What would anyone like about me now?

I decided to start a self-improvement program with weight-loss as the top priority. I wrote down a daily routine and stuck it to my dresser mirror so I'd see it every time I looked at my reflection:

- Wake and check weight on bathroom scale
- Breakfast: fruit and fat-free yogurt
- Exercise: 90-minutes
- Shower and dress
- Flute practice: 90 minutes
- Saxophone practice: 60 minutes
- Reading and studying to prepare for sophomore honors courses
- Backyard tumbling and beam practice for sophomore gymnastics season
- Make dinner
- Stretch, practice splits to prepare for sophomore Drill Squad tryouts.

I took over planning, shopping for, and preparing family meals because I wanted to know exactly what I ate. I substituted low-calorie and fat-free versions of foods whenever I could. I skipped dessert and fell asleep hungry. I became an encyclopedia of food facts, able to spout fat, calorie, and nutrition information for anything consumable. I separated brain from body and let the former make every choice about what I ate and how I exercised.

I also created rules that made sense to no one but me—a hallmark of eating disorders:

- No soda, juice, Gatorade, or other beverages. Water only, eight glasses a day
- No sweets
- No pizza (a former staple when out with my friends)
- No nuts or peanut butter
- No ice cream, but frozen yogurt was OK

- No fried food
- No salty snacks except fat-free pretzels in unlimited amounts
- Popcorn—popped in oil and sprinkled with margarine, but no butter allowed
- Bagels—plain, no spreads.

Later, Sara would help me see that I'd collected hacks instead of acquiring knowledge. Cutting calories and fat helped me lose weight but compromised nutrition. Some effects were immediate: dry skin and hair, hypoglycemia, mood swings. Others didn't appear—or I didn't recognize—until adulthood.

Gymnastics helped with weight loss and fueled my warped body image. I didn't care that my high school teammates and I had lost every meet during my ninth-grade season. Hobbyists with a handful of tricks, we watched other teams perform kips, flips, and twists we had never attempted and never would. More than their talent, I envied their bodies. They stood with perfect posture anchored by a strong core and stomachs as flat as dinner plates. They walked on colts' legs, pivoted from nipped-in waists. Their arms resembled rolling hills, ducking in at the deltoids and arcing in gentle curves from shoulder to elbow. By comparison, I looked like the Pillsbury Dough Boy, but I was determined to change that.

Weekly gymnastics lessons at a club in southwest Omaha ended with 20 minutes of conditioning. My classmates and I breathed like Lamaze devotees to withstand pain as we completed sprints, lunges, squats, cherry pickers, splits with our front leg propped on a mat. From those lessons, I collected skills but also messages about my body: Force of will can subvert the body's signals, which only held me back. Weakness must be overcome.

I subsisted on fruit, fat-free yogurt, dry Shredded Wheat cereal, and whatever family dinner presented for me to pick at. Some weeks I arrived at after-school gymnastics practice so hungry I was lightheaded and sweating before we started warmup. My hands and legs shook when I pirouetted on the beam. My heart pounded and sometimes skipped a beat. My vision wavered. I welcomed it all as signs of progress.

Marching band rehearsals accelerated my weight loss. By Halloween, I had dropped 15 pounds. In my sophomore yearbook portrait, my neck appeared longer, my cheekbones higher, my jawline sharper. My collar bones tented the teal blue turtleneck I'd chosen to set off my eyes. But my thighs defied my authority. A donut of flesh circled the top of each so that they touched. I wanted a gap between my thighs more than anything. That gap was the pinnacle.

My parents and peers noticed that I had shrunk. They began coaxing me to have a few of their French fries or take a bite of their strawberry pie. I refused.

"Wow, that must really satisfy, huh?" a friend carped when she saw me nibbling on dry Shredded Wheat in the school cafeteria.

I shrugged and laughed, pretending it was a joke.

I accepted others' comments with mixed feelings. Compliments about my new size warmed my chest with a happy glow. Judgment about what, when, and how much I did or didn't eat felt like attempts to control me.

"C'mon, eat some real food," another friend coaxed. When I accepted a spoonful of soft-serve ice cream, which I knew was low in fat and calories, a new arrival to the table teased, "Doesn't that break your diet?"

I grew bitter at drawing criticism no matter what I ate—or didn't. *Mind your own business.* They couldn't see that I was climbing toward something better than any food could taste. I wouldn't let anyone stand between me and the summit. I wanted everyone to stop paying attention to my eating. I grew secretive, hiding food and pretending I'd eaten it.

I trained my willpower like I trained my muscles for gymnastics: exercising and stretching to make it stronger and more flexible. I grew proud of how far I could push my body without fuel. Self-discipline felt like the first power I'd ever wielded. I found it intoxicating. I became convinced that the less space I took up, the happier I'd be. But success always lay just over the next outcropping: beyond the next 100 meters sprinted or French fry refused.

By the end of my sophomore gymnastics season in November, I had whittled my body to 123 pounds. Given reserves of fat I saw on every part of my body, it never occurred to me that I might be starving.

I also didn't notice that the hungrier I felt, the better food tasted. In my relentless push to maximize every second for self-improvement, sitting down to eat became a comfort—a break from physical, mental, and emotional stress. The longer I starved myself, the more intricately tied eating became to relaxation and reassurance: a perfect recipe for developing an eating disorder. It also raised B.C.'s peak, guaranteeing me a bigger fall—something I wouldn't begin to understand until I landed in the psych ward at Regions Hospital in St. Paul, Minnesota, at age 29.

After a sleepless first night in the ward that had included admission at 10 p.m. and an intake exam with the E.R. doctor at 2:00 a.m., I dozed in a shared room on the eighth floor. Somewhere between asleep and awake, I registered the whisper of sheets pushed aside, the pad of slippered feet, the rustle of clothes dug from a suitcase and pulled on. Doors slammed in the distance. Silverware clanked.

Someone called my name. "Breakfast. Time to get up."

I opened my eyes. The voice belonged to a small woman in blue scrubs staring from the doorway. I sighed, rubbed my eyes, slid from bed, and waited for the world to right itself in my bleary vision. I smelled eggs and maple syrup.

I stumbled into the commons, which joined a dozen rooms that ringed its outer edge. The orange carpet was threadbare, the walls cracked plaster. The adjoining lounge contained a TV in a car-sized wood console that looked like a holdover from the 1980s. The nurses' station sat opposite the lounge and offered a 360-degree view of the ward, which patients could only leave by obtaining approval from the on-call psychiatrist.

Patients sat at round tables throughout the commons. A few wore hospital garb; most wore jeans and t-shirts. They tried but failed to be discreet about following me with their eyes as I walked to a metal cart and accepted a tray I didn't want.

I hadn't eaten since binging on chips, French fries, and ice cream the previous afternoon, but I wasn't hungry. Given the calories I'd inhaled, I didn't plan to eat for at least 24 hours. Exercise would be impossible in this setting, so maybe I'd put off eating longer than that.

I chose the only empty table, sat as close to the wall as I could, and kept my eyes on my tray, hoping no one would sit by me—or worse, talk to me. I didn't have it in me to be polite. I preferred being an apparition who walked among the living without need for space or sustenance.

I pushed scrambled eggs around with my fork, spreading them out in clumps so it looked like I'd eaten some. I opened a plastic container of orange juice and pretended to sip. I spread butter over two pancakes and watched it melt. Then I shoved a forkful of eggs beneath one doughy disc. I cut pieces off of the other pancake and hid them amongst the eggs. Experience had made me an expert illusionist when it came to making food disappear.

"I'm sorry we woke you," said a deep voice overhead. "We didn't know there was a note in your chart about letting you sleep in since you were up all night."

The guy who'd handed out trays looked down at me. His apology came as a surprise. So did his gentleness. I hadn't expected softness from someone who looked like a nightclub bouncer. He stood well over six feet tall, and though his blue scrubs didn't hide the beginning of a gut, his chest stretched two tray widths across. Tattoos peeked from beneath his sleeves. Everything about his posture radiated stillness, but his dark eyes roamed the room with purpose, like a cop's. Along with a black mustache and stern expression, they capped off an intimidating presence. I pegged him as an enforcer, on staff because he could restrain anyone who got out of control.

"It's OK," I mumbled.

He leaned down and said quietly, "You should eat at least a third of your breakfast." When I looked up, he angled his head toward the corner, where the woman who'd awakened me jotted notes in a file.

Oh, right. They've seen my eating disorder diagnosis.

I nodded. He nodded in return and then wandered toward neighboring tables.

I stared at my tray. I hated eggs. And these had probably been mixed with butter and beaten with 2% milk instead of fat-free margarine and skim. But their protein seemed less dangerous than the pancake's carbohydrates, which would turn to sugar as soon as they hit my system. I shoveled in a few gooey forkfuls and swallowed regretfully. I drank half of the orange juice, ate the fruit cup (*carbs, yes, but complex rather than simple, and low in calories*), and nibbled a sausage link. I even swallowed some milk, though I never drank it otherwise because I hated the film it left in my mouth—perhaps a throwback to my soy-fueled infancy.

I returned my tray to the cart missing exactly 1/3 of its contents. The Bouncer smiled and winked.

I had just folded a leg beneath me and sunk into a lounge chair to read a *People* magazine article about the end of a Hollywood couple dubbed "Bennifer" when the ward's P.A. buzzed with static and announced I had a phone call. I knew it was from Mom and Dad. I took the phone gingerly and hesitated before saying hello.

Dad's voice reverberated from a second receiver once Mom's voice greeted me. "You sound good, hon'," he said, "Are you OK? Are they treating you well?"

"Yeah. Everyone is really kind."

"What happened?" Mom asked.

"I'm just here because of a glitch with my insurance," I said, oversimplifying to ease their minds. "It's not like I was going to, you know... hurt myself or anything." *At least not right away...*

Dad said, "That's OK. Whatever the reason you're there, I'm glad you took care of yourself. I'm glad you're getting help. I'm proud of you."

My eyes welled. I didn't want to cry again. I was sick of crying; it seemed that was all I'd done for 48 hours. I looked at the ceiling to blink back the tears.

Someone tapped me on the shoulder. A nurse said, "You need to hang up." She pointed to her watch and then to a sign on the wall that read, "Calls are limited to two minutes."

"Oh, OK." I put the receiver near my lips and took a breath to speak.

"Now," the nurse insisted. "You need to hang up *now*."

I covered the receiver with my palm. Bolstered by Dad's approval and freed by not caring about anything, I said "Oh-*kay*" with a teenager's snotty inflection—the first attempt at rebellion I could remember.

I uncovered the receiver. "I have to go. They're telling me I have to hang up."

"Listen," Dad said, "I just want to tell you that I get it. I know what it's like. I've been through it, and you'll get through it, too. You'll be OK."

I had forgotten that Dad once had something like a nervous breakdown at work. When I hung up, I thought about how Dad had changed for the better—how his temper cooled and the goofy, gregarious part of him we loved took over more and more of his personality—once he'd begun treatment for depression.

It struck me then that Dad had struggled with his own version of The Trench Coat Guys, ones I imagined in Papal vestments rather than London Fog coats—a vision that would play out in a church-related lawsuit more than a decade later. In fact, I'd seen them in action the summer my eating disorder began.

Freshly showered and wearing pajamas after running at the track, I had stopped to watch from the living room doorway as Dad reviewed tape of an interview he'd given on UPRR's CCTV, which broadcast nationally. The recording had only played for a few minutes when Dad began grumbling about his gut stretching his rust-colored sweater, a smudge visible on his glasses, and a "turkey neck" that moved his jowls as he spoke. He groused about saying "ah" and "um" too often and claimed he held his hands too stiffly at his sides. He was being too hard on himself. I saw in the video a man who was intelligent, passionate about his work, and doing his best while battling demons. I said as much, leaving out the part about demons, but he hadn't been convinced.

That version of Dad, and especially the one I'd just talked to on the phone countered the maniac on the soccer field. I felt certain now that what the Dad on the phone had been telling me was that I didn't need to get out of anyone's way. That I could—that I *should*—take up space, in my life and in others'. I should occupy space in this ward as long as I needed. I should voice my needs and feed my hungers.

That was harder than it sounded, but when Jeneen asked me to move Angie using nothing but my body, I replaced memories of Dad's voice shoving me from a hardware store's aisle with his voice on the hospital phone. "It's OK. You'll be OK."

"C'mon, try it," Jeneen urged me.

I clenched my teeth.

I asked Angie to follow me walking forward and stop before she'd cross Jeneen's line in the sand. Angie crossed the line. She crept up behind me so close that her muzzle's whiskers tickled my nape.

"Ah-ah-ah," Jeneen sang with a note of caution. "Don't let Angie do that. She's invading your space."

I turned to face Angie, positioned myself just left of her nostrils and stepped forward, trying to break through an imaginary wall the way it had looked when Jeneen had gotten Angie to jump back.

Angie didn't jump, but she stepped back. I couldn't believe it!

I tried disengaging her hindquarters, but she seemed confused. She hesitated, then stepped back diagonally instead of rotating her backend.

"Imagine your hipbones are headlights. Shine them at the part of Angie's body you want to move," Jeneen coached.

"Yes! That's it!" she cheered when Angie crossed one back foot over the other.

I did it! I'd made this mysterious animal move exactly as I wanted. Blood rushed to my face. I felt powerful. I sensed a gold cord linking my core to Angie's chest. I looked into her eye again and saw a shift. When I reached out to stroke her muzzle, she didn't pull up her head like she had during grooming.

After that lesson, I started every ride with groundwork. Spending a few minutes taking up space and connecting with my horse before I climbed in the saddle improved everything about my ride. It also put me back in my body after a week spent with academia's intellectual pursuits. It anchored my feet. It centered my core. It encouraged me to stand up straight instead of hunching and to expand instead of shrinking. It reinforced the idea that asserting my will could feel good. Perhaps most importantly, it countered the impatience perfectionism prompted by reminding me that real growth happened one step in the sand at a time.

I'd need every bit of that growth and groundedness when I came face to face with a racehorse named Finn.

Chapter 4 - Finn: Treat Yourself Like Your Best Friend

Seventh Farm Riding School, April 2013

An unfamiliar energy crackled across Seventh Farm's property. I sensed something before I turned from County Road F onto sleepy Glenmont Road, where mailboxes stood sentry for houses that remained dark and quiet on a gloomy Sunday morning. Drizzle jeweled power lines and draped pastures in a veil. The moisture made my shirt stick to my skin when I stepped from the Amigo, but it didn't damper the energy buzzing along my antenna.

The energy originated in the barn. A gelding named Finn had been delivered by trailer that morning, but he wasn't adjusting well to his new environment. He'd stuck his neck through a gap in his stall's bars and was swinging his head in the aisle, tracing a figure-eight with his nose. His movement was so frenetic it blurred the white blaze running from his forehead to his muzzle. Sweat slicked his copper coat and foamed on his neck. It smelled like curdled milk rather than the wet grass and musk I associated with geldings. I could almost feel his metabolism humming. His mass seemed to shrink before my eyes. I pictured soot-smudged men shoveling coal into his furnace's fiery maw and failing to keep it fed.

"Where's he from?" I asked Cate, an advanced rider and college student who worked at the farm.

She stopped sweeping the aisle to rest her hands and chin on the end of the push broom. "A track in Ohio. He retired from racing about a year ago. Tom says he'll be a good lesson horse because his personality is like Charlie's."

"Oh, good." I hoped I sounded more convinced than I felt. I glanced at Charlie, who watched Cate resume sweeping with calm curiosity from his stall across the aisle. On the outside, he and Finn looked like twins except for Charlie's thinner blaze. On the inside, they were foils.

I stepped closer to Finn to see how he'd react. When he didn't flinch, I dug baby carrots from a bag I'd brought and held them out. He paused to sniff my hand. Then he plucked all three carrots from my palm with velvet lips. His breath warmed my skin, but his eyes looked vacant, as if he'd abandoned his body to wander internal landscapes. I wondered if he registered the carrots' taste. I held out two more, but he ignored them. I reached to scratch his neck. He ducked my hand and resumed swaying. I wished I could wrap my arms around his neck and whisper lullabies in his fuzzy ear, though I knew that wouldn't help. His motion hypnotized. My body longed to mimic its rhythm, even as my heart ached at his distress.

"He'll stop doing that in a few days," Tom said.

Cate's sweeping had drowned out Tom's footsteps. He seemed to materialize from the ether, like the steam rising from a cracked white mug in his hand. He saw me glance at the French press dangling from his other hand and asked, "Want some coffee? I can dig up another mug."

I shook my head. "No, thanks. I'm not a coffee drinker."

"Whaaat? Why not?" He sipped, swallowed, winced when the liquid burned his throat.

I didn't feel like explaining how my sensitive system reacted to any stimulant like it was cocaine, so I shrugged. "I dunno. I just never started."

"That's good, don't." Tom took another sip, then gestured at Finn with his mug. "I've seen this before. A lot of track horses do it. They kind of have PTSD. The stall feels like a starting gate, so it freaks them out. Once they've been here a few weeks without having to race, they settle down. He'll be fine."

I nodded and considered what he'd said. I trusted Tom, but it was hard to believe him given what I was looking at.

Finn was still swinging his head when I brought Charlie back to the barn after my lesson two hours later. I paused in front of Finn's stall and wished him well. Then I spent my drive back to St. Paul cursing the horseracing industry.

The following Sunday, Finn was in a stall that didn't allow access to the aisle. Moving him was a good idea, but he'd simply traded swinging his head for marching in place. His steps swept shavings from beneath his metal shoes so they clacked a pattern on the concrete. *Tap-tap,* pause, *tap-tap. Tap-tap,* pause, *tap-tap.* Occasionally, he shook his head, raking his nose along the bars. Blood dotted his muzzle. His new activity appeared less taxing to his body, but I found it even more disturbing.

I tried to keep my voice even when I asked Cate, "There's nothing we can do?"

She looked up from mucking the neighboring stall and shook her head. "Tom's afraid if he lets Finn out now, he'll associate doing that," she nodded at the stalls' shared wall, "with getting out, so he'll do it every time we put him in a stall."

"Oh, right." I shoved my hands in my jacket's pockets and lined up stray shavings with my boot.

"Tom won't let it go on forever though." Cate dumped a pitchfork full of manure into a blue bucket designated for the task. She leaned the pitchfork against the wall, rolled open Finn's door, and kicked shavings beneath his feet. The effect was like muting a TV; he didn't break stride, but the tapping stopped.

Before Cate dumped another full pitchfork into the bucket, the tapping resumed. I couldn't imagine how Finn would join the herd if something as innocuous as a stall sent him careening out of normalcy's orbit.

Finn's tapping haunted me throughout the next week. At some point, its taps and pauses became dots and dashes that rapped a message against my breastbone. They reverberated in a way that felt familiar, but I couldn't decode their message.

I identified with Finn because I'd once reacted the same way to new environments. Before Sara's office had become a safe space, I'd jiggled my knee to burn calories and picked at my cuticles to distract from panic, unable to see anything good in myself or my future.

The first small step in my adjustment to normal resulted from a simple and seemingly random question Sara asked in 2002.

I arrived at The Emily Program that July afternoon disconsolate over a mistake I'd made at work. A student's coach had called and, by pretending she already knew the details, tricked me into revealing that her star player had missed practice because she'd plagiarized her essay for Leanne's class. My revelation was a potential violation of the Family Educational Rights to Privacy Act. More than losing my job, I feared losing my lifeline: a colleague named Leanne.

Dr. Leanne Zainer had taught my graduate school course at Hamline a year earlier. After grading my final essay, which described how trapped I felt in my secretarial job at a Minneapolis construction company, she had told me about a job available in Hamline's Center for Academic Services (CAS). It was a perfect fit for my skills and experience. I'd hoped the job would be a steppingstone to directing a college writing center once I finished my Master's degree.

I worked both for and with Leanne at Hamline while I continued taking graduate classes. After a few months, she'd offered to mentor me. I'd clung to her like a parasite, absorbing knowledge and approval she'd offered freely until I'd inadvertently put both of our jobs in jeopardy three days before I sat across from Sara. I'd barely slept or eaten since. I was terrified Leanne would wash her hands of me. *I deserve to get dropped as her mentee.* My breath caught at the thought.

Sara had been nodding patiently while she'd listened, but before I could continue, she asked, "Who's your best friend?"

"I—" I stopped short, confused. The answer was a no-brainer, but I didn't understand why she'd asked the question.

"My sister, Julie."

My bond with Julie is a theme that unifies my life's story. She appears in nearly every memory. One of my earliest begins with her shriek. I'd convinced her we should explore the narrow space between the shed and the backyard fence. The grass there tickled my five-year-old knees; its feathery tops grazed her three-year-old thighs. I turned to see why she'd screamed and saw a grasshopper the size of my palm on her t-shirt. She flapped her hands in panic and then froze, paralyzed.

"It's OK," I said. "Grasshoppers don't bite or sting."

The creature twitched a folded leg. Its antennae scoured the yellow cotton stretched across Julie's chest. She shrieked again. Tears gushed from her eyes.

The Trench Coat Guys stewed. They hated hysterics. Guy #1 brewed an acerbic comment. In my mind, I held up a hand and said, *No!* He could say whatever he wanted about me, but Julie was off-limits. He looked shocked, then scowled and disappeared.

My skin wriggled as I studied black polka-dots on the grasshopper's pea-green back, but I couldn't bear Julie's anguish. I curled my middle finger against my thumb and flicked, careful not to touch the creature. It leapt from Julie's shirt and bounded through the grass.

"He's gone!" I announced.

Julie unclenched her eyes. She glanced cautiously at her chest, then up at me. She sniffled, then smiled.

I put my arm around her shoulder. "C'mon, Let's go inside."

Bravery had always come more easily when Julie was around. So many adults had told me "You're too quiet" by the time I reached second grade that I thought my voice didn't work, but it never faltered when Julie was nearby. In fact, it grew stronger. I'd never speak to a stranger or ask to break a rule if not on Julie's behalf. It seems appropriate that Nebraskaland Days provided the first opportunity to do so.

Julie and I giggled pulling the Tilt-a-Whirl's safety bar onto our laps. We waved to Mom and Dad as our cab began rolling, then cheered "Wooo!" as it picked up speed. A gap between our scrawny thighs and the metal safety bar sent us sliding across the plastic seat. When our cab began spinning, Julie's smiled faded. Everything beyond our cab reduced to blurred colors.

"I don't like this," Julie said. "I want to get off!"

"We have to wait 'til it stops," I told her.

"I'm scared! I wanna get off!" Her face went pale.

Her fear piqued mine. Instead of thrilling, the ride suddenly felt overwhelming. Dread stirred as my body whipped across the seat once more.

I spotted the grizzled ride operator on our next trip past the entrance where he'd taken our tickets. His smile had made my skin crawl, but Julie was trying to climb from beneath the safety bar.

"Wait." I held out my arm to stop her. "I'll help you."

Hair blowing across my face, I yelled as we passed the operator, "Can you please stop the ride?"

He didn't look up from the panel of buttons in front of him.

Twice more, I timed our pass and yelled, "Please stop the ride. She's scared!"

I marveled when the platform hissed and then slowed.

The operator scolded as we scrambled down the metal steps and into Mom and Dad's arms. I didn't care if I'd been Bad. I'd protected my little sister; that was the only thing that mattered.

Julie and I traded places as sword and shield more times than I could count, able to stick up for each other when we couldn't for ourselves. The lines distinguishing her battles from mine muddied, as did our identities.

Despite our different hair colors—Julie's so white and silky strangers stopped Mom in store aisles to comment on it—no one but our closest friends and immediate family could tell us apart. We took that hint and ran with it, pretending to be twins. We didn't mind when relatives called us by the wrong name because we answered to both. I took their confusion as a compliment, aware Julie was the better of our two halves. Absent my perfectionism and hypersensitivity she breezed into a room like spring: fresh, pure, bright, and mild—a promise of good things to come. I crept in like fall—dry, crisp, and hinting that winter followed. I preferred to park on the couch and read for hours; Julie's piano teacher dubbed her "Wiggles." I feared being laughed at and ducked any suggestion of an audience; Julie was a comedienne at home, performed in plays, danced on drill team, and sang in choir at school. I got lost in a store no matter how many times I'd shopped there; Julie formed a mental map of the biggest mall after a single visit. I dreamed of donning designer suits and attending corporate board meetings; Julie couldn't wait to raise children as a stay-at-home mom. Instead of clashing, our personalities forged an alloy stronger and more versatile than its component parts.

Nothing soldered our bond more securely than having to join a new herd when our family moved from North Platte.

UPRR promoted Dad in 1982, putting him in charge of a national program managed from the copper-colored headquarters building in downtown Omaha. We moved over Christmas break, halfway through my third-grade year.

North Platte and Omaha were opposites, but combining them was corrosive. North Platte sprawled flat and cracked-dry beneath a prairie sun; Omaha crouched in a Missouri River valley and hoarded humidity. North Platte's sandy soil and high water table resulted in rambler homes surrounded by gardens that nurtured everything from potatoes to strawberries. Omaha's clay resulted in two-story colonials on lots hostile to grass and garden. North Platte plodded at a rural pace; Omaha zipped along as if its dizzying I-80 interchanges could fling it into the 21st Century.

We moved into our new house on my ninth birthday. Crackling December cold turned the air to shards that scraped my eyes and nostrils as I watched movers haul boxes from a semi-truck, up a driveway sloped like a C, and into a red-brick and white-sided two-story house.

Julie and I had gushed for weeks about having separate bedrooms but then feared sleeping alone at opposite ends of the second floor's L-shaped hallway. We alternated spending the night in sleeping bags on her teal and my lavender shag carpet until Christmas break ended.

"Students," my teacher said the following morning, "this is Lisa Whalen. She and her family just moved here. Please welcome her."

Silence. Stares.

Why is everyone looking at me like I'm snail slime?

I wore a new outfit—a birthday gift from my Godmother of purple slacks and a striped purple shirt. My North Platte friends and I had agreed that purple was our favorite color, but no one in Omaha was wearing it.

I soon learned that while my North Platte friends and I had rarely thought about clothes beyond their color, my Omaha peers used designer labels to assign rank. Among the most popular kids, even socks bore embroidered logos from Guess or Ralph Lauren. I pleaded with Mom and Dad to visit a boutique called The Stamp Collection, where the popular girls bought everything from t-shirts to Easter dresses. Mom took me there but gasped at the price tags. I sensed her shifting uneasily beside me as I thumbed through racks. We left without buying.

I pouted but then felt guilty. I knew my parents couldn't afford designer clothes and that if they could, buying them would violate values they held dear. And it didn't escape my notice that every time I coveted someone else's clothes, I broke the 10th Commandment. Greed and vanity were deadly sins; more evidence that I needed to work harder at being Good.

Pressure to fit in at Rockbrook Elementary school led me to wage the only prolonged battles I fought against Mom and Dad. My first assault was a temper tantrum when my fourth-grade classmates recognized a coat I wore to recess as a peer's hand-me-down. I burst into tears when I got home, announcing that I would rather freeze to death than wear the coat again. It disappeared from the hallway closet, replaced by a red one from JC Penny that didn't sport a label but imitated popular styles.

Cool girls in my grade paired up with boys to become couples. The couples hung out together after school and bought each other gifts, like lockets and Swatch watches. A few married in ceremonies held on the soccer field at recess.

Lisa Whalen

Newlyweds walked hand-in-hand to secret playground hiding spots for honeymoons. Rumors about who had reached second base dominated lunchtime conversation. The longest-running couple had reportedly "done it" twice. I could conjure only vague notions of what "doing it" meant but knew my parents wouldn't approve.

My novelty led a popular boy named Jake to ask me if I'd "go with" him. I couldn't remember our having spoken, but the popular girls urged me to say yes, so I did. I sat next to him at lunch, wondering what to say, so shy I could barely look at him. I liked that he chose me as his square-dancing partner in P.E., which meant I wasn't left standing alone until the teacher assigned me a partner, but Jake scared me. His blonde hair was too shiny, his eyes too intensely blue. Instead of smiling, he smirked. A flair for sarcasm increased his cache among the boys, but I worried he might turn it on me. I wasn't allowed to curse, and he and his friends swore blue streaks so foul they introduced new words to my vocabulary. Mostly, Jake remained watchful, a lion stalking prey. It unnerved me that I never knew what was going on behind his eyes.

"You're *what?*" Mom said when I asked if I could kiss Jake, since we were going together.

"What do you mean? Where are you going?"

"Nowhere. We're just going *together.*"

"Where?"

"No! Not going somewhere, going *together.*"

We went around and around for several minutes, Mom failing to grasp what seemed obvious to my nine-year-old brain. I sighed. Then I explained that Jake and I were boyfriend and girlfriend.

Mom's eyebrows wrinkled. She shook her head and blew out from between pursed lips, the way she always did when stymied. "Absolutely not. You're too young to kiss a boy. You're not allowed to date until you're 16."

I feared she'd make me break up with Jake, which would erase what little social standing our week-long courtship had bestowed.

She didn't. Mom conceded that I could sit by Jake at lunch and hang out with him at recess, but no gifts were to be exchanged. I didn't dare mention marriage or honeymoons.

There would be consequences for refusing to kiss Jake. I spent a restless night weighing Mom and Dad's disapproval against my peers'. I felt like a plastic bag tossed by the wind, unable to select my own course, not knowing if I wanted to.

When I didn't appear at the spot where classmates declared I would not only kiss but *French kiss* Jake, he dumped me via messenger.

The breakup dominated third-grade headlines. Popular boys performed playground drive-bys, puckering their lips, kissing the air, and yelling "prude!" as they ran past. The teasing stopped when a new drama unfolded, but the breach I'd chiseled into the social scene sealed shut.

Julie struggled in Omaha, too. Her inability to cope ran headlong into mine. She cried every day in first grade. After a few weeks, the school secretary appeared at my classroom door. She called me away from the solar system diagram I'd been labeling and led me to Julie's classroom. Julie's teacher met me at the door and told me to make Julie stop crying.

How? I wasn't faring much better at being dumped like The Little Prince on this strange and lonely planet. Seeing my sister's face chapped red and covered in tear tracks broke my heart. I said I'd try.

Julie brightened when she saw me. We sat on the green carpet in her classroom's back corner. I whispered that not much time was left before Mom would pick us up. I promised she could brush my Twisty Curl Barbie's hair. "Please stop crying, 'kay? We're gonna get in trouble."

She took a shuddering breath and wiped the tears from her cheeks with the back of her hand. "Okay."

My pep talk was like a Band-Aid on a broken bone. Julie began crying again a few days later. Mom gave her a locket with a family portrait inside and suggested she look at it whenever she felt lonely. That seemed to help; I didn't hear about her crying anymore.

As my worries about fitting in grew, my voice shrank. Everyone from babysitters to store clerks complained, "You're so quiet." The phrase's appearance became as predictable as the moon in the night sky.

"Lisa's going to have to learn to speak up if she wants to make it in life," my fourth-grade teacher declared within my hearing.

Great. I'm doomed.

First-grade claustrophobia returned in fourth. Unlike Marya Hornbacher in *Wasted: A Memoir of Anorexia and Bulimia*, who "stayed in bed claiming grave illness" when anxious about school, I gutted out mornings only to succumb during afternoons[6]. Too old to cry, I reported headaches and stomachaches that both did and didn't exist. The school nurse called Mom, who drove me home.

After several such calls, Mom turned to me from the driver's seat as we prepared to depart Rockbrook's horseshoe drive. "I believe you don't feel well, honey, but I don't think you're sick. You can't keep coming home like this. You have to figure out a way to stay at school."

---

6. Hornbacher, 28.

Once I knew I had to, staying got easier. I simply ignored the headaches and stomachaches until they faded.

By high school, I wondered if I'd exaggerated Rockbrook's social pressure. Maybe being new and scared had fed my imagination, made me overdramatize what I'd seen and heard. One tenth-grade experience proved that wasn't the case.

As I settled into my seat for American History and reached into my backpack for a pen, our class's popularity queen breezed into the room. She pinned her eyes on me and announced in a voice loud enough to show how she'd earned her cheerleading uniform, "You wouldn't kiss Jake? What a prude!" Then she convulsed with laughter.

Every head in the room snapped in my direction. Smiles materialized: some puzzled, others amused, a few delighted. I froze, pen in hand, mouth open. *Jake? Kiss? Is she talking about... THIRD GRADE? She didn't even go to Rockbrook. How does she know about that?*

Tendrils of a rumor that she and Jake had begun dating sprouted in my brain. The two must have swapped first-kiss stories.

That I'd come up as a topic of popular kids' conversation crushed my illusions of invisibility. I'd flown low and steady through my first year of high school, content in the belief that I'd never registered on their radar. Discovering I couldn't control whether they talked—or even thought—about me made me feel sick. The back of my neck heated. Sweat broke out in my armpits. I shrugged as if bored and peered into my backpack as intently as if it could explain the universe's Big Bang.

Fortunately, our teacher entered, swinging his beat-up leather briefcase and mumbling to himself. He kicked his chair into place, banged his briefcase on the table, and demanded we take out our notes so he could see how industrious we'd been overnight. I glanced up to find the queen smiling at me from across the room, a malicious glint in her hazel eyes.

My transition to Westside High didn't offer much relief for new-kid angst. I should have expected as much from a place dubbed Hollywood High by kids from other schools. The one good thing about Westside was that Julie and I saw each other between classes. We defied convention by not only acknowledging each other's existence, but seeking it out, gathering with mutual friends to study and gossip during free periods. During and after college, our friends would become so used to seeing us arrive together that upon our entrance, they'd announce in unison, "It's the Sisters Whalen!"

Given the way Julie and I had leaned on each other to get through our hardest times, the answer to Sara's question in the wake of my screw-up at Hamline University was obvious, but the question seemed to come out of nowhere until I answered it.

Sara followed my answer by asking, "What would you say to Julie if she made your mistake?"

Instantly, my perspective changed. *Your intentions were good. Leanne will come around; just give her some time.*

"Now, apply that advice to yourself," Sara suggested.

Whoa. Just like that, I saw that while I thought I had been reciting facts about what had happened at Hamline, I had actually been listing my litany of faults and outlining every option for handling the situation that would have been better than the one I'd chosen. That 180-degree turn blew my mind.

"I'd like you to work on treating yourself like you'd treat Julie. Pay attention to your self-talk. If it's critical, replace it with what you'd have said to her."

Sara's suggestion was simple, but I saw immediately how it could change my life. People had been telling me for as long as I could remember that I was too hard on myself. I'd never believed them. Now I saw what they meant; I wouldn't treat anyone as harshly as I treated myself.

"I'd also like you to set aside 15 minutes a day to relax and do something nice for yourself, something frivolous."

I cringed thinking of what I could accomplish in a week's worth of 15-minute increments: exercise, fold laundry, call a friend, scrub the kitchen floor. "I feel guilty just thinking about it," I huffed, trying to make a confession sound like a joke.

"I know." Sara smiled. "Let's brainstorm so you're prepared. What do you like to do?"

"Well, when I've finished a project at home, I—"

"Nope. This isn't a reward for being good. It's not something you earn; it's a gift you give yourself for no reason. What's something you wouldn't normally consider letting yourself have?"

I bit my lip. I'd grown used to denying myself food, fun, rest, forgiveness, and a host of other things. Treats had been off my radar for over a decade. I struggled to come up with an answer.

"Um, I like celebrity magazines," I said, finally. "Like *People* or *US Weekly*. Maybe I could buy one?"

As soon as I stopped speaking I realized those magazines featured celebrities' perfect bodies and detailed their strict diet-and-exercise regimens, which was why I liked them, of course. *Crap. I can't even reward myself correctly.*

Sara didn't balk at my suggestion. "Good. Why don't you get a subscription?"

A treat delivered by mail every week? The thought set my skin tingling. *I'm on a roll.* "Anything else? I like to have homework, and I can do more."

Sara didn't point out the irony in my request: asking for additional work to battle workaholic tendencies.

"I'd like you to focus on becoming more aware of how you feel throughout the day. Check in with yourself whenever you can. Are you hungry? tired? anxious? content? If you can write it down, that's even better, but noticing is a good first step. And if you feel anxious, acknowledge that and give yourself credit for noticing. Don't try to fix it; see if you can sit with that feeling. Be patient with yourself. If you forget to check in, that's OK. This isn't a test. You're not being graded."

I knew what she meant; just the idea that I might get anxious made me anxious, and my reflex was to reach for whatever would quash the feeling. Often, that was food. Then my brain was off and running: *impulsive, weak-willed, lazy, fat, worthless.*

"Take things as they come, one at a time. Have you ever been on a plane when the flight attendants tell you to secure your oxygen mask before you help someone else?"

I nodded.

"Follow that advice: Take care of yourself before you worry about anyone else, OK?"

I left Sara's office determined to do exactly that, but intention proved easier than practice. A critical comment snuck into my thoughts before Sara's door clicked shut behind me— something about how I hadn't sounded as sincere as I should have when I'd thanked her.

I worked at becoming less critical during my remaining time at Hamline, where Leanne forgave and mentored me. But my efforts came as too little, too late to reverse decades of denial and disapproval.

Starting a new job where I couldn't lean on Leanne overwhelmed my fledgling coping skills. I made it through my first semester as a professor at a Christian college, but before fall transitioned to spring and 2003 turned to 2004, my un-healthy patterns had taken their toll. Tears poured from my eyes the second I sat down in Sara's office one January afternoon.

"I can't do this anymore," I said between gasps. My diaphragm spasmed as I tried to suppress a sob.

Sara's eyebrows furrowed. "I could tell something was wrong when I saw you in the lobby. Did you meet with a psychiatrist for a medication consult like we discussed?"

"I tried." I pulled papers from my purse and unfolded them. "My insurance company farmed out its mental health coverage to a subcontractor. I scoured the Internet for contact information before I finally found a phone number. The company's receptionist said she'd mail me a list of covered psychiatrists. It took two weeks to arrive, and the numbers on it are so out of date they don't include the 763 or 952 area code."

Sara frowned and shook her head as the implication sunk in: Six years had passed since Minnesota had added those area codes; the list hadn't been updated since then.

I handed her the creased sheets covered with my notes. "In some cases, I had to try all four area codes with a number before it would connect. Then, I still got wrong numbers." I leaned forward and pointed to numbers as I described them. "That's a Kindercare. That's a law office. That's a warehouse. Only three are psychiatrists' offices, and they have six-month waiting lists for new clients." I sniffled as my tears began falling in earnest. They dotted my khakis with a scattershot pattern, like data accumulating on a graph.

Sara placed a Kleenex box on the chair beside me. "Hmmm," she said, studying the list. "Can I make a copy of this?" She smoothed the pages against her lap.

"Sure." *You can keep it for all the good it does me.* That thought sent fresh tears dripping from my chin onto the purple sweater I'd worn to a meeting on campus that morning. Its tag scratched my nape, and its synthetic wool itched my arms where my t-shirt's sleeves ended. I wore it only because it was baggy enough to hide my size and heavy enough to disguise sweating caused by hypoglycemia.

"I can't wait six months. I don't want to live like this."

"No, you can't," Sara agreed. She stood and pulled a binder from her bookshelf.

"I—" My breath hitched again, and I whispered, uncertain whether I wanted to be heard. "I don't want to live anymore."

"It's going to be OK; I promise." Sara flipped through the binders' pages. Then she looked at me intently. "What I'm going to propose might sound extreme, but it's not. It will get you seen by a psychiatrist, OK?"

"OK." I dabbed my eyes with the growing wad of damp tissues crumpled in my fist, wondering how much I'd smeared my makeup. My lashes felt sticky, my cheeks stiffened by salt.

"What county do you live in?"

"Ramsey."

"Good. That's good. Ramsey's public hospital is Regions, which isn't far from here. It has to treat you, regardless of insurance." As if speaking to herself, she added quietly, "And if I remember correctly, it's the only hospital in the metro that separates patients with depression from the rest of the psych ward."

Psych. Ward. The phrase chilled me. Even my tears stopped, as if the ducts were shocked into submission. My brain conjured scenes from TV dramas like *ER* and *Scrubs*, where patients needing psych consults were wacked out of their minds: hallucinating, attacking staff, damaging property, and injuring bystanders. *Oh, God.* My heart skidded like flat rocks I'd skipped across lakes during family vacations.

Sara laid a hand on my wrist. "It's not like the movies. You'll go to the ER and tell them what you told me. They'll admit you, and you'll see the on-call psychiatrist. I can even call ahead and explain the situation if you want."

"Yes, please," I whispered, sounding to my own ears like a girl who saw poltergeists. "I'm so scared."

"I know. But this will help."

"Can—" I cleared my throat. "I don't think I can drive there like... this. Can I call my sister to give me a ride?"

"That's a great idea!" Sara jumped up, grabbed the receiver on her desk, and began pressing buttons to get an outside line. "Do you need a phone book?"

I shook my head. I took the sleek black handset she handed me and punched in numbers I knew by heart.

Julie left work. She drove me east on ice-rutted University Avenue. My teeth chattered, though not from the bitter temperature, which made snow squeak beneath the tires when we slowed for red lights. Night was already chasing dusk at 4:15.

A bruised sky was fading to black by the time we reached Jackson Street. When Julie turned right, Regions Hospital sprawled across several blocks on our left.

An ER doctor sent us to a psych holding area. We waited in one of several exam rooms lining a hallway. Nearby, someone howled like a werewolf. Hair rose on my arms and neck.

Just as I reminded myself that a St. Paul police officer stood at the reception desk outside our room, he replied to a call on his radio and disappeared.

Then a man lurked in our doorway. He appeared to be in his mid-20s. His clothes were clean and unrumpled, but his eyes shone glassy as agates. He rocked side to side, leering at us, and stroked his crotch. "Are you virgins?"

"What?" Dazed, I was sure I'd misheard.

"I need 12 virgins for…" The man's speech trailed off to mumbling.

"Um, I think you should leave?"

Before he could reply, Julie slammed the door hard enough to shake the wall. *Why didn't I think of that?*

I examined the doorknob for a lock, but it didn't have one. I looked for something to push against the door, but everything, including the chair I sat in, was bolted to the floor. I watched the knob, waiting for it to turn. Shadows the man's feet cast beneath the door disappeared.

I jumped when the door swung open a few minutes later. The cop stuck his head in and looked us over. "This door has to stay open."

I wanted to beat his chest for leaving us unprotected, but I didn't even have the energy to explain why we'd closed the door. I perched on the edge of my chair and kept quiet, flicking my gaze nervously from the floor to the hallway while I waited to be seen by a doctor.

Once admitted, I tried to grasp how a narrative that began with an unremarkable girl from small-town Nebraska could lead to her being escorted by security through an inner-city hospital's underground tunnels. I knew policy was policy, but the idea that I required delivery via guard would have made me fall over laughing under any other circumstances. *I'm harmless, scared of everyone and everything.*

When the elevator's doors opened on the 8th floor, the guard told Julie, "You can't go any further."

I sucked in a breath at the thought of Julie leaving. Tears flooded my lower lids.

"Don't cry. It'll be OK. I'll call you and visit as soon as they'll let me," Julie said.

The guard ushered me through a heavy metal door. It locked behind me with an electronic hum.

I blanked out until tingling in my right arm brought me back to the present, where a blood pressure cuff tightened around my biceps.

"Your pressure's a little high. Are you nervous, Lisa?" asked the nurse whose hand squeezed the cuff's rubber pump.

I nodded.

The cuff deflated with a hiss. Heat rushed past my elbow and into my hand.

The nurse patted my arm. "You'll be OK."

Everyone kept saying that, but I wasn't so sure.

"Follow me." The nurse led me to a cabinet. She pulled out a gown, pajama pants, and slippers. "You'll have to wear these until the psychiatrist says you can have your clothes back."

She led me to a dorm-style bathroom. "You can change in there."

I changed and handed my clothes to the nurse. She put them in a cloth bag tagged with my name and the patient number printed on a plastic band around my wrist.

"Just a couple more tasks to complete, then I'll show you your room."

I nodded but couldn't meet her gaze.

"Read this and sign at the bottom if it's accurate." She handed me a list of everything I'd had with me when I was admitted. My face burned at seeing my identity laid out so matter-of-factly. My life boiled down to so little.

I scrawled my name.

The nurse pointed to lockers in the far corner. "Your things will be kept in there. If you need any of them, you can ask one of the aides."

I have to ask permission for my possessions? I have truly fallen to rock bottom.

And yet, relief surged through me. I was no longer responsible for a single thing outside my skin. Someone would tell me when and what to eat, when and where to sleep. I would not have to answer a phone, attend a meeting, vacuum my house, or adhere to an eating disorder's demands that I do all of that perfectly while resisting hunger until I grew faint.

The nurse led me through a commons. Adults of varied ages and races perched in twos and threes at round tables. They looked like overgrown children in the hospital's shapeless gowns and reminded me of the orphans in *Annie,* a movie Julie and I had reenacted repeatedly as kids. "It's a Hard Knock Life" flitted through my head.

Tour complete, I climbed onto my assigned bed, curled into a ball, and pulled the sheet over my head. *I'd give anything to be invisible.* Then I remembered I had nothing to give because my possessions resided in a locker I couldn't access. I wanted to laugh but cried instead.

I missed my watch. My room didn't have a clock. Not knowing the time left me unmoored. At home, I kept at least one clock in every room. Not knowing the time felt like sliding on ice. Time gave me traction, carved my day into orderly increments I could measure, control, or if need be, endure.

I studied the sheet's threads and focused on breathing. Inhaling wasn't easy inside my shroud. The air grew hot, wet, and stale, but I didn't care. Suffocating didn't seem the worst that could happen.

A voice chirped hello from the end of my bed. I lowered the sheet past my nose and saw a woman whose golden hair fell in waves down her back. She wore jeans, a maroon University of

Minnesota sweatshirt, and tennis shoes. *She gets to wear clothes?* For a second, I hated her.

"Hi," I mumbled.

She walked to her side of the room (the side with a window, I noted) and changed into pajamas. Apparently, she was my roommate. I flashed back to nights spent sleepless on friends' floors, chased there by my college roommate's mean streak. I'd feared roommates ever since. But at least this woman didn't resemble the zombies in the commons.

I rolled so my back faced her and pretended to sleep.

"I'm Laverne. How'd you end up in here?"

I didn't turn but answered, "I'm Lisa. My therapist sent me to the ER. The admitting staff sent me up here."

"It's overwhelming when you first come in, isn't it?"

I rolled to face her. "Yeah." *Why is she being so nice? I don't want kindness; I don't deserve it.*

Laverne described the other patients, then confessed her husband and children hadn't come to visit during her four-day stay. "He's telling everyone I'm in the hospital for high blood pressure." Her chuckle faded to a bitter sigh.

"I'm sorry." Anxiety fluttered in my chest. I didn't know how to comfort her. I'd be devastated if my family shunned me, but I understood her husband's reasoning. I'd die from shame if anyone else learned where I was. "He's probably scared because he's powerless to help you and doesn't know what to do."

"Hmm... maybe." Laverne explained that her friend had found her lying on the Mississippi riverbank and driven her to the ER. "I wasn't going to drown myself or anything, but in retrospect it probably wasn't the best thing to be doing in January."

She pulled her hair into a ponytail and secured it with a cloth band. "To everyone else, I have it all: a successful business, a husband, two beautiful kids, a church community, friends and neighbors who care, but sometimes it's too much and still not enough, you know what I mean?"

"Yeah, I do."

She turned off the light and climbed into her bed. Then her breathing slowed and deepened.

I craved sleep, but it wouldn't come. I wondered what Julie was doing. I stared out the window, where the only sign of life was the red glow of an exit sign in the parking ramp across the street.

I looked for an exit the first time I rode Finn, too.

After his rough start at Seventh Farm, I worried that he'd never settle in and Tom would sell him. He and Liz were selective about the people they sold to, but I'd heard of Thoroughbreds in other states going from the track to the slaughterhouse. The idea sickened me.

Fortunately, a best friend named Cash helped Finn adjust to Seventh Farm.

The two geldings arrived on the same morning, though from different states and to different effect. I left Finn swinging his head in the aisle to look at Cash and was startled when a brown head lunged at me. Despite the iron stall bars between us, I jumped back from what looked like a fire-breathing dragon.

I recovered to find Cash's ears flat against his ebony mane. White half-moons rimmed his eyes, forming bookends for the white star on his forehead. He bared his teeth and glared at me without blinking—a challenge laid at my feet. I glanced away to avoid riling him further and waited for my heart to stop pounding.

When I looked back, Cash studied me with a calculating stare. His sides heaved. I tightened my core and slowed my breathing, hoping to convey confidence.

He didn't take his eyes off me, but he cocked a hip and rested a rear leg. That slight softening was enough to make the dragon disappear. Something about the smug glow in his eyes and his fierceness while confined to a 12-foot cube reminded me of The Grinch Who Stole Christmas: menacing, yes, but also comical and, ultimately, misunderstood. That impression would prove accurate; with time and training, Cash's heart grew to three times its size, beginning with his treatment of Finn.

The first time Cash and Finn were turned out together, they moved away from herd members grazing in the adjoining pasture. Finn stuck by Cash's shoulder, and Cash let Finn shadow him, treating the larger, skinnier horse like a wingman rather than a rival. Finn's devotion primed Cash's confidence, and Cash's confidence comforted Finn. Their posture relaxed. They startled less often. Their tails stilled.

When it was time to meet the herd, Cash strutted through the paddock gate in a bluster of bravado and challenged the herd patriarch, who was significantly larger. The patriarch put Cash in his place, but Cash's effort made an impression. He moved up the ranks quickly, if not unscathed.

Finn sidled up to Cash and sheltered in the wide berth others awarded his new best friend. When Cash wasn't around, Finn skirted the paddock's periphery, keeping his head down and settling for hay scraps rather than venturing toward lush piles in the center.

I hated that Finn would have to take some licks to be accepted. I imagined stomping into the paddock, pointing at the ground, and yelling, "All right, everyone, listen up! This hay is Finn's. You are not to touch it or a single hair on his hide. Do I make myself clear?" I wasn't sure which parts of that fantasy stemmed from affection for Finn and which from a desire to revise my own history. I could only feel encouraged that I'd progressed from identifying with him to casting myself as his protector.

I was assigned to ride Finn one spring morning in 2014 after weeks of watching more advanced classmates work hard to collect his long stride and control his lightning-fast canter.

Finn didn't move when I lifted the gate's metal latch and felt its lock release with a satisfying *thwack*. I relished the safety chain's clanking and the hinges' squawking; in my mind, they signaled the start of rare and precious time with horses. I swung the gate closed behind me and took a second to calm my excitement about riding a new horse. I didn't want him to interpret it as apprehension.

In truth, I *was* a bit apprehensive. Finn was among the sweetest, gentlest horses in Seventh Farm's herd, but I'd never had direct contact with him. I was practically a stranger, and therefore a potential threat. I avoided pinning my gaze on him the way a predator would, letting my eyes flit from my feet to the fence and from his hooves to the halter in my hand. He watched me cautiously.

I ditched the brisk pace that drew comments from strangers when I walked campus hallways and meandered in Finn's general direction. He knew the drill, though, and scooted closer to Cash. A few steps later, he turned and shuffled Cash and T-Bird like cards in a deck to keep them between us.

Slow down. Breathe. This is a treat, a gift; don't forget to enjoy it. I inhaled to a count of four and studied my surroundings. The horses seemed especially serene, enjoying a respite from flies that kept them swishing their tails and stomping their hooves in late summer. Beyond the split-rail fence, the pasture's rolling hills glowed green. Flickering sunlight made the occasional dewdrop sparkle. Dew had also batted down paddock dust without soaking the rich, rusty-red dirt. It was nice not having to pull my boots up from sucking mud with each step.

I used the ground's give to gentle my footsteps as I started toward Finn again. I took it as a good sign that he didn't move when I clucked my tongue and waved the other geldings away. But just as I neared his shoulder, he trotted away.

In the past, this was when I'd have become frustrated. Sensitivity would lead me to take Finn's reticence personally, to interpret his reluctance as contempt. Perfectionism would deem a failure anything short of capture on first attempt. I'd have worried about falling behind my classmates, whom I could hear greeting each other, laughing, rolling open stall doors, and leading horses down the aisle toward the outdoor crossties. I'd have fretted over lost lesson time, which was expensive. My energy would have betrayed what I felt, no matter how carefully I tried to conceal it.

I pictured my brain a chalkboard swept clean: no demands, no judgments, no clock, no to-do lists. Cash had made inroads with Finn by letting Finn be himself, so I'd try the same. I said hello to Cash and patted his neck. *It's OK, Finn. There's no rush. Whenever you're ready.*

Getting Cash's seal of approval boosted my credibility. I talked to Finn in the same voice I used to approach scared cats when I volunteered at the Animal Humane Society. "It's OK, buddy. You're all right."

I channeled sympathy and affection. After a beat, Finn planted his feet and lowered his head. When I held up the halter, he pushed his muzzle through its nosepiece. I wanted to pump my fist to celebrate the victory once I'd secured the halter's clasp, but I didn't. Instead, I patted his neck and concentrated on embodying gratitude.

Finn's skin was as thin as his coping ability. A nervous nature and preference for hay over oats meant he rarely gained weight, even with supplements mixed into his food. Bones closer to the surface turned every nip and kick into open wounds. I used the curry comb's metal teeth gingerly, watching for twitches that indicated sore spots, but he didn't flinch. I ran my hand over withers that arced like Everest from the base of his neck. I placed pads over the spot where three walnut-sized callouses had developed from saddles rubbing against his hide. The calluses had disappeared thanks to an extra-narrow saddle Tom had purchased. Now, only white hair marked where the mounds had once risen. I Velcroed a nose net to his bridle to prevent wind from tickling his nostrils and whiskers, which made him toss his head. Other riders had complained that sensitive gums made him difficult to bridle. *I get it, dude. We're one of a kind.* I cupped the rubber snaffle in my palm to keep it from touching his gums as I slid it between his teeth. He accepted the bit gracefully and lowered his head so I could pull the crown piece over his ears.

From the first step, I loved riding Finn. A slight frame and long legs made his canter feel even faster than its winged pace; each stride's swell and trough left ground in our wake. He jumped like a sprite and shared my preference for light contact in the reins.

The warmup had made me practically giddy. Lining up by the gazebo to receive Liz's instructions burst my bubble.

"Lisa, I put you on Finn because you and he both need to work on contact. We'll do some leg-yielding, which will force you to take a stronger pull on the reins."

I groaned inwardly and wished for an escape. I was terrible at leg-yields. Liz had explained the maneuver, which asked the horse to move diagonally while facing forward, but I'd never mastered moving each of my limbs independently to get the desired result. Something broke the line that connected the picture in my mind to its execution in my body.

"Your leg and hands are too quiet," Liz said once we started the exercise. "You look like you're trying to move a cat instead of a horse. Finn weighs 1100 pounds, not 11. Be louder! Turn up the volume."

I squelched a rueful laugh at the gameshow bell that sounded in my head: *ding, ding, ding!* I thought I'd left declarations that I was too quiet behind in my 20s, but apparently not. Maybe that had been the message in Finn's *tap-tap* pattern: Taking up space is a good start, but it's not enough. To be my own best friend, I had to let my body speak.

"Slow down, Lisa. That's too fast," Liz said for the third time in 20 minutes once we switched to cantering. I had slowed Finn a few times already, but his speed crept up just like the Amigo's when I let my foot, rather than the speedometer, set the pace.

"You need more contact to keep Finn slow. If you can't maintain a slow, rhythmic canter, I won't let you jump him."

I'd joked with my family that my Irish heritage was to blame for my longing to gallop long lines and jump everything in our path. Ireland had invented the Steeplechase, after all. But treating life like it was a steeplechase had brought me crashing down more than once. It was time to learn a new discipline. I sighed and took a firmer hold on the reins.

The hunter/jumper riding Seventh Farm taught countered my worst impulses in the most frustratingly gratifying manner. It reminded me over and over that health and happiness require *slowing down*. The more frequently Liz repeated, "Slow down; that's too fast," the more I understood why Sara had begun my eating disorder treatment by suggesting that I spend 15 minutes a day being frivolous. In her gentle way, she'd been saying,

"Slow down. Live in *this* moment. Stop anticipating and rushing toward the next."

It sounded eerily similar to Liz's mantra: "Speed hurts horses, especially over the long-term."

"Lisa, look at the reins!" Liz scolded. "You can't keep Finn slow with slack reins. How do you expect to jump without any contact?

"Sorry," I said, feeling defeated.

"I know you're worried about hurting Finn's mouth, but having consistent contact is kinder than allowing slack. The reins are going to pull taut at some point, like when he jumps or falls out of balance, and you'll end up popping him in the mouth. Then he won't trust you. If he starts avoiding the bit, you'll *really* have problems."

My brain followed Liz's logic, but my body balked. The second I felt tension in the reins, I heard my childhood horse camp instructor yelling, "Don't pull on the reins! You'll hurt the horse's mouth!" This was different: different discipline, different (much softer) bit. But my hands were faster than my mind. They let up on the reins before I could stop them.

On the way home and at work that week, I imagined my triceps resisting the reins' pull, my calves pushing a horse to leg-yield. I repeated in my head, *Loud and slow is kind.*

I got to test the effects of my mental practice the following week. I felt the difference immediately. When Finn and I jumped, the difference showed. Consistent contact made cantering's 1-2 rhythm pulse through every cell, as if my heart-beat matched a cadence Finn's feet tapped against the ground. I couldn't tell where Finn ended and I began. I knew when and where his feet would land a stride before they met the sand. We crested small fences with an ease that conjured images of caramel I'd once pictured stretching from a Snickers bar.

"Who *are* you?" Liz asked when I stopped. "That was great! Bring *that* version of yourself to class every week."

Liz's compliment was gratifying, but experience had taught me that I'd try to be that version every week and rarely succeed. For once, I felt OK with that. I was beginning to accept that such peaks and valleys were inherent in riding—and in life. Experience had also taught me that over the long-term, my efforts' wavy line bent toward progress.

I untacked Finn and led him to the paddock. He'd never gotten comfortable with stalls, but given his overall success, Tom hadn't forced the issue.

Finn crossed the paddock to stand beside Cash. I smiled seeing both geldings happy and healthy.

Their status stood in sharp contrast to that of a horse named Caramel I met the next fall.

Charlie relaxes in shade between lessons in August 2018 © Lisa Whalen

Lisa Whalen

Finn soaks up the early-morning sun in July 2017 © Lisa Whalen

Chapter 5 - Scruffy and Caramel: Choose Your Transformation Trajectory

St. Paul, Minnesota, September 2014

This must be a fire code violation. Uneasy, I tried to avoid stepping on toes while I edged past rows of lawn chairs that lined Leatherdale Equine Center's back wall. Air scented by coffee and popcorn hummed with voices and shuffled pages as people poured over programs identical to the one in my hand. I scanned the crowd for Becky. She'd convinced me to attend this competition. I didn't see her, but I spotted one of only a few open seats. Once I determined the second-row stadium seat wasn't saved for anyone, I shuffled apologetically past my neighbors' knees and slid into it.

Sunlight shone through an open garage door at the arena's far end, where horse trailers dotted a knoll still intensely green despite leaves winking like medallions as September sun lit the U of M's St. Paul campus. Turning onto the campus from Larpenteur Avenue, I'd passed the apartment where a neighbor had complained about my constant crying almost 40 years earlier. Sitting directly across a cornfield from its living room window prompted a weird sense of having come full circle.

I checked my watch and stood to look for Becky. *If I can't find her, I'll just stay for an hour.* I'd been reluctant to sacrifice this first Saturday after classes had begun at the college where I taught. My yard needed raking, my house winterizing. Sitting indoors seemed an even bigger sacrifice when ducking through the arena's entrance meant leaving behind a crystal blue sky. Becky had promised the event would be worth it.

I studied the program, which told twelve equine Cinderella stories—or at least the stories' exposition, inciting incident, and rising action. Today would present the climax and, I hoped, a resolution. Horse trainers from across the Midwest would advertise their skills while competing for cash prizes. Each had donated months of training time to horses that a local rescue had saved from abuse or neglect. Busy or not, I was excited to replace horrifying "before" pictures of the horses with more pleasant "after" images. I was confident the endings would be rosy because pre-screened members of the audience would bid on the horses in a silent auction. The endeavor reminded me of my dashed hopes for Boxer, the horse in George Orwell's *Animal Farm*. Both the novel and the teacher who'd introduced me to it had shaped my life's trajectory, not unlike volunteer trainers had shaped the lives of horses I would watch at that morning's competition.

A P.A. announcement indicated the contest was starting. I gave up trying to find Becky and followed along with the program's horse and trainer profiles as their real-life counterparts were introduced.

Two pairs stood out immediately. The first, a Saddlebred gelding, elicited a collective "Oooh" from the audience. His caramel coat glimmered as if dipped in oil. His neck curved from shoulder to muzzle like a candy cane. A buttercream mane frosted his neck. It matched a tail as fine as spun sugar. With each step, he confirmed his Saddlebred genetics, lifting and placing his front feet like he aimed to set a teacup on a saucer. His former owner had given him a nonsensical name typical of breed registries. It seemed beneath his dignity, so I called him Caramel.

I soured when I noticed Caramel's trainer: a dark-haired woman in a quilted Blue Vest and designer breeches. Blue Vest led Caramel by a lead rope but also held a leather crop over his head, where cliché dictated a carrot should dangle. Already high-strung by breed, Caramel looked electrified. White slivers showed at his eye's edge. *A new environment, loudspeaker, crowd, and unfamiliar horses aren't enough for him to deal with, so she adds the constant threat of a whack? Why would she use that tactic with an abused horse?* Even my amateur eye saw that the crop was a crutch she was using to make Caramel hyperflex his neck, which strained his spine and front legs, to look like fashionable show horses that usually burned out within three years.

The second standout pair was Blue Vest and Caramel's opposite. A trainer who looked 16 but the program said was 22 ambled in on stork's legs. An oversized silver buckle seemed the only thing that kept his jeans from pooling around his ankles. His brown cowboy hat looked oversized. He was followed by a short, squat, mutt of a mare. Her dun coat looked scruffy, though I knew she'd been bathed and groomed. Not a single characteristic distinguished Scruffy. The two would have been easy to write off except that talent oozed from the trainer's pores. His lowkey presence filled the arena and drew the eye. When he acknowledged their introduction to the crowd, a spark lit in Scruffy's eye. Her gait twinkled with joy. She followed him absent a lead rope, giving the impression the two were linked by invisible thread. *I'm watching the Mozart of horse training.* I decided that's what I'd call him.

As the other pairs were introduced, I glanced at Scruffy. She stood beside Mozart looking content. Caramel shifted his weight, pawed the dirt, and swung his backend to stand parallel with the rail instead of remaining beside Blue Vest. She guided Caramel back into position without raising the crop, but her smile looked strained. Trainers on either side of her eyed Caramel warily, gripping their lead ropes every time he moved.

Blue Vest returned to dangling the crop over Caramel's head for Round One's halter class. Saddlebreds excelled at dressage, a complex, nuanced discipline, so halter classes, which equated to equine ABCs, shouldn't require threats.

Mozart led Scruffy through Round One like a potter shaping clay. Her legs, designed for efficiency rather than glamour, were all business, but coupled with her attitude, they made her gaits comically endearing. She wasn't just in on the joke that she was competing against Saddlebreds and Thoroughbreds, she played it to full effect.

The crowd and I grew increasingly nervous at Caramel's unpredictability. I worried something would startle him, setting off a chain of spooked horses that shuddered like a freight car coupling to a train. I held my breath and sat on my hands when Blue Vest led Caramel through Round Two's obstacle course. When asked to walk between two planters of marigolds, Caramel galloped. He nosed PVC pipes reluctantly but stepped over them without fuss. He crossed the wood platform with only a small start at hearing his hooves. I thought he might be OK going over a blue tarp spread on the sand, but after trotting to it, he skidded to a stop. Blue Vest pulled on the lead rope. Caramel locked his knees and leaned on his haunches. Blue Vest stood behind him and waved her arms. Caramel moved his backend left and then right, willing to move in any direction except forward. When Blue Vest waggled the crop, Caramel reared. Ultimately, they timed out and ended the round without finishing the course.

Scruffy's Round Two efforts raised my spirits. She and Mozart seemed to meld minds. She danced through the course like a kid in her first pair of tap shoes. She didn't look twice at the tarp, even after sand skittered across it, sounding like a snake. She hopped into the trailer and backed out again without hesitation. Then she turned to the crowd and nodded as if to say, "You may applaud me now." So we did.

Scruffy's only slipup came on her way out of the arena. As she followed Mozart toward the exit, she startled at the marigolds, arching her back and springing up from all four feet like a cat. She recovered and resumed meandering after Mozart without a care. If Mozart hadn't already won me over, his response to a silly mistake that capped off their perfect round would have. He checked to make sure Scruffy was OK, shrugged, put up his hands, and looked at us with a "What can you do?" grin.

Difficulty increased in Round Three, along with Caramel's apprehension. Under saddle, he shied, crow-hopped, and almost collided with another horse during the warmup. Blue Vest asked him to canter, but he bolted. I swapped hoping the pair would place for praying they'd finish unharmed. I longed to see Caramel calm and free to be himself instead of forced into a limiting frame for a showy effect.

Caramel's situation called to mind my own after my family moved to Omaha, where I contorted my identity trying and failing to fit in. Even books thwarted my efforts. My classmates favored the "Choose Your Own Adventure" series, but I hated the novels' formulaic plots. Narrated in second-person point of view, the books turned the reader into the protagonist and then prompted a choice: Enter the abandoned house? Cheat on the test? Shoplift the candy? That choice led to others and then one of several possible endings. The point of view jarred my ear. The simplistic morality insulted my intelligence. Choices that led to a happy ending announced themselves from page one because "wrong" choices involved bad behavior.

Most of all, I resented the books for depriving their characters of a resolution. Protagonists and antagonists alike remained suspended between parallel worlds, forever in limbo. Voicing my dislike for the series would have sealed my outcast fate, so I kept quiet. I checked the novels out from the library but skimmed or ignored them in favor of books like *Dear Mr. Henshaw*.

I maintained a similar *modus operandi* in high school, where I spent the first 15 minutes of every day mute during homeroom. The only good thing about four years of those daily meetings was Mr. Kolterman.

He'd proven less frightening than his reputation as the district's toughest teacher implied. Throughout my ninth-grade year, he'd starred as Daddy Warbucks in a community theater production of *Annie*, and began several mornings by belting out the song "Tomorrow" from down the hall. Then he slid open the glass door to our room, coffee mug in hand, and boomed, "Good morning, ladies and gentlemen! Welcome to another fine day!" He held the mug up in salute and took a hearty swig before settling behind his desk.

Cobbled together from disparate elements that shouldn't have jived but did, Mr. K supplied homeroom with its only noteworthy moments. Tall and long-legged, he got away with wearing sneakers and jeans because both remained spotless and because he paired the jeans' dark wash and military creases with sports coats. He knew exactly how far he could push school convention and student perception, wearing a gold hoop in his left ear so thin and inconspicuous it seemed less rebellious statement than appendage. A pendant that hung from a silver chain around his neck matched the turquoise on each ring finger. Thick lenses set in chunky black frames made his eyes difficult to read but somehow balanced his goatee and bald pate.

Like his appearance, Mr. K's personality kept students intrigued and therefore engaged. He rolled into the parking lot on mild mornings with his black, IROC-Z's T-top open and its stereo booming. In winter, he traded the IROC-Z for a black Suburban he called "The Beast" in tribute to his favorite novel, *Lord of the Flies*. His vehicles, strict standards, and ability to pivot within the same breath from slang to Shakespeare kept meathead guys who thought nothing of slinging the word "fag" at each other from applying the slur to him.

Though an avid reader, I'd disliked literature until Mr. Kolterman showed me in sophomore honors English that mining the text's layers made meaning rise from the page, beginning with *Animal Farm*. I sympathized with Boxer the horse immediately, unaware that like him, I operated from a flawed belief that I could solve any problem by working harder. Little did I know that his friends' betrayal would cause Boxer's unhappy ending and foreshadow my lead-up to A.C. a month later.

Mr. K's comments, scrawled across my essays in red felt-tip, offered the first evidence I believed that I might be more than an average student. When he showed my work as an example in class, I began seeing myself as a potential scholar. He helped me recognize that George Bernard Shaw's *Pygmalion* was more sophisticated than comparisons to *Cinderella* implied and more nuanced than *My Fair Lady*. I liked listening for echoes of its ancient foundation: Ovid's *Metamorphoses*. Had I an inkling of what was coming in my junior year, I'd have been more intentional about enjoying Mr. K's class.

As it was, stories of transformation appealed to the perfectionist in me, and Shaw's carried the added sparkle of challenging messages about economic class and social status I'd been running into like fences since my first day at Rockbrook. I'd already begun transforming, thanks to my ninth-grade diet. I took inspiration from Eliza Doolittle, followed Boxer's example, and intensified my efforts at transforming by adding to my daily workouts a nightly routine of sit-ups, leg lifts, and stretches.

In October, my plan bore fruit. My friend Gretchen grew tired of my predictions that I'd end up a spinster like Miss Havisham in Dickens' *Great Expectations*. She announced, "I know a guy who's perfect for you. I'm going to set you two up."

Gretchen pulled a compact from her purse and dusted powder on freckles sprinkled across her nose. Though they highlighted, rather than compromised, her creamy complexion, she tried to hide them by distracting with wild eye shadow and changing hair color. She used a palm to smooth strands that were the shy pink of blush champagne that week. Once satisfied, she snapped the compact shut and stowed it in the purse on her lap. She settled me with a "now, pay attention," stare and declared, "You don't know this guy. He's a senior. You'll like him."

Before I could ask for details, the bell rang, sending us to separate homerooms.

A senior? My parents wouldn't like that. They'd probably nip Gretchen's plan in the bud before it could bloom. The idea didn't devastate me. I couldn't help but flash on my disastrous third-grade relationship with Jake. I was curious about this new guy and excited about having a date, but I knew I'd never live up to a senior's expectations.

Buoyed by Westside's rare football victory two weeks after Gretchen's decree, I ditched my flute and marching band uniform to don a carefully selected outfit: black jeans to slim my thighs and a blue ribbed turtleneck to emphasize my eyes. I flipped my head upside down, scrubbed my fingertips against my skull to reanimate curls that my uniform's hat had flattened, and checked my reflection in the locker room mirror. I didn't have time to do more than swab gloss on my lips before I squished into Gretchen's backseat.

Pizza Hut's warmth relieved late-October's chill. Steam fogged the windows. Def Leopard's "Pour Some Sugar on Me" drifted from the kitchen to mix with Pac-Man's *wocka-wocka-wocka* from the arcade. The air smelled of baking dough. My stomach rumbled.

Gretchen helped upperclassmen I didn't recognize pull together tables so we could join them. I stood at the periphery, bit my lip, shifted my weight from one foot to the other. My arms felt gangly in the letter jacket I'd earned for gymnastics. I folded them across my chest, then worried I appeared closed off and clasped my hands instead.

When I sank into a chair beside a long-time friend named Molly, Gretchen leaned in from behind me and whispered, "We should have put you at the other end." She looked down the table and waved at a lanky guy in a blue sweater. That was *him*—the senior she wanted to set me up with: Collin.

"Yeah, too bad," I said, secretly relieved. The scene felt like too much: crowded setting, unfamiliar people, inside jokes I didn't get. My brain's circuitry sizzled.

I snuck a peek at Collin and caught the impression of thick, black hair starting to flip up at the ends from natural curl. Olive complexion. Broad forehead narrowing to a firm chin. *Cute.*

Hair prickled on my arms and nape. Something felt odd about others' surreptitious glances and stage-worthy gestures. They were watching me. *They all know I'm here to meet him!* Gretchen had told everyone, of course. My palms grew clammy.

I couldn't flirt under scrutiny. Experience had taught me how that would go: My face would burn, my brain would melt, words would wither in my throat. I'd giggle nervously at every utterance, then stare at my fingernails or tuck my hair behind my ear repeatedly like I had a tic. I scrabbled for an excuse to leave, then remembered Gretchen had driven me.

Waiters delivering pizzas and soda provided a distraction. I picked at a slice of pepperoni, pulling it apart to make it look like I'd eaten. The guys competed to stretch the longest strand of melted mozzarella while inhaling one slice after another. Once the focus shifted away from me, my muscles unclenched. Soon, my cheeks ached from laughing at the guys' antics.

Gretchen and Molly announced they were going to the bathroom. I rose to tag along, but Gretchen shook her head. Hurt, I sipped water, ignored my stomach's howling, and wondered how to avoid looking like a loser while sitting alone.

I didn't have to wonder long. Collin slid into Gretchen's empty chair.

"Hi, Lisa. How's it going?" He smiled and drummed graceful piano-playing fingers on the tabletop.

What would Gretchen say? I searched my mind for a witty response but came up blank. "Um, hi. Good. How're you?"

I wouldn't have expected such deep chocolate irises to be ringed with flecks of gold. They gave his eyes a warm glow. The effect was hypnotic. His neck—too long and elegant for a teenage boy—was balanced by a strong nose and a square chin. His smile revealed a dimple in his right cheek and a sliver of space between his front teeth.

Collin asked where in the flute section I'd stood during our band's halftime performance. "I heard you were the only ninth-grade flutist selected for Warrior Concert Band last year," he said.

Wow. I was impressed by his memory and the dossier Gretchen had evidently prepared.

I nodded, then asked Collin about his college and career plans. Suddenly, we were talking easily, though he carried the conversation.

Gretchen tapped me on the shoulder 20 minutes later. "We've gotta go. Jenny has to be home by midnight, and I'm her ride."

I nodded, surprised to feel disappointed that I had to end my conversation with Collin.

Gretchen peppered me with questions on the drive home. What did I think of Collin? Wasn't he hot? Smart? The sweetest guy I'd ever met? I agreed but played it cool. I feared his replies to the same questions would adhere to a familiar theme: "Lisa's too quiet." Quiet girls didn't pique boys' interest.

In the cafeteria on Monday morning, Gretchen insisted that Collin wanted to date me. The news kept me floating dreamily through the day's classes.

Scheduling our first date was complicated by Collin's job and my commitments to sports and music. I worried he'd lose interest. Gretchen hectored me about asking him to Christmas Prom, a dance that reversed boy-asks-girl tradition. She promised he would say yes. I agreed but fell mute every time I tried.

On Thanksgiving Eve, Gretchen grabbed my hand and pulled me toward the school's main staircase. I had just reached the bottom when Collin turned the landing's corner. He stopped short when he saw us, grinned, then descended to meet us.

"Lisa has something to say." Gretchen pushed me forward.

I gasped and shot her a look.

Collin flashed an amused smile. "Oh?" he said, coyly. "Is there something you want to ask me?"

Heat spread from my cheeks to my temples. "Oh," I started. "Um, yeah, I was wondering— I mean, do you want to go to Christmas Prom? With me?"

"Yeah." Collin's smile widened. "That sounds fun."

I swooned.

When he left, Gretchen nudged my shoulder. "That wasn't so hard now, was it?"

Collin and I managed to meet for dinner and a movie the weekend before the dance. Despite feathery snowflakes that slicked roads and soaked our shoes, the date went better than I could have hoped. We returned to my house at 9:30 to slouch on the basement carpet, our backs against the recliner, and watch a rented movie. A single corner lamp bathed the beige walls in creamy light. Dark paneling lent the room a sense of intimacy. I couldn't stop smiling. Every time Collin reached for the Mountain Dew I'd offered him, his thigh brushed mine. My body's right side felt electrified. Current surged between us. I curled my toes to keep from trembling and poured concentration into sensing every millimeter of skin where Collin had laced his fingers through mine.

I had just begun calming when Collin turned to face me and leaned forward. His eyes grew until he looked like a cyclops. His lips touched mine before I recognized what was happening. *You're supposed to close your eyes when you kiss!* I remembered, glimpsing a family portrait on the wall behind Collin's shoulder. I blinked my eyelids shut a split-second before we parted. *So that's what they mean by fireworks...*

Already my favorite season, Christmas surpassed all expectations even as I counted the days until I'd turn 16 on New Year's Eve. I also counted the minutes until Christmas Prom, but when it arrived, I didn't allow enough time to get ready. Using hot rollers for the first time took longer than I expected. I had yet to put on a fake emerald necklace and earrings when the doorbell rang. My stomach flipped. I fumbled with the necklace's clasp. *This is it.* I gave myself a final onceover in my dresser mirror. I felt gripped by otherworldly certainty that my life was about to begin.

Air collected beneath my dress as I raced down the stairs, surrounding my thighs with a rippling taffeta halo.

"You should have seen Collin's face," Mom reported the next morning. "When you came floating down, he looked utterly smitten—just blown away. It was like a movie. I've never seen anything like it."

I took the fact that our chemistry left the most pragmatic person I knew starstruck as a sign Collin and I were meant to be.

We stopped at Collin's house for pictures and then visited someone whose significance I wouldn't recognize until that fall. In the moment, I suspected nothing. Collin led me into Hy-Vee Supermarket, where he had ascended from bagger to customer service representative. Cashiers fawned over my dress. A manager wished us well. Then Collin brought me to checkout lane 13 and the person he most wanted me to meet.

"I'm Tonya," the woman replied, gripping my icy fingers with a firmness that belied her size. Baggy khakis and a Hy-Vee vest couldn't disguise how petite but well-proportioned she was—exactly the way I wanted to look. "It's nice to meet you."

When I returned Tonya's greeting, she added, "I was hoping Collin would stop by. We're pretty fond of him around here. I wanted to see you two all dressed up."

Suddenly, my dress seemed childish. I felt stung by pangs of envy at the time Tonya spent with Collin—far more than I could. Though hairspray had turned her ebony bangs into a sculpture more elaborate than mine, closer inspection revealed crow's feet forming at her temples. I suspected she was at least a decade older than Collin. *She's no competition*, I thought, relieved.

Collin noticed my involuntary shudder when the store's automatic doors released us into a subzero night. He pulled me close and rubbed my bare arms, making my refusal to wear a coat worth the argument it had provoked with Mom.

The evening flew past in a blur of color and music: tealights flickering on white tablecloths, jewel-toned dresses shimmering beneath spotlights, bass beats thumping from car-sized speakers, my arms tingling when they brushed Collin's sleeves. Friends cooed about how cute Collin and I were together—how utterly, sickeningly, adorably, perfect we were as a couple. They kept using that magic word: perfect.

Weight I'd lost since buying my dress caused its bodice to slip from my shoulders repeatedly. I tugged at my neckline, worried about showing too much cleavage. When my efforts grew too frequent and obvious to disguise as casual gestures, I cracked a joke about my dress's refusal to stay up.

Collin put his mouth near my ear and shouted over the music, "I'm not complaining." He faced me again and smiled, waggling his eyebrows suggestively. His eyes were glazed with lust.

I froze. I'd never felt desired, didn't think myself desirable. My heart pounded. I suspended, paralyzed, between fear and pleasure.

Collin saw my expression and panicked. "I'm sorry," he mouthed. He studied my face, his own clouding with uncertainty. He leaned toward me, hesitated, then put his lips near my ear. "I shouldn't have said that. I was just kidding."

His breath on my neck sent a shiver down my spine. My body flooded with adrenaline. I felt slithery and strong, like I could curl around a car and lift it—my first taste of the power sex grants a woman.

I touched Collin's sleeve and flashed a sly smile. "It's OK. I liked it."

When Collin's features relaxed, I felt more commanding than I ever had—and than I ever would again.

Two weeks before my birthday, I knelt on my bedroom's lavender carpet and slid my 116-pound body into left-leg splits I would hold for two minutes to prepare for Westside's upcoming Drill Squad auditions. I'd dreamed of joining the dance team that was limited to juniors and seniors since seventh grade. I breathed through the strain of elongating muscles like gymnastics had taught me.

Someone knocked on my door.

Mom stuck her head in. "There's someone here to see you."

The clock on my nightstand read 10:12 p.m. *Who would drop by this late, even on a Friday? And why is Mom OK with it?* I shot her a puzzled look.

She pushed the door open and shrugged. "You'll have to come downstairs to find out."

I traded bike shorts for black jeans I'd worn to school, tucked in my red turtleneck, and bounded down the stairs.

Gretchen stood in the front entryway, her cheeks deep pink. She pulled off her gloves, shoved them in her coat's pockets, and then shivered as she handed the coat to Mom. Behind Gretchen, Molly and both their boyfriends also gave Mom their coats. Then Collin stepped through the door and shut it behind him.

"Happy Birthday!" they shouted in unison.

"What? But... You all said you had plans tonight."

"We lied so we could surprise you," Gretchen explained. "Your Mom invited us. Collin had to work until 9:30, so we met him there and... here we are. Surprise!"

Mom grinned like a Cheshire cat, clearly pleased with herself. *This means Mom and Dad like Collin!* I hadn't thought their fears about me dating anyone would allow that to happen.

"Come in, come in." Mom waved everyone down the hallway. She swung open the dining room's French doors to reveal a table covered with snacks, soda, and a cake bearing the image of a car and driver's license.

My mouth hung open.

"You all have fun!" Mom climbed the stairs. "I'm going to sleep."

My hands began shaking, so I stuck them in my back pockets. "Dig in!" I encouraged everyone.

Collin bumped my hip with his and whispered, "Hey. Happy birthday."

I bumped him back and whispered, "Hey, yourself. Thanks."

He kissed me gently on the lips.

"Awwwww!" the others crooned.

"You guys are too perfect," Molly declared.

I grinned like an idiot, Eliza Doolittle in my own version of *Pygmalion.*

Collin and I saw each other every chance we got, which wasn't as often as I'd have liked. I never took off the gold necklace he'd given me for Christmas. I loved how it made me feel connected to him, though not enough to erase worries that he'd dump me for one of many thin, leggy girls who walked Westside's halls with confidence I didn't have and without inhibitions I did.

Insecurity fed my dysfunction. I analyzed female bodies, comparing their every line and angle to mine. I even compared my limbs to Collin's, which were long and ropey with muscle. He and his buddies fueled nuclear metabolisms with Taco Bell but never gained an ounce. Collin expressed nothing but appreciation for my body, but I was convinced that to keep him, I'd have to get thinner.

I'll have to settle for powder and mascara, I decided one evening in March. I didn't have time for more than that. I leaned toward the mirror to coat my lower lashes. Even in the bathroom's flattering light, my skin looked sallow and my eyes glassy. Purple ruts had formed below my eyes. I sighed at my reflection. *At least I washed my hair.*

The day before I hadn't left bed to bathe. The thermometer had read 103.7 when I'd pulled it from beneath my tongue. The doctor had diagnosed simultaneous ear, sinus, and respiratory infections. I'd been sick a lot since the school year had begun. A voice at the back of my head whispered that my poor health had something to do with how little I ate. I ignored it.

I bent at the waist to fluff my hair. A squeezing pressure cinched my forehead. Pain exploded behind my eyes. I grabbed the towel bar to steady myself and straightened one vertebra at a time. Once upright, I closed my eyes and waited for the wallpaper's pink and yellow flowers to stop quivering.

Collin had called a few minutes earlier and asked to visit since I'd been absent from school all week. Mom had stunned me by agreeing to forego a longstanding family rule that any kid too sick for school was too sick for fun. Maybe she was relieved I was showing signs of life.

I'd eaten only an apple and a cup of soup while home sick, claiming illness staunched my appetite, which wasn't true. I just liked the stage of hunger where my stomach stopped growling and shrank. Emptiness made me feel light, clean, and pure.

I shivered. My toes were tinged blue and felt cold to the touch. I pictured Dad rolling his eyes and shouting, "Put some socks on! No wonder you're sick!" But my painted toenails looked delicate against my pale skin and bony ankles. *I'll risk getting yelled at.*

Collin and I cuddled on the basement couch. My head felt wrapped in cotton, my body like a germ factory. I could almost trace the microorganisms' paths as they wandered through my internal organs. Still, I nearly levitated with happiness. I'd warned Collin on the phone that I might be contagious, but he'd wanted to see me anyway.

I interrogated him about school: Which couples had broken up? Who was flirting with who?

He opened his mouth to answer, then gasped. He held his hand a few inches from my biceps. "God! You're radiating heat. I can literally feel it coming off you. Are you sure you're OK?"

I waved him off. "I'm fine. So, you were saying… ?"

He started to speak. Then he leaned in to kiss me.

"Don't!" I put my hand in front of my mouth. "You'll get sick!"

Gently, he pushed my hand away. "It's worth the risk."

It was the most romantic thing I'd ever heard.

While Mr. Kolterman made me a smarter student, Collin made me a better person—funnier and more outgoing, sexier and more confident. Group dates were fun, but my favorite times were those we had to ourselves. On one such date, we left a basketball game to watch *Days of Thunder* at my house. Aside from a scene in which Nicole Kidman ripped off her helmet and shook out her golden curls to accept Tom Cruise's kiss, I didn't know what the movie was about. I'd been suspended in the present for what—an hour? 90 minutes? I noted only Collin's Polo cologne, the taste of tacos on his tongue, the tickle of his lips against my neck, the heat of his hands beneath my clothes. I had no idea being in my body could feel good. That countered every message I'd absorbed from religion, gymnastics, and dieting.

Collin pulled back. He cradled my chin with his thumb and index finger. "You don't have to wait for me to initiate everything, you know. You can kiss me first."

"I know. I'm sorry." I looked at my lap. Then I remembered that I was supposed to stop apologizing all the time. I started to apologize for apologizing and caught myself.

The truth was that I *didn't* know. I still waited for Collin to reach for my hand, sending telepathic messages instead of grabbing his.

"Try it," he suggested. He ran his thumb over the pink paint on my fingernail.

"Now?"

"Yeah. If you want to."

"I do. I just..."

"What?"

"I don't know. I'm afraid you'll pull away or I'll do it wrong or something."

"You can't do it wrong. And I won't pull away. I promise. I *want* you to kiss me."

I stared into his eyes. His dilated pupils sucked me in and swayed me.

"OK, you better not." I poked him in the ribs to underscore my point. I closed my eyes and leaned forward. The distance felt like a chasm. I felt his breath on my cheek and prepared to meet his lips when I heard him swallow a laugh. I opened my eyes to discover he'd pulled back and was watching me.

I slugged his shoulder. "You promised you wouldn't do that!"

He laughed. "I couldn't resist. You looked so cute I couldn't help it."

I laughed, too, but to hide embarrassment. Something squeezed too tightly around my chest.

"Try it once more. I won't do that again."

I couldn't move, couldn't speak.

"I'm sorry," Collin said, sounding sincere.

I snuggled into his arms, loving the feel of his chest against my back and his chin atop my head. But I couldn't relax. The exchange unsettled me, and I didn't know why.

My weight's plateau unsettled me, too. No matter how many calories I cut or how much I exercised, I struggled to lose more weight. As March ticked into April, I spent more time running sprints up Westside's stadium stands. I worried about Collin seeing me in a swimsuit and wanted to look good for the year's peak event: Prom.

Prom was inherently tied to sex, especially for virgins. The couples Collin and I hung out with made no secret of their sex lives or the hotel rooms they'd booked. Collin and I preferred discretion, but everyone teased us anyway. We didn't really mind. We knew where we stood and where our relationship was headed; that was all that mattered.

I wore my first strapless dress. Its fitted bodice of pale pink silk hugged my shrinking torso perfectly. My ivory skin looked delicate rather than pallid. Pronounced collarbones framed the gold necklace Collin had given me.

Despite my dyed-to-match two-inch heels, Collin dwarfed me by almost a foot. A fresh haircut and the tuxedo I helped pick out made him even more handsome. But his smile in photos seemed reluctant—almost a smirk.

He's always hated having his picture taken. I was too busy hopscotching from one cloud to the next to notice warning lights blinking from the ground.

After dinner at Caniglia's Venice Inn, slow dances, a Post-Prom Party in the school gym, and a make-out session in the car, Collin and I headed to my house to make breakfast. Batter sizzling on the griddle filled the kitchen with its cakey scent. My stomach growled. Ignoring it was easy. We bumped into each other purposely, then joked about the tight space between stove and sink. I bustled with energy yet felt deeply content.

While I waited for the pancakes to brown, I spun from the griddle, spatula in hand, and planted a kiss on Collin's lips.

"Wow! What was that for?"

"Just because." I smiled and kissed him again.

"Mmm, I love it," he said.

I scooped pancakes from the griddle and piled them on plates. Collin doused his with syrup and fed me a bite. The sugar hit my bloodstream like a drug. My skin hummed.

A voice at the back of my head whispered that this was the happiest I'd ever be. I didn't know where it came from, so I shook it off.

The harder I tried to lose weight, the faster I slid into melodrama. I didn't know what brought it on, though it seemed to intensify as I grew stingier with calories.

Sometimes jealousy turned my chest into a sucking wound. I feared losing Collin to someone thinner, prettier, less socially awkward. I knew showing my insecurity made me less appealing, so I swallowed it.

A few times I overreacted to something Collin said and lapsed into pouting. Later, I couldn't remember why I'd been upset and felt embarrassed by my behavior.

"Are you cold?" Collin asked as we hung out at my house one night. He pulled a blanket from the back of the couch and wrapped me in it. I nodded, grateful for the ruse. I *was* cold all the time, but my trembling when we made out had nothing to do with temperature. By Friday or Saturday night, hunger and its insomnia had worn me down. I anticipated seeing Collin to the point of distraction, then felt pressured to make the most of our time together. Mostly, though, my trembling was caused by overloaded circuits. I craved physical contact but also feared it: where it could lead, what I'd lose if I followed it—or if I didn't. Nothing would disappoint my parents more than knowing I'd had sex at 16. Without sex, I feared Collin would tire of me.

The closer Collin and I inched toward sex, the louder a voice in my head shouted warnings. If we slept together and our relationship ended, I'd crack into a million jagged shards. Yet an end—or at least a pause—seemed inevitable. Collin would leave for college in August. He'd enter a world I couldn't access or understand. Few relationships survived that separation.

Still, I expected we'd marry, probably once we both finished college. How could we not end up together, if he loved me a fraction as much as I loved him?

We were talking about sex. How almost everyone we knew was having it. Whether we should. Whether we would before he left for college. We were running out of time.

Collin wore a favorite blue t-shirt and nylon soccer shorts, but he looked better than ever: solid, confident, mature.

Our feet pushed off in synch and kept the patio swing swaying. I stared at his familiar blue boat shoes beside my white sandal's crisscrossed straps and willed myself to enjoy the moment. The scene should have been idyllic. The magnolia tree's branches arched overhead like a protective umbrella. Dusk had turned the sky purple. Crickets chirped. Fireflies winked. My hand rested in Collin's. His touch had become familiar, too; the pressure of his fingertips on my knuckles comforted. I didn't know what I'd do without it. I tried to remain upbeat, but sorrow draped my voice. My mind felt cloudy. I couldn't think, didn't know what else to say. He seemed preoccupied, antsy. I noticed that a lot lately but chalked it up to the same moroseness clinging to me and to nervousness about college.

He turned, tucked a loose strand behind my ear. His watch slid from his wrist to his forearm. I smiled at our shared habit: I wore mine loose, too.

"I don't think we should," Collin said, softly.

I searched his eyes to see whether he was saying what he thought I wanted to hear. He seemed sincere.

"OK. Me either."

I'd have agreed no matter what he said.

A squall gathered force inside me. I wanted him to love me with a fierceness that didn't allow resistance to any part of me, body or soul. I wanted confirmation that my love was strong enough to overpower pledges made to God and family. I wanted him to prove what I suspected: That having sex wouldn't make me Bad. Most of all, I wanted fate to confirm what I knew to be true: That nothing could keep us apart.

"What do you think of this one?"

Collin stretched out his arms and turned a circle.

I drank in the shirt's fit. Its navy neckline made his eyes look darker and more mysterious. A wide green stripe showed off his broadening shoulders. Thinner white stripes below the green emphasized his trim waist.

"I like it," I replied. I glanced around to make sure no one was near the dressing rooms, adopted a breathy, Marilyn Monroe voice, and added, "It looks *very* good on you."

He tipped his head and smirked. "Yeah? How good?"

"Realllllly good."

He flipped the price tag over and considered. "OK. I'll get this one. I have one more left to try on."

I wandered away from the dressing room entrance and rifled through a rack of t-shirts. *Definitely more blue. And maybe some black to show off his tan.*

Normally I hated shopping, but aside from freezing in air conditioning that felt arctic, I was having fun. I loved that Collin wanted my input. It confirmed the identity I clung to proudly as more and more people referred to me as Collin's girlfriend rather than by my name. Only a serious girlfriend would be asked to select clothes her boyfriend would take to college. I liked that the clothes would remind him of me while he was away. Still, something squeezed the air from my lungs every time I thought about him leaving.

We bumped hips and shoulders strolling the aisles. He grabbed an arrangement of silk daisies, narcissus, and blue iris from a shelf and imitated a gallant English gentleman when handing it to me. I fluttered my eyelids and purred, "Why thank you, Mr. Darcy."

The best thing about the afternoon was its ordinariness. We combed racks side by side, agreeing on everything, except when I grabbed a polyester shirt of orange and brown paisley and held it up to declare, "This is *sooo* you!"

"Nice," he replied, voice dripping with sarcasm. He laughed, showing the sliver of space between his teeth that I loved so much. My heart lurched.

This is my favorite date. I preferred its casual intimacy, its blend of silliness and tenderness, to Prom's rigidity. I pictured more of its sweet mundanity seven or eight years down the road when I'd be Collin's Wife. We'd work as a team: shopping for groceries, picking up dry cleaning, balancing checkbooks, raking leaves, attending family BBQs.

I couldn't wait to greet that future with open arms. I had no idea how perfectly that posture positioned me for a fall.

At the Leatherdale Center more than 20 years later, Caramel seemed set for a fall, while Scruffy ascended toward success.

Mozart rode Scruffy for Round Three as skillfully as he'd led her for Rounds One and Two. He held the reins loosely in one hand but could have been in a boat on a windless day for all he moved. Only his shirtsleeves' flapping hinted at how fast Scruffy could canter, how high she could jump, and how precisely she could halt.

For the freestyle category in Round Four, Blue Vest followed 15 minutes of tedious prop setup with a reenacted fairy tale. Caramel wore a costume—the handsome prince come to save his damsel in distress. Their routine didn't include a single skill Caramel hadn't already shown that day. Its gimmicks seemed designed to show off the trainer's creativity instead of Caramel's suitability for a new owner. He looked less anxious than he had all day, but only because he had seesawed in the other direction, seeming resigned. Annoyed, I crossed my arms and sighed as the pair's five minutes dragged.

Caramel never placed in the top five when the results were announced. Scruffy earned first place in Rounds One and Three, second in Round Two.

I contemplated leaving. It was 2:00; I'd arrived at 9:00. I'd talked briefly with Becky between Rounds One and Two, but she was sitting a mile away. Hearing a country song blare from the speakers sealed my decision. I stood to make my way out but paused when Scruffy cantered into the arena virtually sparkling with excitement. She didn't slow as Mozart hopped from the saddle, touched his boots to the ground, and leapt back in facing backward. I plunked back into my seat, mouth open.

Mozart repeated the maneuver, alternating in quick succession from Scruffy's left and right sides like she was a pommel horse. He scooted onto her rump, grasped the back of the saddle, and flew like Superman. His face hovered inches from Scruffy's churning hooves, but I never doubted his safety. They'd become a single organism. Mozart leapt back into the saddle facing forward just in time for Scruffy to leap a barrel. They drew a spiral, turning tighter and tighter until Scruffy slid to a stop at its center.

With the song's last chords fading, Scruffy leapt onto a flatbed truck backed into the arena's center. Mozart waved at the driver. Scruffy didn't flinch at the engine's diesel growl. The driver shifted into gear and drove from the arena with Scruffy still as Buddha beneath Mozart.

The crowd and I jumped to our feet. Whistles pierced the air. We clapped and stomped until Mozart led Scruffy in for an ovation. He doffed his hat and bowed; she curled a front leg and curtsied. We burst into vocal cheers and continued clapping as they walked from the arena once more.

Mozart's confidence and ability to draw out the best in Scruffy reminded me of Mr. Kolterman. I could tell both men approached teaching by identifying a student's strengths. They dug for possibility as if searching for treasure, then held the jewels to the light and let them shine.

Blue Vest had been awarded the richest raw material, but she'd begun by identifying deficits. She sought to hide them by forcing Caramel into a beautiful but rigid—and ultimately harmful—frame.

The two pairs embodied what Sara had taught me, what I'd understood but was still learning to live. For too long, I'd treated myself like Blue Vest treated Caramel. *What if I'd treated myself like Mozart treats Scruffy?* I'd never know how a different choice might have changed my life's trajectory, but I could hold the pair in mind as a model for shaping my story's resolution.

Both Scruffy and Caramel went to good homes. In updates posted online, they looked happy and healthy. In fact, Scruffy looked a lot like my equine nemesis, Penny.

And I was on the verge of finding out that my battles with Penny had barely begun.

Lisa rides Penny through a bounce (two fences with one stride between them) in August 2018. © Julie Dettinger

Part II: IMPACT
Chapter 6 - Penny: Fight for Yourself

Seventh Farm Riding School, May 2012

Waiting for The List felt like playing roulette. I imagined that a black and red wheel began spinning in Wisconsin as the Amigo's tires began rolling from my garage in Minnesota. But in the months leading up to May 2012, anticipating The List became more like watching Mr. Summers draw names from the black wooden box in "The Lottery."

My classmates agreed. As we leaned against the tack room's rough-hewn walls ahead of our lesson, Becky asked, "Who do you think you'll ride today?"

Once the others had placed their bets, I said, "probably Penny." I tried not to show displeasure when I added, "I've ridden her exclusively for months."

"Yeah, thanks for that," the lawyer replied with a laugh. "I've enjoyed having a break. I still dread Liz saying I'll ride her."

"Me too!"

As if our conversation conjured her, Liz entered carrying The List. She read off riders' names and the horses they'd be paired with for the day's lesson. "And Lisa, you're on Penny. Pull them out of their stalls and let's get going, ladies."

The lawyer chuckled. Becky shot me a look of commiseration and shrugged.

Objecting would only result in Liz repeating her teaching philosophy: "You may not get the horse you want, but you get the horse you need."

I didn't understand why I needed a bully. I was convinced Penny had inspired movies like *Heathers* and *Mean Girls*. She had the same lustrous hair, haughty expression, and ability to sniff out vulnerability those movie characters shared with Westside's track star. The sprinter had sat behind me in several classes and liked to single out shy students for public derision. One afternoon, she drew back the eraser end of her pencil like it was a slingshot and let it smack my head. The *thwack* and my startled reaction to it elicited snickers from the popular guys sitting near us. I glanced back and saw her laughing with them, soaking up their approval. Too stunned to speak, I returned to taking notes and pretended to be unfazed, though my face blazed. I spent the following weeks tensed for a repeat attack that never came.

Like Westside's star, Penny had honed her bullying technique. She dragged riders' legs along the rail. She'd once lurched away from the rail to bite a gelding's butt, straightened, and continued cantering without missing a step, while Liz reprimanded me for letting it happen. The most scathing reprimand I'd ever received came when Penny refused my requests to go forward and backed into another horse. Fortunately, the horse's rider thought quickly enough to smack Penny's rump with a crop until she moved out of kicking range.

Kicking was a genuine concern because Penny's herdmates also suffered her scorn. One of the few times she'd been allowed in the paddock between lessons, she cornered a larger mare and kicked until Liz ran in and shooed her away. Even geldings who topped the herd hierarchy gave Penny plenty of space.

I grabbed Penny's halter and peered into her stall. She pinned her ears and glared.

I sighed and rolled open the door, resolved not to put up with diva behavior. I backed Penny into the corner without trouble, but when I lifted the halter, she turned her head and snapped at me.

So, it's gonna be that kind of day, huh? Wonderful.

Penny had never bitten me, and I didn't think she would. Chomping at the air beside me was her way of saying, "I hate having my morning interrupted. I shouldn't have to put up with you."

Her tail lay still, so I didn't expect outright defiance. That could change once I got in the saddle. I smacked her chest to let her know she wouldn't get away with threatening me. She raised her head and glowered down her nose.

"Don't be that way," I said, softly. I reached beneath her neck, rested my palm against the soft hair on her cheek, and guided her head into position above my shoulder.

Were Penny human, she'd have rolled her eyes. But she snorted and held out her nose, acknowledging that the show must go on despite her contempt for the amateur with whom she was cast.

"Thanks." I pulled the halter over her ears and scratched her neck.

When I led Penny to the outdoor crossties and hooked up her halter, she snapped at me again.

"Hey! Knock it off." I shoved her head out of my personal space. My mood darkened.

Then I remembered that riding with a negative attitude wouldn't work. I'd read in *Horse Speak: An Equine-Human Translation Guide* that horses' unwanted behavior is often a reaction to what they sense in a person: angst, anger, trauma, or even mild melancholy. Before anyone enters a horse's environment, she should "return to zero," as in zero emotion, zero distraction, zero agenda[7]. Only a quiet mind and open heart would foster positive interaction. I exhaled and tried to let go of resentment. Penny stilled.

---

7. Sharon Wilsie and Gretchen Vogel, *Horse Speak: The Equine-Human Translation Guide*, (North Pomfret, VT: Trafalgar Square Books, 2016). 8.

I hoped she'd remain pacified enough that I could groom and tack her without holding a crop the way beginning riders had to. I grabbed a curry comb and ignored Penny's dramatic head nodding while I worked the teeth through her brown hide, which looked sprinkled with red and yellow glitter in the sunlight.

Penny's looks and talent kept her at Seventh Farm despite her troublemaking. Show judges underestimated her until she started moving. Within her compact frame lay an athlete's power and a dancer's grace. Barely larger than a pony, she jumped as high as most Thoroughbreds, yet her short legs covered less ground per stride, which made her gaits dreamy to ride. Her ebony tail, even thicker and shinier than her hide, added dramatic flair to every jump. A long forelock framed oversized eyes as slick and wet as black paint, giving her the wistful beauty of a character in Japanese Anime. She was exquisite, and she knew it.

Groomed and saddled, Penny followed me down the gravel path leading from the barn to the outdoor arena. The morning marked our first lesson outdoors after a long winter. Penny flared her nostrils, eager to sample the season's scents.

"Keep on your toes," Liz warned. "The horses might be spooky until they're used to being outdoors again. They might want to run."

Good! I'd tired of indoor sluggishness. Some Sunday mornings my legs ached with fatigue from reminding Penny to keep moving.

Penny echoed my sentiment. She studded our warmup with raspberries blown through puckered lips—a sign of contentment. When I stopped to adjust my stirrup length, however, she wouldn't stand still. Once trotting, she wouldn't halt. She cut the arena's back corner no matter how hard I tried steering her toward it. I gritted my teeth, caught myself growing frustrated, and tried returning to zero.

I shouldn't have let down my guard once Penny started cooperating. On our second attempt to canter over a pole, she juked like a Heisman-winning running back at the last second and went around rather than over it.

"You didn't fight for it!" Liz said, disgusted. "Pull Penny up and come over here."

I wrested back control and slowed Penny to a walk. I asked her to turn around. She corkscrewed her neck, insistent on turning the opposite direction. Knowing Liz wanted to keep class moving, I gave in and let Penny lead.

"Never cut out on a jump," Liz admonished. She shaded her eyes with one hand and grabbed the reins with the other to stop Penny's fidgeting. "You just taught Penny that it's OK to cut out in front of a fence, so she's probably going to try it again. She doesn't trust you. Without an active, engaged core, you're a pushover, and she'll take advantage of you. She's taking charge because you aren't. When she tries to carry out her own plan, use your core and spine to push her forward.

"Next time, fight for what you want. The tougher you are, the happier Penny will be. Do you think I'm timid when I ride her?"

I shook my head.

"Right. And she's an angel with me. Don't be a passive passenger. Be an active rider."

I nodded.

Liz waved me toward the rail, where my classmates had lined up to go over the same pole.

I thought about Liz's instructions while I waited for my next turn. She was right: I wasn't a fighter. Conflict set my nerve endings tingling. I preferred to stand back, go with the flow or do my own thing. Asserting myself contradicted every message I'd absorbed growing up. Good girls didn't ask for what they wanted. Wanting was a sign of greed, gluttony, or lust. Good girls worked hard, followed rules, and waited for someone to acknowledge their efforts. They didn't disagree, and they certainly didn't fight. Most importantly, they strove to be selfless.

Selflessness had been a family cornerstone for as long as I could remember. My parents had modeled it at every turn, never hesitating to go without so we kids would have what we needed. I loved them for that. Selflessness had formed an effective foundation for family interactions because we all subscribed. Its steps had become a dance we knew so well we didn't need music.

It didn't dawn on me until well into treatment with Sara that people didn't function that way in the outside world. They voiced needs, pursued wants, acted naturally, and assumed that if someone objected, he or she would say so. Everyone had figured I'd been doing the same. The realization turned my worldview upside down and shook it like a snow globe. I'd always done the opposite, looking out for what others needed and either supplying it or getting out of their way so they could find it. When my needs reared their ugly heads, instead of voicing them, I gulped them back, then worked harder to empty myself of wants. That figurative habit became a literal eating disorder. No wonder I'd viewed relationships as a series of one-way exchanges that depleted my goodwill. I'd set myself up to feel taken advantage of, to grow increasingly resentful until I broke off contact. Or, until I cut out.

Penny's refusal to go over the pole and my inability to make her do it shed new light on the way my life had split into B.C. and A.C.

Omaha, Nebraska, September 1991

"Collin slept with someone else."

The words hit with a force that almost sent me sprawling.

Collin's best friend, Keith, delivered the news, then watched for my reaction.

I resettled on the edge of his parents' living room couch, needing the pain of its frame pressing against my tailbone to counter numbness spreading through my body.

Keith moved closer until our knees nearly touched. He started to lay his hand on mine but rested it beside his leg instead. I wanted to inch away but didn't.

The air conditioning clicked on. Air whooshed through the vents. Silverware tinkled as someone unloaded a dishwasher. The sound reminded me of bells the altar boy chimed during Mass. Dad had explained half-jokingly that the bells woke up sleeping parishioners and alerted those who didn't understand Latin that the Mass was reaching its climax: transubstantiation, the moment when wafers and wine became body and blood. *How appropriate*, I would think later, since Keith's announcement marked the moment I transformed, hollowing from the person I'd been B.C. (Before Collin) into the shell I became A.C. (After Collin).

Dishwasher empty, the house suspended in weighty stillness.

"Was it...?" I faltered, tried again. "Um, with... who?"

"Tonya."

Her? I'd expected a peer, one of the juniors who'd flirted with Collin. Yet, my breastbone vibrated like a tuning fork, suggesting I'd known all along.

Tonya. The coworker Collin had introduced me to at Hy-Vee grocery store before Christmas Prom. The divorcee 10 years

Collin's senior. The mother of a young boy. The woman Collin danced with at a coworker's wedding, while I sat alone, the only attendee who didn't know a soul. The woman who'd shot me withering looks at Collin's going-away party six weeks ago.

God, I'm an idiot. I sucked in a breath. "Oh, right."

Mind reeling, I logged the room's contents as if collecting crime scene evidence: aloe plant on a side table, yellow carnations in a glass vase, blue brocade upholstery, heavy gold drapes. *Why would someone pick those?* The drapes didn't match anything, including plush carpet I gripped with my toes.

I floated near the textured ceiling and watched someone named Lisa pose questions in monotone. Keith's answers set altar bells ringing in my head again.

When?

Two months ago, while I was on a family vacation and Collin housesat for my parents. *Ding! That's why neighbors had said Collin was never around.*

Who knew?

Everyone. *Ding! That's why Gretchen shushed our friends when they made cracks about Collin just quietly enough that I couldn't understand. That's why everything had felt weird at his going away party: Everyone had known except me.* I thought I might be sick.

I wanted to ask where but couldn't form the words. *Please, not in my house.*

The room felt suffocating. *I have to get out of here.* Something feral was building in my chest. I swallowed. "Well, thanks for telling me."

I stood, hesitated, spotted my sandals on the entryway tile, and walked to collect them. Keith followed. "Are you OK to drive? Do you want to stay for a while and talk?"

I fumbled with my sandals' straps. "No, that's OK. Thanks."

I have to get out of here. Gorge rose in my throat. I gave up and shoved each foot into a shoe, leaving the straps unbuckled.

Heat smacked me when I swung open the door. The air smelled of sweat. The sun blinded. I pulled sunglasses from my head and put them on, grateful for their protection from glare but also scrutiny.

"See you…" I gave a half-hearted wave. *When? He'll leave for Army basic training soon.*

Keith picked at gray paint peeling from the doorframe. "I'll write… if you want me to." He looked from the frame to me. His gaze held more hope than seemed appropriate. I recognized its saccharine glaze from mirrors I'd looked at while prepping for dates with Collin: lovesickness.

Ding! That's why Keith was willing to narc on his best friend. That's why he kept rubbing my shoulders and offering to get me a drink at Collin's going away party. That's why he'd insisted we talk face-to-face today, instead of over the phone. Keith's motives for telling me about Collin's betrayal were no purer than my friends' for keeping the knowledge to themselves. *I've been a pawn this whole time.* Panic clawed at my lungs.

I forced a smile and told Keith, "Sure, letters would be great!" My belief that he'd follow through on his offer to keep in touch would become one more foothold I'd grasp for and feel disintegrate beneath my weight as I tumbled into depression.

My lower lip quivered. *Do not cry. Don't gift Collin with a report of how thoroughly he duped you, how completely you fell apart on hearing the news.* For a girl steeped in Catholic catechism since birth, I ignored with surprising ease the fact that pride is the worst of all seven deadly sins. And it always comes before a fall.

I waved to Keith through the windshield of my parents' car, backed down his driveway and into the street.

Construction signs along West Center Road mocked my formerly rosy view of the future: Road closed. Detour. Rough road ahead. They piled up as I drove east, as did clues to Collin's betrayal that I'd missed. Clues that were suddenly as obvious as orange cones.

I braked for a red light at 108th Street. Shade cast by a pedestrian overpass I'd walked as a kid did more to cool the car than its laboring air conditioner. I drummed my fingers on the steering wheel and counted betrayals.

Ding! My parents let Collin housesit as a favor, not because they'd needed someone present. His own parents had moved from town, leaving him with nowhere to stay while he worked to earn as much as he could before he left for college.

Ding! My parents paid Collin $100 for housesitting, knowing he would shoulder college tuition on his own. He'd accepted the money from me without a word.

Ding! Collin had invited me to his going away party, where I'd been the only attendee who didn't know he was sleeping with the woman sitting in the kitchen while I flitted around the living room.

Ding! Friends who'd known me long before they met Collin had looked me in the face and lied about his infidelity.

Ding! Collin had written to me from college, spouting gratitude for the five-page missals I sent him weekly. He'd laced his letters with compliments, inside jokes, and claims that he missed me, as if nothing had changed.

The traffic light switched from red to green. I caught a glimpse of my forearm as I turned onto 108th Street and blinked in surprise: Somewhere between Keith's house and the overpass I'd scratched my skin raw.

At home, I lay on my bedroom carpet and cried until spent. Then I put a favorite CD on repeat, ripped pages from a notebook, and navigated the chasm between what I wanted to say and what I allowed myself to put on the page.

Three drafts later, I recopied a final version of my letter to Collin, starting over each time I made a mistake. The letter seemed like a historical document, a record of the day I cracked and my life split. I wanted Collin to feel the punch words could deliver, the way I had at Keith's house.

"This is the last letter you will ever receive from me. I know about Tonya. Who told me isn't important. The only thing that matters is that it wasn't you..."

I closed with, "Have a nice life."

I didn't sign my name or put a return address on the envelope. Collin would know who sent it.

Three nights after I'd launched my letter through the mail like a missile, I curled on the family room carpet to watch a favorite TV drama called *Life Goes On*. The show featured a family like mine: white; middle-class; two parents, two daughters and a youngest son. That night's episode resolved the teenage daughter's love triangle, which had been building all season. The irony didn't escape me. But then everything seemed fraught with heightened significance. I couldn't tell what meant something and what didn't. Terrified of missing more clues but too numb to decipher what I took in, I walked the world snow-blind, grappling for any landmark that indicated where I was, how I'd gotten there, and how I'd get out.

I no longer trusted my antennae. How could I? They had failed to detect betrayal bubbling beneath the surface surrounding me.

The tuning fork buried beneath my breastbone had cracked, too. That's how I'd always pictured the internal decision-making tool I would recognize in adulthood as intuition. It had guided me like a faithful companion since childhood. Thoughts, feelings, and information my antennae collected pinged the tuning fork. The resulting vibrations' peaks and valleys separated fact from fiction and right from wrong. Since I'd learned of Collin's betrayal, however, my fork's tines warbled with a wonky tone that distorted rather than clarified. I doubted my capacity to read people and situations, to identify motives or evaluate sincerity.

Even my favorite TV show rang flat.

Still, tears leaked from my eyes while I watched. My stomach ground unceasingly. I couldn't remember the last time I had eaten, but food offered no comfort.

I was so lost in my misery that I didn't register the phone ringing until Julie tapped me on the shoulder. "It's for you."

My greeting came out as a grunt.

"Hey," said a familiar voice. "It's me."

"Hey." I wiped my eyes with the heels of my hands and told Julie I would take the call in my room.

"I got your letter," Collin said when I'd shut my bedroom door and Julie had hung up the receiver downstairs. "How are you?"

Are you serious? How do you think I am? "Not good."

Collin spun a tale about him and Tonya that cast him as the victim and put me at fault. He was hurt that I'd written in my letter about throwing away the necklace he'd given me and the pictures we'd taken.

I put my forehead in my hand and bit my cheek. *I won't beg for an apology.*

When I didn't sympathize, Collin added, "You didn't say anything about how I'd gotten glasses when you came to my going away party."

His whiny tone stoked my fury. *I'm the inconsiderate one here?* I thought about reminding Collin that he'd been well into cheating on me by the time I came to his party but decided it didn't matter.

"You were the one who said we shouldn't have sex," I sputtered. "You said we weren't ready—that *you* weren't ready—that it wouldn't be good for us. Then you slept with *her!*"

"It wasn't like that." He paused.

Like what? I considered voicing my thoughts but didn't want to make this easy for him.

"It wasn't just sex. There was more to it than that."

Is that supposed to make it better? For a second, I thought I'd spoken. Later, I'd wish I had. My cheeks stung as if slapped. *Who is this?* Nothing in Collin's words or tone sounded familiar. Their emptiness seemed to suck up air until only a vacuum remained. *Was this... vampire who he was all along? How did I miss that? I must be dumber than I thought.*

"Aren't you going to say anything?" Collin demanded.

"You didn't even have the decency to tell me. I had to hear it from Keith." The edge in my voice surprised me. I pictured skates hanging in the closet opposite my desk and the way their blades etched the ice. Rather than strong, however, my voice sounded brittle—more ice than blade. "You turned my friends against me—friends who were mine before they met you. I was the only person at your party who didn't know. And *she* was there! Do you have any idea what that feels like?"

Collin sniffled. *Is he crying?* I hoped that meant an apology was coming. That was all I needed. Then we could have a real conversation. We'd decide how we'd move forward together from where we found ourselves now. *Just say "I'm sorry,"* I telegraphed along the phone line.

After a minute in which the line's hum was all I heard, Collin sighed. "I guess that's it then."

"I guess so."

I didn't believe that was the end until I heard a click and a dial tone.

I waited for Collin to come to his senses even as I feared he wouldn't. I was equally certain that I would never see him again as I was that we would end up together. It felt like he'd died. He was gone suddenly, without explanation or goodbye, but I was so mad at what he'd done that I couldn't mourn the loss. Happy memories turned sepia, overlaid by doubt about their authenticity.

Everything in my life diverged. I became incapable of making decisions about anything—from what movie I should see to how far out of state I should go for college. I longed to leave high school behind, to wipe out and replace every memory, but I didn't want to be too far from my family.

I walked Westside's halls feeling flayed. Everything abraded: fabric, air, light. I'd been laid open. A diagram of the human figure from my biology textbook overlaid my reflection in mirrors: a genderless, featureless, collection of sinew, lidless eyes bulging. Yet I was also numb—as stiff, cold, and weighty as the ivory sculpture in Ovid's *Metamorphoses*.

Collin and I could have been cast in a play, the way we entered and exited the same stage throughout the years to come. But our timing had fatal flaws. We came closest to crossing paths in October, a month after our phone call.

My friend Barbara and I waded through trigonometry homework in study hall, hoping to finish it before the upcoming fall break. We worked too intently to notice the room's door creaking open and clicking shut as students came and went until Gretchen plunked into a chair across the table from me, her hair the color of lilac that month. She pulled a sucker from her mouth and announced, "Collin's in the cafeteria right now."

I waited for a punchline. Gretchen popped the sucker back in her mouth and watched me. When I didn't react, the sucker came out again with a crisp pop. "He's home for a long weekend and stopped in to see a few people."

Oh my God, she's not kidding! My pulse beat in my ears. I'd missed another signpost, taken another wrong turn. *Why didn't I go to the cafeteria?*

I set down my pencil, wiped my palms on my jeans and clenched my fists beneath the table. "Oh, that's nice."

"Well, I just thought you might want to know. I'm gonna head back there and say goodbye to him." Gretchen paused a beat before standing.

"OK," I replied.

She shoved the sucker between her lips and headed for the exit, pausing again after opening the door. She looked back at me. I waved. She shrugged and disappeared into the hallway. The door clicked shut with a finality that made me flinch.

I wondered if Collin had come home to see Tonya. I pictured him surprising her at Hy-Vee, her face lighting up when she spotted him walking toward her bearing roses, and felt sick. "Maybe I should just walk past—"

"NO!" Barbara's raised voice and vitriol drew looks from students at surrounding tables. She lowered her voice. "Don't give him the satisfaction."

"I just want to see if—"

"No! I don't know why you can't get over him. Move on. Forget he ever existed."

I didn't know why I couldn't let go either, but Barbara's bluntness stung. Every cell in my body cried out to get up and move—if only to catch a glimpse of Collin through the cafeteria's windows. I imagined how his face would look if he saw me. What I'd say if we came face-to-face. Did he miss me—even

163

a little? Had he ever really loved me? What had I done wrong? How could I fix it? Those questions and dozens more tortured me daily; they trailed me from the shower to the car, heckled me from Spanish class to band rehearsal.

Barbara returned to solving equations. I fidgeted, unable to concentrate.

"I have to go to the bathroom," I announced.

Barbara rolled her eyes but didn't comment. She flicked a strand of red hair over her shoulder, pushed up her glasses, and punched numbers into a calculator with her pencil's eraser.

I stepped gingerly into the hallway and saw them: Collin and Keith walked away from me down the hallway, then turned a corner. I tiptoed so my boots' heels wouldn't give me away. I peeked around the corner and spotted them again. I hesitated, trying to decide what I should do.

Before I could choose, they pushed open a door that led to the parking lot and disappeared.

It didn't cross my mind until I wrote about the experience for Sara more than a decade later that maybe, just maybe, Collin had come to see me.

October waned. Leaves the color and shape of almonds fell from the magnolia tree beneath my bedroom window. I missed the blossoms' lush scent, which had turned sour once the petals fell and browned. I perched on a cedar chest inherited from Grandpa and watched Mom rake the backyard, too tired to do anything else.

When Mom tied the last bag closed and dragged it toward the garage, I threw my homework onto the lavender carpet I'd loved in third grade but now thought childish. As happened often that year, I lay beside my homework to study, then woke two hours later with the carpet's pile impressed on one forearm and my notebook's spiral binding biting into the other. I fantasized about sleep all day, then chased it around corners at night. Staying awake during daylight hours felt torturous. I forced my eyes open again and again until I couldn't anymore. Sometimes I skipped the homework façade and crawled beneath the covers to the foot of my bed. I curled up, submerged in a cocoon of lavender cotton, and savored oblivion's approach. I hated that my parents woke me for dinner. I slung daggers across the table with my eyes and grumbled replies to only the most pointed questions, unaware my parents would one day face similar responses when they mentioned concerns about their parish priest to the Archbishop. I blamed Mom and Dad for playing a part in Collin's cheating. Even though I knew that was ridiculous, I clung to a belief that if they hadn't forced me to go on the family vacation I'd asked to skip, Collin and I would still be together.

Another blow I didn't see coming landed in fall. One Wednesday morning, Westside's principal slid open the glass door to our homeroom. I set down the pencil I'd used to fake solving equations while obsessing about another near-miss with Collin. The principal's appearance made me straighten in my seat, though I'd done nothing wrong. He hung his suitcoat on the back of Mr. K's chair. *Is he planning to stay?* I wondered who was in trouble.

Instead of sitting down, the principal put his hands on his hips and glanced around the room, taking in the motley crew perched in (or, in some cases, on) study carrels. Then he drew in a slow breath and announced that Mr. K wouldn't be returning to homeroom. He wouldn't be returning to Westside at all. He had cancer. His prognosis was 4-6 months.

"You'll have a substitute starting tomorrow. Do you have any questions?"

Yeah, a million, like how could anyone "substitute" for Mr. K?

No one spoke. Our eyes flitted around the room, leaping away when they met someone else's.

We won't get to say goodbye? I missed having Mr. K as my English teacher that year but had taken comfort knowing I'd enroll in his infamous senior seminar next spring. I looked at the *Beowulf* projects he hung in the window behind his desk each year after grading them.

I knew we students were blips on the radar of Mr. K's life, that he had family and friends who would play a crucial role now, but I couldn't fathom the fact that he'd disappear from our lives overnight.

Passing for normal and pretending to care about anything sapped my energy. By the school day's end, I was sucked dry. I rattled around the house as hollow as a gourd.

Still, I studied harder than ever. *Heartbreak or not, the work must be done,* nagged a voice in my head. *And only a 4.0 GPA is acceptable.* I wanted to match the image of myself Mr. K had introduced. I wanted to be the scholar he'd thought I was. Besides, college shone like *The Great Gatsby's* green light, *The Wizard of Oz's* Emerald City; the better my grades, the farther I could escape from Omaha. I couldn't wait to leave my gray life for a world of full color. I'd start over as someone else—anyone other than Collin's Jilted Girlfriend. Each A grade I earned mortared another yellow brick into the road out of Nebraska.

My relationship with food swung even more wildly between love and hate than my relationship with sleep. I couldn't make the simplest choices. How hungry did I have to be before I could eat? Could I push it for one more hour? Two? Would I eat egg whites like I should or cinnamon rolls like I wanted? At what fullness should I stop eating? Eventually, I'd think, What does it matter? Every choice led to the same unhappy ending.

Except I wanted to look perfect so I could win Collin back next time our paths crossed. I knew they would. They had to. I couldn't fathom any other resolution.

No matter how hard I tried, I couldn't find a middle ground. Sick with dread at having to get through the school day surrounded by traitors, I couldn't choke down breakfast. Too humiliated to enter the cafeteria, where Collin's friends hung out, I skipped lunch. By the time I got home, I was shaky, sweating, irritable. My head spun. I pledged to eat just a few bites, but I lost control once food crossed my lips. I checked out, then came to, horrified to discover I'd eaten a week's worth of calories.

Not eating when Mom woke me for dinner would arouse suspicion that I didn't have the energy to evade, so I tucked in.

Dessert? Why not? I had destroyed a perfect diet day and would have to compensate anyway. I might as well make it worth my while.

My stomach bloated and stretched painfully. My fingers swelled. I felt filled with muck from crown to calf.

I drove to the gym and spent 60 minutes on a stair-climber set to the highest level, aware my efforts would barely make a dent in the damage I'd wrought.

I swore the next day would be different.

It wasn't.

Nights, I woke from recurring nightmares. Two rotated in sequence.

In one, I lost my flute; in the other, I misplaced my purse. I tore apart house and car, looking for the missing item. I searched school hallways, racing against a clock, knowing I'd never spin the right combination for every locker before the timer went off. I envisioned my driver's license, credit card, and school ID—my identity—in someone else's grasp and panicked. No one I asked would help me search.

I mentioned the dreams while gathered with friends before the homeroom bell one morning. Jenny had asked for examples to include in a research paper she was writing for her psychology class.

"Oh, that's easy," Jenny replied. "They mean you recently lost something important."

Silence blanketed the group. My friends glanced at each other and then became engrossed in the table's surface. My face burned.

Eventually, Barbara changed the subject. Conversation resumed, and I longed for the itch of lavender carpet impressed on my forearm.

Mr. K. did return—just once. He hobbled through the door leaning on a cane and carrying a box of donuts. His ponytail, goatee, and eyebrows were gone. His jeans hung limply from a belt. His skin was gray, his cheeks sunken. But he greeted us with a hearty, "Hello, homeroom!"

He watched the guys suck down donuts with a mixture of joy, sorrow, and envy.

"Miss Whalen," Mr. K. said, bowing as if greeting a foreign dignitary. My eyes filled. I couldn't speak, so I smiled and gave a dignitary's nod.

Melancholy hooked its bony fingers around my diaphragm and squeezed so hard I couldn't breathe. As the hand tightened, India Ink seeped from its grasp and spilled into my torso. My heartbeat sent it shushing through my arteries, where it thickened into tar. Like it, I grew stiff, sticky, and toxic. I lost the ability to adapt. If cold, tired, thirsty, I couldn't carry on a conversation. I met friends' teasing and teachers' inquiries with a blank stare.

And I began to rot. Some days, I could smell it. When I nodded sympathetically at Barbara's heartbreak over unrequited love, I caught a whiff of grass clippings bagged and left in the sun. When I ran into Gretchen at the mall and swallowed questions about Collin, asking instead how her boyfriend liked college, something like overripe strawberries wafted from my pores. When I heard my laughter's brittle edge, my voice's flinty sarcasm, I wondered when my skin would begin to mottle.

I covered the rot with coiffed curls, pleated slacks, dangly earrings, and mild expressions. But sometimes it escaped in emotional belches—usually scathing comments about myself that I wrapped in humor to deflect concern. If a cut-down aimed at someone else snuck past my antiseptic veneer, I curdled with shame.

I became convinced calories consumed hastily and in secret were putrefying my insides. Post-binge, I felt dirty from mouth to colon, gummy from palm to sole. I showered in water hot enough to turn my skin raw, but it didn't help. Hunger was the only thing that cleansed. Emptying my torso felt like house-keeping, so I ate as little as I could stand.

What's happening to me? My dreams expanded to include one in which Westside's principal confronted me about having skipped homeroom for a year. I climbed the main staircase—the one where I'd asked Collin to Christmas Prom—sick with dread at having to face Mr. K after avoiding him for so long.

The most terrifying dream became the most frequent. In it, I stood in my bedroom, dressing to go out, when I was jolted by a gritty crunch. I tested the spot with my tongue, and a tooth gave way, hanging from my mouth by strands of tissue. I tasted blood.

I clamped my lips shut and ran to the blue half-bath down the hall. The loose tooth dropped into my palm. I stared at it, disbelieving. A sticky mixture of blood and saliva dribbled down my chin. Another tooth wiggled free as if alive.

I looked in the mirror and pulled down my lower lip. Exposed roots hooked through my jaws like earrings. Another tooth worked its way out and plinked into the sink.

I screamed.

By the time Mom and Julie stood in the bathroom's doorway, I was bent over the vanity, spitting mouthfuls of red-tinged saliva into the sink.

"Let me see," Mom said. She cupped my chin. My bottom teeth unraveled like a hem with a wayward string. "I'll call 9-1-1." Mom ran for the phone.

I spit more blood into the sink. A tooth followed.

Sirens sounded in the distance.

"It'll be okay," Julie said, staring at me like she saw a ghoul. "They can fix it. They can fix anything."

"Not this!" I wailed. Each syllable sent blood splattering onto the faucet. "No one can fix this!"

I woke, sweat-soaked and panting.

I'd learned in Catechism that praying for something I wanted and bargaining with God was selfish, so I sent up 20-minute prayers every night thanking God for every blessing in my life and asking only for grace. Faith helped people stamp out vice; it led them away from Bad toward Good. I hoped it would rid me of gluttony. *If I can empty myself of everything but faith, I'll be OK.*

I must not have done it right because praying didn't work.

Mom suggested I see a psychologist. I'd need a referral, but I'd aged out of the pediatric clinic at 16, so Mom made me an appointment with her physician.

I sat on an exam table in the clinic, shifting my weight from one butt cheek to the other and swinging my legs. I felt naked. I didn't understand why the nurse made me put on a paper gown to ask for a referral. I dreaded telling a stranger about my failings, but I was desperate to fix whatever was wrong with me. My stomach tangled itself in an increasingly complex knot while I waited. I stared at the chipped red polish on my nails with disgust and picked at a cuticle until it bled.

Finally, the doctor entered. I flashed on an image of someone taking an eraser to the crown of his head and failing to finish the job, leaving a ring of white hair around the base of his skull. More white hair sprouted from his nose, which held reading glasses. He looked like Santa in a white coat and seemed friendly, so I relaxed.

"What seems to be the problem?"

I pulled my finger away from my mouth and explained in halting sentences that I'd been depressed since I found out my boyfriend cheated on me. I told him how I couldn't sleep, couldn't eat or ate too much, felt lethargic, didn't care about anything. For good measure, I added that Dad, a licensed counselor, recognized symptoms of clinical depression and thought I needed treatment.

"I was, uh, wondering if you could, like, give me a referral to see a psychologist?"

"Well." The doctor scribbled his signature across a chart. "You don't have depression."

"I don't?" *What a relief!*

He leaned in and over-enunciated like he was talking to a dolt. "What you're experiencing is an *adolescent adjustment problem*. Your hormones are making you feel all kinds of new things. You need to get a grip on your emotions. Exercise some self-control. You'll be fine."

I flinched.

"Anything else?"

I shook my head. He scribbled comments on a file labeled with my name. He said something else that my ears failed to decode. Then he pulled the door closed behind him, chuckling at the idea that I might be depressed.

Don't throw up. Don't throw up, my mind chanted as I dressed.

At home, I climbed into bed and pulled the covers over my head. I remembered my lumpy body shielded by a paper gown and heard the phrase "adolescent adjustment problem." My mouth filled with saliva.

A knock sounded on the door. Mom and Dad came in and asked what happened. Dad's face flushed as I explained. His jaw clenched tighter and tighter until a muscle twitched in his cheek.

"I'm gonna call that place," he growled.

He thundered down the stairs. Bits of his conversation floated up: "... HMO crap. Since when do insurance companies diagnose?... malpractice."

After several minutes, Dad called from the bottom of the stairs. I rolled from bed and slouched down the steps to stand beside him. He wanted to know if I would talk to a legal representative; she needed a deposition to file a complaint.

"Noooooooooo!" I cried. I melted into a puddle on the bottom step.

Dad pleaded. "The guy's irresponsible, a quack. The clinic needs to know so we can get you treatment and so he can't hurt anyone else."

"I DON'T WANT TO! Leave me alone!"

I had never raised my voice to Dad. I braced for an explosion, though I barely cared what happened.

Dad sighed. "It's OK," he said gently. "You don't have to." He put the phone to his ear and walked toward the kitchen, where I couldn't hear him.

I fell asleep immediately that night but woke from a nightmare at 4:00 a.m. I stared at the ceiling until it was time to shower and dress for school.

I hadn't attended a funeral since early childhood. My only memory of that one was sitting in a wooden pew beside a second-cousin I idolized, then peering into the casket when she lifted me. Mr. K's funeral came sooner than I was ready for.

I crossed the soccer fields with a friend after school, sweater tied around my waist so my arms could soak up sun and soft spring breezes. I worried wearing jeans was disrespectful, but the principal had said students were welcome and could wear what they'd worn to school.

I entered the church that neighbored Westside and was directed to the choir loft. Seeing familiar faces in an unfamiliar context heightened the event's surrealism.

Lisa Whalen

Mr. K. lay in a casket lined with purple silk. He wore a conservative suit that contradicted everything I remembered of his personality. He looked so restful that I expected him to pop up and belt out *Annie's* "Tomorrow."

His partner spoke in a subdued voice. I didn't register a word. After a few hymns, the pastor dismissed us. I ducked the receiving line, unsure what to say, certain that if the roles were reversed, the last thing I'd want was a bunch of teenagers thinking they understood such a loss.

At home, I filled out the form for selecting my senior-year classes. My pen hovered over a box labeled "Senior Seminar." It wouldn't be the same without Mr. K. I hesitated, wishing fate would force my hand. Then I put an X in the box labeled "Composition." Before submitting my form, I drew a thick, black mark through the words "Senior Seminar."

Weeks before summer's reprieve from the hell of 11th grade, I watched a confetti of red, white, and yellow plastic fly at me from beyond the windshield. That image would return when I watched arena sand arc into the air as I fell from Smitty's back nearly 20 years later. But when I was 17, broken headlights were the first sign that something was wrong.

Plastic crunched. Metal screeched. Our forward progress halted.

I'd been driving Barbara home from the academic honors banquet we'd attended at the University of Nebraska at Omaha. Neither of us knew or understood the spaghetti of roads that tangled around the campus.

"Can you see what it says?" I had asked Barbara about a street sign just before I'd hit the gas. She'd screamed, "Oh, my God!"

174

Then I'd felt the impact. It shocked me dumb.

Barbara yanked at the passenger door handle, rocking and chanting, "I can't get the door open!" She yelled in a panicked voice, "I think we should get out of the intersection."

Huh? I turned to look at her.

Anger overtook panic. She repeated for what may have been the third time, "We need to get the car out of the intersection."

I nodded. *Right. That sounds familiar.* A carousel of memories clicked through my mind: *Sweltering trailer. Window air conditioner rattling. Images projected on a screen. A boy chasing a ball into the street. Stomping on the brake. Red warning light— too late.* The driver's ed simulator had claimed my classmates and I were too slow every time. We'd suspected it was rigged to make a point.

"We have to *move the car* so no one else hits us," Barbara yelled.

"OK." I turned the key. The engine shrieked; it was already running. *Who put the gearshift in park? Barbara?* I couldn't remember having moved.

I shifted into drive and pulled into Hardee's parking lot.

Where are we? I didn't recognize anything in sight. *Wait, were we just in a car accident?*

"We should find a phone. Um... there." Barbara pointed at a pay phone in Hardee's vestibule.

I opened the driver's door, stood, and examined my body for injuries. *My nylons didn't even run,* I marveled, dumbly. I smelled French fries. I had only picked at the banquet's calorie-laden dinner, and now my stomach roared.

Barbara crawled over the gearshift to stand beside me.

"Look what you did to my car!" An elderly man barreled toward me from the corner, where a damaged car had jumped the curb. He pointed at me and shook his fist. "You wrecked my

175

car, you fucking kid! My car's destroyed! This is your fault! You *bitch!*"

His Buick's backend had crumpled like an accordion. Its bumper lay in the street. My hands began shaking, then my legs.

Barbara walked up behind me. "The police are coming."

"Huh?"

"I called 9-1-1."

"Oh."

"We should call our parents."

I followed Barbara to the vestibule on soupy legs and dug in my purse for quarters.

"Are you OK? Is anyone hurt?" Mom asked.

"No, but I wrecked the car. An—And s-some old man is ye-yelling at me." My breath hitched, and I burst into tears.

"Don't worry about the car. It's OK. Did you call the police?"

"Stay right there," Mom said, when I told her they were on the way. "We're coming."

Barbara's face looked ghoulish in the squad car's flashing lights. An officer opened its rear door and told me to take a seat. *Am I being arrested? Am I going to jail?* My throat croaked guttural noises that sounded inhuman. I sobbed. It was too much—all of it: Collin, Mom's doctor, Mr. Kolterman, rotting, the weight I couldn't lose, the car, and now the police. The cop asked if I wanted a sack to breathe into so I'd stop hyper-ventilating. I shook my head and cried harder.

Mom crouched beside the squad's open door. She put a hand on my knee. "Lisa, it's OK. No one is hurt. You have to calm down so you can answer the officer's questions. Take a slow breath."

"I'm TRYING!" I wailed. Then I hated myself for being a brat.

Mom rubbed my arm and waited while I got myself under control.

Time slipped again. The next thing I knew, the police had let me out of their squad car. Barbara's parents had picked her up. A tow truck had hauled away my parents' sedan. The old man had driven away. I was in my parents' minivan.

Mom turned to face me while Dad drove. "What were you doing in this area?"

It sounded like an accusation. I sniffled. "I was lost."

I longed to hear Collin's voice, to feel his arms around me, his chin atop my head. He was the only person who could fix the mess I kept making of my privileged life. My hysteria started winding up again.

"Shhhh, it's OK," Mom said.

"B-But I was going to be a perfect driver. I'm careful. I wasn't going to get even a parking ticket. This will be on my record forever."

"But, Lisa..." Mom hesitated. She sighed. "You can't control what other people do."

Her words boomed in my head. It had never dawned on me that someone else could mar my driving record. Full of teenage self-absorption, I'd assumed that if I did the right things, I'd be a perfect driver. As if I didn't share the road with people who got distracted, made mistakes, or ran red arrows, like the man whose Buick I'd smashed. That I couldn't prevent strangers from impacting my life was a terrifying prospect. I shuddered. *I can't trust anyone to make the right choice, including myself.*

The sense of being stuck—in my obsession with Collin, in my eating disorder, in my depression—was more than figurative. The thick, black mark that divided B.C. and A.C. became the point where my development arrested. I kept pace physically and intellectually from that point on, but psychologically and emotionally, I remained 16.

Hospitalization acted like a catapult. With medication and Sara's help, I hurtled through 13 years' development in three, beginning at age 28 and arriving at an age-appropriate outlook in my early 30s. I felt that snap and fast-forward but couldn't articulate what it was until my tuning fork pinged faintly for the first time in ages while I watched TV in 2013. In one episode of a show called *Rectify*, a psychiatrist treating a character for PTSD records him describing his trauma's cause and tells him to listen to the recording over and over until it bores him. *That's it!* Exposure creates familiarity. Familiarity breeds acceptance. Acceptance allows reintegration of a split life and self.

Writing did for me what recording did for the TV character. At Sara's suggestion, I wrote about A.C. Years later, I revised, clarified, and shaped the pages as part of writing my life story. Each revision dulled the trauma's impact. Betrayals lost their sting. Memories lost their pull. A.C. became material I employed for a narrative. In other words, I described the trauma until it bored me.

Writing was great for reintegrating mind and emotions, but it left out a key component of eating disorder recovery: my body. Horses supplied that piece.

If I wanted to jump fences, I had to toughen up. If I wanted to jump fences on Penny, I had to strengthen my core in every sense of the word.

The universe responded as if it had read my mind. On a whim, I joined a friend who was taking a yoga course focused on intuition.

I was intrigued but skeptical about metaphysical claims the instructor made during the first five weeks. On the last night, I was glad she said we'd end with a guided meditation; I needed the relief from school-year stress.

"Get into a comfortable position," she coached.

I sat in lotus position and savored my yoga mat's cool and tacky surface against my calves, but my mind jumped like a spider, from lesson plans for tomorrow's classes, to the Amigo's nearly-empty gas tank, to plants in need of water at home.

"Imagine roots sprouting from your seat bones to ground you to the earth's core. Imagine a thread at the crown of your head lengthening your spine into outer space."

I filled with details the scene she sketched: an outdoor setting, a journey, a dwelling, a stranger, a message I needed to hear.

The air is damp and smells of wet leaves. Sequoias disappear into low clouds. Fog mutes everything but wings flapping in the distance as a flock takes flight.

I follow a dirt path that narrows until I'm in a copse with no idea which direction is forward.

Two cartoon bluebirds appear overhead, identical to the birds who helped Cinderella sew her ball gown in the Disney film. They survey what lies ahead with googly eyes, warning me about raised roots and sharp bends. Their song burbles like laughter.

They lead me to a cottage and flutter figure-eights in front of its door. They'll wait outside while I cross the threshold.

Inside, Paul Bunyan gestures for me to sit. His legs don't fit beneath the table, so he pulls up a bench and straddles it. His eyes are the size of Frisbees.

"What do I need to know?"

He pulls a titanium rod from behind his back. Fear zings through me, but he smiles gently. "This is your spine. You're stronger than you think."

I nod solemnly, as if I've received a communion wafer.

He gestures toward the door, so I walk outside.

The bluebirds deposit me at the yoga studio's door. They tweet a reminder that I can call on them anytime.

I opened my eyes and blinked at the overhead light. *A titanium spine.* Energy danced across my skin.

"Find a partner," our instructor said. "You're going to tap into your intuition, to become *in-tune* with your core self."

I turned to my friend and smiled shyly. We'd met only two months earlier but had hit it off as if rediscovering someone we'd always known. Her blue eyes twinkled beneath henna-red bangs.

As instructed, I handed her something of value: a ring Julie had given me. She clasped it between slender fingers, closed her eyes, and stilled.

After several seconds, she opened her eyes and looked chagrinned. Her face flushed.

"This is going to sound dumb, but the only image that came to me is a cartoon bluebird."

I gasped. "What?" A sound like rushing rapids roared in my head.

Her eyes widened. She glanced around, looking nervous. "I kept seeing a... cartoon bluebird. I don't know why."

"I can't believe you said that!" I gawked at her.

Her eyebrows knitted. "What's wrong?"

"Nothing. It's just... There were two cartoon bluebirds in my meditation." My nape prickled. "They led me to the figure who gave me a message."

Her face relaxed. She put two fingertips on her chin and nodded slowly. "OK, now it makes sense. I almost didn't mention the bird because it just seemed so... random. I thought my brain was being flighty." She clapped a hand over her mouth.

We erupted with laughter.

"I didn't choose that word intentionally—I swear! This is *weird!*" She rolled my ring between her palms, then realized she still held it and gave it back.

"Did the birds have big, googly eyes?" she asked.

"Yes!"

I slid the ring on my finger. When it finally juddered over my knuckle, I spun it a few times for good measure, but I didn't feel my usual need to fidget with it. My body felt held together by rubber bands, each piece of my anatomy joined to my core with perfect tension.

I thought of my bluebirds as Penny battled me and I battled the urge to give up throughout 2012. I pictured my titanium spine while she and I waited behind classmates to ride over a series of poles.

Well, *I* waited. Penny tossed her head, pranced, turned perpendicular to the rail, and crept closer to the gelding ahead of us, angling to bite him. I vowed to stay calm. Each time she moved out of line, I led her in a tight circle the way Liz had coached me and lined her up behind the gelding again.

We repeated that process. I thought of her as a challenging student in a classroom and refused to rise to her bait. I repeated what I wanted from her as clearly, assertively, and calmly as I could.

By our third turn at the end of the line, I could sense Penny's intent to move before she tensed a muscle. I tightened my core and closed my fingers around the reins to create a boundary. *You may not move beyond this point unless I ask you to.*

She pushed against the boundary, raking the sand with a foot, turning her head, shifting her backend from side to side.

I held firm.

Penny's ears twitched. She considered moving but hesitated. I could almost hear her weighing options. At last, she relaxed and stood still.

I let the reins out to their full length—a reward for good behavior.

We trotted over the poles without a hitch.

I kept the reins long when we cooled down at the lesson's end. Penny plodded along, head bobbing gently with her gait. For once, we were content with each other's company.

Then a squirrel rustled pine trees that lined the rail. Penny startled as if stung. She spun 180-degrees. She shied, wrenching me sideways in the saddle, and leapt from all four feet. My classmates gasped. From the corner of my eye, I saw Liz turn to see what had caught their attention.

I kicked out with my right leg, threw my weight into my left heel, and stretched its stirrup away from Penny's body to counter her sharp tilt. The move sent me leaning out over the sand like an aerialist, but I didn't waver. I centered my core over the saddle, bent my knees, and rode out Penny's undulations.

Contact with my seat grounded Penny. She stilled. She scanned the arena, as if hoping no one had seen the Mean Girl frightened. She snorted, shook her head, and returned to plodding as if nothing had happened.

"That's why you develop a strong core," Liz drawled. She looked purposefully at each of my classmates to see that they absorbed the message.

I inventoried mind and body: No adrenaline. No tension. No doubt. I'd known from the moment Penny startled that I wouldn't leave her back. *Titanium spine, indeed.*

My victory was short-lived. The next Sunday, I struggled to get Penny trotting correctly over the same four poles, but I brightened when Liz said we could end the lesson by cantering. That was my favorite way to ride: with ground and throttle wide open.

Penny and I zipped along the home stretch, faster than I'd ever felt her go. Her speed thrilled.

Mid-lap, a freak gust swirled the sand at Penny's feet, twirled through her mane, and sent air up my nose with a heady rush. Penny surged forward. Her muscles churned beneath my seat. I smiled, giddy.

Instead of continuing forward, she angled toward a fence. Its pole sat only 12 inches off the ground, but it looked as tall and solid as a bus. I'd never left the ground on horseback.

Stop or go over? Stop or go over? I had less than a second to decide. I knew I shouldn't let Penny carry out her plan, but Paul Bunyan whispered in my head, *It's too late to stop; you'll crash. You're going over, so don't freak out.*

I tried rising into two-point position and came up short, but the attempt engaged my core enough that I didn't bounce out of the saddle when we landed. I stopped Penny on the fence's far side and exhaled. *That was... FUN!* Exhilaration swelled my chest.

I walked Penny to the gazebo and braced for a scolding, but I didn't get one. Liz merely tossed off a distracted, "Hey, don't go over those fences," before ending the lesson with some closing words. Her lack of concern told me everything I needed to know: I could trust my core.

I swung my leg over Penny's back, hopped to the sand, and secured the stirrups.

"I can't tell you how happy I am with how you rode today," Liz said as she walked up behind me.

I turned, Penny's reins in my hand.

"You didn't put up with any of Penny's crap. Good for you."

"Thanks!" I led Penny from the arena. *Liz was right: Penny may not be the horse I want, but she is the horse I need.*

Willow takes a break in her stall after riding lessons in June 2015
© Lisa Whalen

Chapter 7 - Willow: Rise from Your Roots

Seventh Farm Riding School, July 2014

That must be a mistake. I tried to temper my excitement at seeing The List. I dropped my duffel bag on a tack room chair whose left front leg, which grew more precarious every week, was the subject of a running joke among my classmates. I missed them. The barn was unusually quiet that Tuesday—almost a different place than the bustling village I was used to on Sunday mornings. Stall and garage doors stood open. Tidy piles of dirt and wood shavings dotted the aisle where riders had picked the horses' hooves. Dust hovered in sunlight filtering through a small, barred window, as if waiting for someone to stir it.

Twenty minutes later, three other riders and I led our horses from the barn. I greeted Tom as we passed him but stopped when he spoke.

"You're riding Willow, huh?" He sounded as surprised to see me with the mare as I felt to be leading her. He also sounded less happy than I was about my pairing with the horse who'd won nearly $1 million on the racetrack before coming to Seventh Farm and becoming Liz's show-horse-in-training.

"I've never ridden her. Anything I should know?"

"Yeah. You have to ride her really well. You'll be the only person on her today, so when I train her tomorrow, I'll feel everything you did. Don't screw her up."

Oh. That wasn't the kind of advice I'd had in mind. *No pressure, ha-ha.*

"Wait here until I put Saphira in her stall."

Uh-oh. On my left, the three riders and Liz receded into the distance. On my right, Saphira distilled to hooves clopping on concrete. I suddenly felt like the lone tree on a hilltop.

Beside me, Willow blinked placidly. I backed her up so we could stand in the barn's shade. I hadn't seen her up-close for so long I'd forgotten that what looked silver in the paddock was actually a white coat spattered with brown freckles. She looked healthier than I'd ever seen her. Her ribs looked less like xylophones, her hipbones less like wings. Her black eyes glowed with dewy shine, reinforcing the vision I'd always had of them as Kohl-lined and her as Cleopatra.

She turned an ear in my direction but stood with an ethereal calm I'd come to expect. Unlike Penny, who projected every emotion as if on a stage, or Angie, who crackled with ambition that stall walls couldn't blunt, Willow was an enigma. I wondered nervously if that would make her harder to ride. *Maybe I shouldn't have been so excited to see my name with hers on The List.*

"Let's go." Tom walked past, having traded the fringed leather chaps he wore to ride for faded Levi's and the coffee in his cracked white mug for water. His boots crunched along the path to the arena.

I'd barely closed the gate behind Willow, when Tom pointed at the mounting block and said, "Get on."

He led Willow past Liz's class and into a desert that lay between the gazebo and the road. There, he stopped, squinted up at me, and said, "Willow is going to want to run. Don't let her. Keep her slow. She's still figuring out how to use her back-end to stay balanced and uphill. And she's sensitive, so you have to follow any pressure with immediate release. As soon as she does what you want, let up with your calf or loosen your fingers on the reins. She wants to please you, so constant pressure without release will make her crazy."

"OK." I fiddled with my sunglasses, trying to get their frames over my ears and under my helmet's straps without pressing painfully into my scalp. Something told me I couldn't afford any distractions for what was to come.

Tom grabbed one rein to get my attention. "I mean it. Don't let her run. You don't want to make her lame, do you?"

"No."

"Good." He let go of the rein. "Walk Willow in a circle. Once you've walked two laps, you can trot. A *slow* trot. If you keep Willow slow, you won't piss me off."

Alrighty, then. I gulped, less worried about pissing off Tom than screwing up so badly I'd never ride Willow again. I liked everything about her already: her calm nature, light step, long stride, gliding walk.

Tom walked to the corner, where a maple reached just enough over the rail to provide the only shade. He leaned a boot's sole against the fence and sipped from his mug while calling out rapid-fire commands. I hoped I'd learned enough from previous experiences where my name had appeared on a list unexpectedly that I could keep my nerves in check.

The only other list more indelible in memory than Liz's had been typed and taped to chicken-wire glass in Westside's band room on a Monday in 1989. Blind auditions held the previous Friday whittled our 180-member marching band to a 70-member Warrior Concert Band. I didn't expect to make Warrior Band as a freshman, so I'd walked into my audition with little to lose. Low expectations had kept me in my body instead of watching myself from outside. Paired with a perfectionist's preparation, that lack of pressure resulted in an audition strong enough to earn Seventh Chair in Warrior Band's flute section. Elated, I slid into my seat for the first rehearsal and subsequently became my own worst enemy.

My freshman friends couldn't hide the resentment cloaked in their congratulations. Close quarters during rehearsals highlighted the precariousness of my position: Chairs One through Six considered my presence an incursion; Chairs Eight through Thirteen churned with bitterness at my having overtaken them. Both groups murmured that I better not try to move up when the challenge period began. Challenges were the last thing on my mind. I was too preoccupied with keeping my profile low and my head above water. The music was harder than anything I'd played in middle school or studied in individual lessons. I was so afraid of making a mistake that during difficult passages, I stopped blowing air through my mouthpiece and moved my fingers over the keys without producing sound.

My friends joined me in Warrior Band as sophomores, the same year I became Collin's girlfriend and Mr. Kolterman's student. My life seemed headed in the right direction. Audition pressure that mounted each year once I had a target on my back seemed like my biggest music-related obstacle. Then my name appeared on the list of audition results for my senior year.

I didn't believe friends who said I'd earned First Chair until I saw my name in black and white. In the throes of A.C., rehearsals became the high point of each weekday. The same orange plastic seat I'd occupied for three years felt like a throne once it became first chair. Finally, I'd done something right.

My elation didn't last. Every time I unzipped my case and twisted together my flute's segments, I braced for the moment our conductor would pull me aside and confess that my placement was a mistake. When that didn't happen, I became convinced my audition had been a fluke.

I wasn't the only one who suspected I wasn't First Chair material. Outrage wafted from the junior in Second Chair. Envy tightened her smile every time we negotiated our shared music stand's ideal height. Third and Fourth Chair mirrored the junior's expression, though more subtly. All three circled like wolves. Once rehearsal ended, they shapeshifted back into my closest herdmates.

I grew terrified my every sight-reading error confirmed my misplacement. I lengthened my daily practice from 90 minutes to two hours. Tension in my fingers caused tingling and then numbness in my right hand. My teacher for individual lessons warned me that if I didn't loosen my muscles, especially around my jaw, I'd develop TMJ, a condition that causes chronic pain and locking. I didn't tell her my jaw already clicked when I chewed. I didn't care about injury. I had already lost so much: Collin, Mr. Kolterman, friends, gymnastics (cancelled by the administration because of insurance costs), Drill Squad, and my sense of self. I clung to First Chair like a lifeline.

The tighter I hung on, the faster First Chair slipped from my grasp. Solos I had fantasized about for three years loomed like crevasses in the sheet music. I lost count mid-measure, tried to find my way in but misread cues and joined at the wrong spot to discordant effect. Even in the correct measures, I couldn't get my flute to speak like it used to. My tone grew spindly. My tense embouchure made notes in the upper register crack or split into ghostly harmonics. Without breath support, my tone went flat, so I pushed in my flute's headjoint to raise the pitch. Then I remembered warm metal skews sharp, so I pulled out the headjoint. I adjusted so frequently that I forgot what I was listening for and stopped trusting my ear.

Three weeks into my First Chair tenure, the junior in Second Chair challenged me. Our director selected a passage, he turned his back to us, and we played it for him. Fear sent my fingers rogue. He picked the junior as the winner.

I locked a smile in place as I took my seat in Second Chair amongst stares and whispers the following morning.

I continued cobbling together a thin façade of nonchalance through the end of my senior year, but the effort exacted a price. Parts of me continued cracking off and falling away with each real or imagined defeat.

I gave a repeat performance during college. I auditioned for and won a music scholarship but blundered through rehearsals, intimidated by the exposure of an orchestra's two-flute section. The conductor grew tired of telling me to play louder. I wasn't well rooted enough to voice my part when our First and Second Flute lines diverged. I lost solos and eventually First Chair to my more confident peer.

Like horses wearing a trench along an arena's rail, I dug a rut every time I faced life's challenges: heighten the stakes, increase the pressure, choke, feign placidity while beating myself up. My eating disorder formed its own loop: starve, binge, over-exercise. The two circles linked to form a figure-eight that ran on its own momentum. Hunger amplified my anxiety; anxiety made me choke; failing made me depressed; depression drove me to eat; eating made me anxious about gaining weight; exercise launched me into starving. I didn't see the overlap, though. I couldn't. Desperation to be someone better acted like blinders. Numbness acted like draw reins, keeping my head tucked so tightly that all I saw was my footsteps on endless sand. When I finally crossed the threshold of Westside's front door for the last time, the air smelled sweeter, like the Magnolia blossoms outside my bedroom window, though no Magnolia trees grew near school grounds.

I thought of a post-graduation trip that Dad proposed as a palate cleanser for college—better yet, as a blast of sun that would clear gray clouds, halt my centrifugal motion and set me straight, like the I-80 roads we'd travel, but the trips' atmosphere turned dark as quickly and unexpectedly as a Nebraska sky.

Dad, Julie, and I tore across Nebraska's desert-prairie headed for Denver, where Grandpa had moved, reluctantly, from his house to a nursing home. We pointed a teal blue Chevy Cavalier toward Rocky Mountains that oriented Colorado natives like Dad and opened the throttle.

Leaving Omaha felt like loosening bindings. Julie and I sang along to Michael Jackson's greatest hits, flinging words against wind that gushed through open windows. I stuck out an arm and rolled waves with my wrist while the sun thumped my skin, adding freckles as it charged my internal battery.

Eight hours later, we swapped shorts wrinkled by dust and sweat for fresh slacks, combed tangles from our hair, and followed signs through endless beige hallways to find Grandpa's room.

Grandpa's transformation stunned me. He'd withered from the stout oak I remembered. His arms, once as solid as the pedestal beneath his antique dining room table, looked like matchsticks draped in crepe. His ruddy cheeks had turned ashen. His voice, a baritone that drew looks when he recited prayers during Mass, whispered a scratchy greeting.

"Hi, Grandpa." I raised my hand in a timid wave.

Instead of lighting up the way I was used to, Grandpa scowled.

"How ya doin'?" Dad asked, his voice inflated with false cheer. He laid a hand on Grandpa's shoulder.

Grandpa shook him off. He waved an arm dismissively across his chest. Then he pointed at my midsection, and said, "fat."

I blanched.

Grandpa repeated the charge in a clearer voice: "Fat."

I stared at the floor's gleaming tile while my face heated and my gut contracted. I flashed on songbirds that had crashed into our dining room windows in Omaha one spring and fallen like little brown stones.

Grandpa pinched my side. "You've gotten fat." He pointed at Julie. "You, too."

I stepped beyond his reach, uncomfortable but afraid to speak.

Silence pooled. The air flattened and thickened like a can of soda abandoned after being opened.

I couldn't remember Grandpa criticizing my siblings or me. He'd always sung our praises to a point that embarrassed me. Everyone in his life, from his mail carrier to his pastor, knew who we were, which instruments we played and hobbies we pursued. He'd never remarked on our appearance.

This must be the father Dad had to reckon with when he left the priesthood. He's lucky a first grandchild had been enough to graft their split relationship. While that relationship had since borne fruit, its rootstock hadn't changed. Grandpa forgave, but he didn't forget. He'd scoffed at Dad's every suggestion, from restaurants we could try to new neighbors we could meet. When Dad attempted to cull, clean, or repair Grandpa's house, which had remained a museum of early 1900s America until Grandpa moved out, Grandpa had said things like, "What'er you doing, Doofus?"

James, Julie, and I had loved exploring the house's dresser-sized radio, foot-pedal sewing machine, metal ice cream maker, and ornate oak highchair—the one both Grandpa and Dad had eaten in. We were too young to notice how cluttered the house was, how its development had arrested the day Julia died, how the only way through its rooms was via paths worn into threadbare throw rugs. We also didn't fully register how mean Grandpa could be or how his criticism spun a tight spiral that sought out Dad exclusively. No matter how urgent the task, how efficiently or cheerfully Dad completed it, everything he did was wrong according to Grandpa. He'd repaid Dad's efforts to rid the back porch of decades-old newspapers by looking at us kids, shaking his head, and rolling his eyes. Those conspiratorial moments had thrilled but also sickened me. I couldn't articulate why, but intuition hinted that chastising a father in front of his children violated some universal rule.

I didn't understand until Grandpa turned his critical eye on me how being raised by fathers—both heavenly and earthly—who held unreasonable expectations had shaped Dad's life as well as mine.

"How'd you get fat?" Grandpa asked once I'd moved out of his reach.

The answer was so long and complex I wouldn't have known where to start. Since A.C., I'd gone from 116 pounds to 136. I hadn't panicked much about that gain, because I planned to lose it and more once I started fresh at college.

Before I could reply to Grandpa's question, Dad flipped a switch and guided our conversation onto a safer track.

But Grandpa's assessment reverberated in my head long after we drove east again, absent wind, music, and conversation, each of us lost in thought.

I continued traveling east for college, which couldn't start soon enough. I began filling the dining room with supplies the minute we returned from Denver. My excitement grew alongside the room's mountains of spiral notebooks, highlighters, bed sheets, deodorant, shower shoes, and storage bins. By late July, the detritus prevented anyone from using the table for its intended purpose, as only a single-file swath of carpet allowed passage through the room.

I tingled with anticipation the morning my family and I piled into the minivan and headed for Minnesota, where I would attend an all-women's college. With each green interstate sign that flicked past, I stretched and yawned to release tension. My certainty that college would fix me just barely outweighed my fear of living 400 miles away from family.

Dad lined the van up behind trucks loaded to the hilt and pointed at the cinderblock rectangle I'd live in. The dorm's unloading zone looked like an anthill. Strangers wearing purple t-shirts scurried in every direction and then funneled through the front door. A few climbed into our van, grabbed plastic totes, and carried them away. I didn't know whether I'd see my belongings again.

I met my roommate in our first-floor room. Our parents peppered us with questions and suggestions about what furniture should go where. They recommended getting a TV and offered to split the cost. *No distractions,* I pleaded internally. I planned to transform through a solitary focus on study, music, and weight loss; anything else wasted time. I kept quiet and was saddled with a TV that my roommate left on 15 hours a day. Coupled with hunger and nervousness, the afternoon's chaos felt overwhelming. I snapped at family members who tried to help me unpack while they digested their own emotional cocktails. Once they'd left, I berated myself for being a brat.

Three weeks into the semester, my roommate turned on me. She stopped speaking, slammed doors and drawers, whispered "bitch" when we passed each other in the hallway. Our mutual friends followed her lead. I was bewildered. For days, I cowered from hostility that hovered like a specter in our room. I began leaving at 7 a.m. and returning at 10 p.m. When my friends down the hall said I could sleep on their tile floor, I accepted gratefully. By the time my obsessive replaying of events revealed her anger's cause—I'd joked with Dad on the phone about me being a "preacher's kid"; she'd thought I was talking about her because her Dad was a pastor—the divide had become a mote we didn't have the tools to cross. She moved out a week later. *Bliss!* With a clean slate and full control over my life, I chased the dragon of my first diet's high.

I detached my body from my head and made it a secondary concern, a junky collection of mechanical keys and springs I was saddled with but could make perform. Free from high school's strictures and my parents' supervision, each day presented a series of options from which I could choose my own adventure. I was convinced that every correct choice would become a foothold I could use to climb toward a version of myself so perfect that Collin couldn't resist.

I knew but couldn't admit that Collin was no longer Collin. He'd become superhuman: an idea, a standard, a meter to measure my happiness. Retellings had made our story a myth and him a god—an uncanny parallel to the Gospels and Jesus, which I studied in theology classes. Any short-term pain required for transformation would be well worth the long-term reward, so the New Testament proclaimed. I pushed my body harder than ever, following with military precision a regimen I designed:

7:00 a.m.

Wake, dress, walk to the cafeteria. The scent of bacon and freshly-baked bagels beckoned before I descended the stairs. I stared longingly at egg burritos oozing orange cheese and pancakes that steamed the line's glass divider. My stomach clawed like a wild animal, but I selected half a banana and three ounces of strawberry yogurt.

7:45 a.m.

Practice. I freed my flute from its padlocked cubby in the music building and ducked into the practice room furthest away from offices, classrooms, and rehearsal halls so no one would hear me. Soundproofing screwed into the concrete walls didn't damper noise as much as I liked, but paper taped over the door's narrow window prevented people from seeing who was making all those mistakes. To burn extra calories, I paced while warming up on scales and stood while reading sheet music.

9:30 a.m.

Class. I fidgeted in my seat, clenched and unclenched muscles, pointed and flexed my toes in pursuit of weight loss. Gum distracted from hunger, but my stomach occasionally roared, drawing sympathetic looks from neighboring students.

One afternoon, I grew so lightheaded climbing four flights to a class that I stopped on the third-floor landing. I leaned my butt against a wall, braced my hands on my knees, and breathed deeply to stop my head's spinning. My backpack fell to the floor with a thud. I ignored it. I cared only about delicious warmth drifting from the clanking radiator beside me. A persistent chill had invaded my bones. I suspected that cutting calories had slowed my metabolism, but I was still losing weight, so I tolerated the cold.

When red orbs faded from my vision, I heaved my backpack over my shoulder and looked up. My legs trembled. *Just one more flight. I'll take it slow.*

1:30 p.m.

Study, write, work in the campus writing center. In the computer lab, pulling my mind from hunger-induced fog and back to the essay I was writing was like swatting a typewriter's carriage at the end of every line.

"Focus!" a voice yelled in my head. "Stop wasting time and concentrate!"

I typed, printed, and then carved away paragraphs, cleaving phrases and rasping words from the page to get below the assignment's length limit. I couldn't shut up about what I was learning. *Where is this impulse during class?*

In classrooms, I was a spider suspended in the back corner, trapping and ingesting information unnoticed, except in theology classes. My favorite professor, a nun named Sister Jean, liked to call on me. The worst part about it came right after she said my name, when every head snapped in my direction. I stiffened, gulped a breath, then said, "Um, I think that—"

"What? We can't hear you, Lisa," Sister Jean interrupted, her voice gentle but insistent. "Please speak louder."

"I think Paul's epistles were intended to—"

"Class? Did you hear her? No? OK, say it again, Lisa, but project your voice."

By the third go-around, I wanted to scuttle from the spotlight, so I cut my answer short.

6:00 p.m.

Dinner. While friends crunched on tacos and took agonizingly small forkfuls of chocolate cake, I picked at a salad, trying not to stare at French fries they left untouched. On special occasions, I treated myself to a small portion of pasta with meatless red sauce. The next morning, I skipped breakfast to make up for the splurge.

7:00 p.m.

Exercise. Four nights a week, my friends and I went to aerobics class. On weekend mornings, I ran along Mississippi River Boulevard and did calisthenics in my room.

8:30 p.m.

Shower, then study or attend meetings. My stomach felt exquisitely flat and empty, but so did my head. I struggled to keep pace with conversations and couldn't wait to lie down. Impatience and irritation I knew came from hunger thrummed in my cells. I clenched my fists or picked at my cuticles to keep from snapping at people.

11:30 p.m.

Lights out. When hunger prevented sleep, I plucked a fat-free yogurt from the mini-fridge. Still, I woke during the night to glance at my alarm clock and gauge how long I had to wait until the cafeteria opened for breakfast. I dreamt about swimming in chocolate pools and serving feasts I wasn't allowed to sample.

Then I woke the next morning and started my regimen from the beginning.

My regimen made the semester fly past. I couldn't wait to spend Christmas with my family, but six weeks in Omaha with no boot-camp schedule loomed like a war. If I got bored, I'd eat, and mediocrity would win. I couldn't afford to retreat; I'd lost ten pounds since September—a good start. I needed to keep up my transformation's pace.

When my theology professor offered a chance to earn credits by spending January in Israel, I seized it.

I realized my mistake before I boarded the first airplane. Sitting between Mom and Dad in an empty gate at Eppley Airfield, I felt like a toddler who'd crawled into her parents' bed on a Saturday morning: warm, safe, loved, content to hide for as long as the cocoon allowed. I jiggled a knee to stave off encroaching dread.

The setting did nothing to ease my fear. The only sign of life was a custodian pushing a mop across the terminal. Automated announcements echoed through empty space as if to remind me that I was the only person foolish enough to leave Omaha on January 2, 1994. They also reinforced the sense I had of being suspended between worlds. My home was in Omaha, but my life was in St. Paul. Neither existence felt complete. At the thought of uprooting myself again—this time to a foreign country—

homesickness wrapped my ribs so tightly I could barely breathe. I didn't know any of the 22 people I'd travel with; I'd meet them when I arrived at Minneapolis-St. Paul International Airport. From there we'd fly to Tel Aviv. Fall semester had been my first extended separation from home and family. Spring semester lay just ahead. Jamming a Middle East itinerary between the two suddenly struck me as not only foolish but frightening. Israeli-Palestinian clashes had cooled, but the region never rested easily for long.

In Minneapolis, I discovered I was the group's youngest member and the only one traveling without family or friends. Hunger hyped my anxiety and sapped my energy, leaving nothing to fuel my social skills. Loneliness mushroomed.

The trip progressed the way it had begun: with me lonely but withdrawn, starving but afraid to eat, determined to make the most of seeing another country but desperate to go home.

Israel's desert raised the first sign I noticed that my self-improvement efforts might be dangerous. Our silver bus trundled over the packed-earth roads that slithered through a Martian landscape. Dust kicked up by the bus' wheels marked our progress in vanishing ink; I wondered how we'd find our way back to Haifa.

The desert's vastness prevented me from measuring our journey by time or distance. Finally, our bus hissed to a stop at the base of an outcrop called Masada. We exited, squinting and blinking, beneath a cloudless sky. The air smelled like a library book: sunny, fresh, and dusty all at once.

Ruins we'd come to study lay scattered across a mesa at Masada's 1500-foot summit. The only way to see them was by climbing a single-file, switchback trail called The Snake. With the Dead Sea's coastline a fingernail in the distance and no sign of life in any direction, I struggled to comprehend that we stood at the root of human civilization.

A guide explained that Masada's infamy sprouted from New Testament narratives. Herod the Great, the king who'd put a price on the infant Jesus's head, constructed a palace on the site to escape increasingly violent clashes between Jews and their Roman rulers. When the Romans defeated the Jews in 70 A.D., survivors fled to Masada, a site whose Hebrew name means "strong foundation or support," and lived peacefully until the Roman military arrived.

Our guide's description of the ensuing battles' swings in momentum mirrored my internal struggles. Their familiarity, combined with my lightheadedness, led me to imagine events as clearly as if they played out in front of me:

Legions stretch to the horizon in perfect formation. Bronze helmets glint in the sun. Dust clings to soldiers' legs. Sweat drips from their temples. Sunburned and weary, they await a signal to attack.

Their commander kicks his mount with gristled calves, raises his arm and brings it forward. The ranks become a churning mass that bellows with a guttural roar and begins to climb.

Jewish settlers hurl rocks and roll boulders down the cliffsides until the soldiers retreat.

Soldiers build a wall around the mount's base and post sentries to prevent escape. The commander considers waiting for a surrender but suspects correctly that settlers have preserved crops, bred livestock, and filled cisterns; their supplies will outlast the military's.

When soldiers haul in a battering ram, settlers douse them with boiling water.

When soldiers construct a ramp, settlers coat it with oil.

Finally, soldiers build a tower on a natural rise beside the cliff. They attach a ramp, catapult rocks into the settlement, and charge the fortress, increasing the pressure until its walls collapse.

They spill onto the mesa and discover that settlers have committed suicide to avoid becoming slaves.

The siege's senselessness left me achingly weary, but what I kept coming back to, what the story seemed to emphasize, was that settlers chose their own adventure and then decided how their story would end.

Two hours of exploring Masada used up the meager energy provided by a croissant I'd picked at for breakfast. By the time we began our descent from the peak, I was weak and unsteady on my feet. Halfway down The Snake, I slipped. Pebbles rolled beneath my boots' soles and skittered down the trail. I put my hand against the sun-warmed rock beside me but still went to a knee. My heart galloped. The money belt beneath my jeans' waistband grew clammy. If I fell, I'd tumble like a ragdoll down the cliff's jagged side. And I *would* fall. Adrenaline left behind a hunger beyond anything I'd ever known; it threatened to consume me from the inside out. I couldn't fathom how I'd get to my feet, much less to the bus. My legs quivered when I stood. I wanted to cry, but tears required energy; the effort to produce them seemed monumental. *If I fall, I better die.* Drawing everyone's attention and answering questions about what happened would be too humiliating to bear. I bargained with God. *Please, don't let me faint. I'll eat whatever is put in front of me at dinner.*

I locked my eyes on the ground and put every ounce of concentration into placing one foot in front of the other.

Twenty minutes later, I sank into my seat on the bus. I sipped water from a bottle with the hope it would extinguish the fire in my stomach. My body rebelled. I gagged on the third mouthful. I wrapped my arms around my abdomen, closed my eyes, rested my forehead against the seat in front of me, and didn't move until we reached our hotel 60 minutes later.

Chairs on either side of me in the dining hall stayed empty. I didn't care; conversation required reserves I'd depleted.

As promised, I ate everything I was served, though my mind screamed protests. When the waiter replaced my empty dinner plate with a piece of cheesecake, I winced but lifted my fork. *A promise is a promise.*

Study time followed dinner. I returned to my room to stand in front of its mirror again. My belly had already grown. *I won't be such a pig at breakfast.*

"You're so *skinny!*" Mom gasped when I stepped from behind the car door in the driveway, home for spring break. She didn't sound as pleased as I felt.

We hugged, then lifted my suitcase and backpack from the trunk. Mom looked me up and down. When she saw me notice, she tried to hide what she was thinking, but a telltale wrinkle showed between her eyebrows. My jeans, though baggy, were a size eight—nowhere near my goal—so I didn't understand Mom's concern.

"Let's celebrate your homecoming at The Garden Café."

I couldn't remember the last time I'd eaten at that restaurant, whose trendy menu and upscale prices usually made it off-limits.

Worried that sitting in the car for six hours would stall my calorie-burning, I hadn't eaten all day. Home lifted the pressure I felt at college, so I ordered my favorite splurge: a grilled cheese sandwich, French fries, and chocolate milkshake. *It's a one-time indulgence,* I assured the commander in my head. *I have all week to exercise.* Besides, I felt like a new person: thinner, happier, more in control of my body and life than I'd been since B.C. I ate every bite.

I spent that night and the following morning warring with an internal dictator who pledged retribution for flouting his laws.

I had just fallen asleep on the couch the next afternoon when a crash jolted me upright. The noise sounded like someone knocking over metal garbage cans in the garage. I'd thought nothing of leaving the garage doors open after parking in the driveway an hour earlier—nothing ever happened on our cul-de-sac—but now that choice seemed careless. Only a flimsy service door stood between the noise and me. Mom and I were the only ones home. She was ironing clothes in the basement, which now felt miles away. From the stairwell, I heard James Earl Jones call out CNN's tagline and knew Mom hadn't heard the crash.

I crept to the dining room window, flattened myself against the wall and peeked out. I hoped I'd see a raccoon running from spilled garbage cans—anything but an intruder.

What I saw was a tree.

One of three 70-foot oaks that normally stood like columns in our front yard lay prone. The crash had come from branches swiping the garbage cans as the tree missed falling on the garage by an inch.

I scanned up and down our avenue's steep incline. Nothing moved. Even leaves on the trees left standing dangled limply.

"What do you mean? What tree?" Mom asked when I explained what I'd seen. Her face wrinkled with confusion. "If it's a branch, I'll take care of it when I'm done here."

It took convincing to get Mom upstairs. When she saw the oak, her mouth fell open. "What on earth...?"

"It was a perfect storm—no pun intended," a tree trimmer told us before he and his partners donned earplugs and set upon the oak, chainsaws snarling like a wolfpack.

Lisa Whalen

The trimmer meant that a microburst had downed the behemoth because burlap remained wrapped around its base from when it had been hauled in as a sapling. While we had kicked soccer balls against its trunk and tried unsuccessfully to climb it, the tree had been anchored by a single root running straight down into the earth. Although the oak had available every nutrient it needed to thrive, one event from its past had stunted the growth necessary to keep it upright during surges in downward pressure.

In the oak's absence, sun warmed more of the lawn, which greened and thickened, but the yard looked bare, the empty space a reminder of something missing.

I returned to campus certain I would finally lay siege to my high school self. I would rise from the ashes reborn. I pushed myself harder than ever. I joined the honors program and earned a 3.9 GPA. I tutored in the writing center. I played flute for Sunday Mass and in the orchestra. I became features editor for the campus newspaper. I joined one organization after another, trying to quiet the voice in my head that proclaimed I was never enough. My grades belied my ability to learn outside a classroom.

One night, I returned from dinner feeling an internal itch that I couldn't scratch. I paced my room's confines clenching and unclenching my fists to escape a rebellion I sensed fomenting. *I should practice my flute or do sit-ups and pushups.* I knew I wouldn't. I needed something. Its absence gnawed at me. Finally, I admitted what I'd known since I had turned the key in my room's lock: I needed a break. I needed comfort. I needed food.

I pulled a box of graham crackers from my closet shelf. My hands shook when the plastic wrap crinkled between my fingers. The package ripped open to reveal scents of sun-dried bran, sugar, and something like maple syrup. I let the first wheaty-nutty bite melt to gruel on my tongue. I ground the second between my molars.

The first cracker was gone before I registered another bite. As if beyond my control, my fingers reopened the package and slid out a second cracker. I bit and chewed, barely swallowing before biting again. Cracker shards scraped my throat, but I didn't slow down. I crunched faster and faster. Only glue sealing the second package offered enough resistance to snap me from my trance. Realizing what I'd done, I closed the box and slumped on my bed, disgusted and frightened.

A knock sounded on my door: my friends coming to get me for aerobics. I wiped crumbs from the corners of my mouth, ran my tongue over fuzzy teeth, and opened the door.

I tried to beg off, claiming I felt sick without admitting why.

"C'mon," they persisted. "You'll feel better once you get there."

I demurred. They insisted.

I surrendered and spent the next hour holding down gorge that threatened to rise.

My resistance crumbled one Sunday after a weekend visit to my Grandma Galvin's house 70 miles north of St. Paul. She'd filled me with pot roast so tender it peeled apart on my tongue, potatoes so creamy they stuck to my soft palate, apple pie with a crust that flaked like baklava and melted ice cream on its golden surface. I tallied calories, devised penance for skipped exercise, and hatched a plan for redemption. But I couldn't quiet my mind. *I'll just peek.* I peeled open the Tupperware Grandma had placed on my car's passenger seat before hugging me goodbye. *I just want to know what's in it. Then I'll give it away.*

Inside, eight varieties of dessert bars lay in tidy rows. Their scents stoked memories: Christmas lights casting rainbows on our cat's fur as he dozed beneath the tree, baskets and pastel eggs hidden in closets. Grandma's bars had accompanied every holiday. Now, the smell of peanut butter and chocolate, brown sugar, marshmallows, and strawberry jam, muddied the distinctions between comfort and guilt, autonomy and loneliness. My regimen required concealing how I felt and lying about what I ate. I couldn't ever let down my guard because I might let something slip that revealed my weak and gluttonous nature. Constant subterfuge left me isolated; no one knew the real me.

I watched, hypnotized, as my fingers plucked a square from the Tupperware and raised it to my lips.

"No!" my brain commanded. "Put it down!" I didn't want past habits to taint my future.

My hand wouldn't heed. A survival instinct laid siege to my self-control. Before I realized I'd finished the first bar, I pinched a second between my fingertips. I took another bar. And another. Tears pricked behind my eyes. I glanced in the mirror and searched for signs I'd already gotten fatter, certain I could feel it, but I kept going. My stomach expanded uncomfortably: a warning. I should drink water and cleanse my palate; that would slow me down, but I couldn't pause long enough to reach for the bottle on my dresser.

I finished one layer. I pulled up the wax paper, knowing more family relics lay beneath it. By the time I'd finished half of the second layer, pain rippled through my stomach. I replaced the Tupperware's lid, threw the container in the closet, and slammed the door so I wouldn't have to see what I'd done.

My abdomen grew hard. I couldn't bend at the waist. I stumbled to my bed and lay on my side, legs drawn up, arms curled around my midsection. I fell into fitful sleep fully clothed.

I woke to sun screaming through the blinds. My head pounded. My mouth prickled with thirst. I guzzled water, felt my stomach stretch again, thought I might vomit. I welcomed the idea but couldn't follow through. Instead, I dressed and resumed the regimen that would send me careening toward Regions Hospital 10 years later.

After my discharge from Regions, Sara helped me narrow the chasm I'd cleaved between mind and body, but my afternoon with Willow in 2014 revealed why it hadn't closed.

Tom called out commands faster than I could process. "Inside rein back; outside rein forward! Sit back through the turns. Feel her mouth through your fingers. She's leaning to the inside; don't let her shoulder drop."

Willow was only walking, and I was already losing track of which command to follow with which limb and in which sequence.

We had just found a rhythm at the trot when I noticed that Liz and her students had gathered near the gazebo to watch. Having an audience reminded me of faking my way through passages as First Chair flutist. My legs clenched. My knees became a fulcrum, and I pitched forward. The pressure sent Willow running.

"Slow her down!" Tom shouted. "Steer her in a spiral. Tighter."

He set his mug on the rail and walked to the spiral's center. "Come closer. She can't sprint in a circle." He rotated to watch our orbit. "When Willow does what you want, release your fingers. Only hold for the time it takes to say 'finger.' Say it. Out loud. Say 'finger.'"

"Finger," I mumbled, feeling silly.

"Did you say it? I didn't hear you. Louder!"

"Finger!"

"That's better. Willow has to associate release with doing the right thing. If it's not immediate, she won't understand." Tom stuck a hand in his jeans' pocket and nodded while turning in place.

Willow was so responsive to the slightest cue that I understood immediately why she'd been so successful on the racetrack. Sensitivity, as much as speed, had made her a champion. I could tell she'd intuited her jockey's intent and broke from the pack at the perfect moment. Though it was taking her longer than expected to adjust to show jumping's slow pace, she *was* adjusting. *If she can do it, so can I.*

Tom continued firing commands, so I decided I'd release the pressure on myself. *Whatever happens, I won't mime performing this time.* I sank my weight into my heels and spread my toes, picturing my feet as roots that would keep me upright no matter how much Willow resisted slowing.

Regulating Willow's speed with my posting made the relationship between my internal and external struggles concrete. I would continue to rise and fall in both eating disorder recovery and in life, but I didn't need to fear that falling would break me. If I learned to fall and rise reliably, I'd avoid feeling hammered by the impact of every trot stride or life setback. In fact, without posting's small falls, I *couldn't* rise.

I liked the idea of emphasizing the rise, so I reversed the usual posting description and repeated *fall and rise* as I sought to match Willow's steps to my contact with the saddle's valley.

Tom's comments grew more positive.

"Uh-huh. Now, let your hands come forward when you turn. Outside rein and inside rein should match the curve you want. Good. Stop."

I halted Willow and patted her neck. She sighed but showed no signs of exertion. I sighed, too, feeling drained but happy.

"Now," Tom said, "do all of that in the opposite direction."

Going to the right was tough for racehorses, who made a living going left. The right side was also my weaker one. Though right-handed, I'd led from my left arm and leg for every vault, dismount, and tumbling pass in gymnastics. *Fall and rise, Lisa. Fall and rise.*

The longer I rode Willow, the more I realized that being worthy of riding her was less about perfect technique than intent and integrity. As long as I kept my mind clear and my heart open, she forgave my mistakes and seemed to know what I meant even when it didn't match my cues exactly.

We drew larger and larger circles in the desert, expanding each time I steadied her uphill trot. Then we graduated to straight lines. By the time we cantered, riding felt like floating.

"OK, you're fine," Tom said. "Go join Liz's class." He lifted his mug from a fencepost and turned to leave the arena.

I patted Willow's neck, leaned toward her ear, and whispered, "Thanks. You really *are* Queen of the Nile."

Willow snorted and licked her lips. Then she did a full-body, wet-dog shake. Her ears flapped, the sound—like wet paint against a wall—among my favorite in the world. I laughed like a kid on a trampoline as her body shook mine.

Tom heard the commotion and turned. Once Willow stilled, he said, "You know what? You're actually a good rider."

I smothered an indignant gasp. *Try not to sound so surprised.* "Thanks." *I think?*

"You made my day. You should ride Willow again."

"I'd love to." I ran my fingers through her mane.

"I mean it. You should ask Liz about that."

"OK. I will."

Tom ducked between the fence rails and headed for the barn.

My success with Willow continued in Liz's class. I felt none of my usual disappointment about not jumping. Cantering on such a fast and sensitive horse provided plenty of challenge. My cues took on subtlety I'd never displayed.

Just when I thought the day couldn't get better, Liz said, "I like you on Willow. I might have you ride her again."

"I'd be happy to!"

I couldn't stop smiling as I led Willow toward the barn. There, I slid damp saddle pads from Willow's back and hung them in the foyer to dry. I knew she'd roll in the dirt as soon as I turned her loose, but I brushed her anyway. I didn't want to end my time with her.

I hoped I'd ride her again, but I wouldn't count on it. If therapy and riding had taught me anything, it was how dangerous rigid expectations could be. I'd accept today's gift and be grateful.

As it turned out, I didn't ride Willow again for two years, but I liked stopping by her stall to say hello and soak up her eyes' liquid light. Spending a few minutes with her helped orient me when I felt lost. And I had to build on that sense of orientation because my last ride on Buck before he left Seventh Farm would threaten to knock me out of balance and threaten to nudge me off-track.

Chapter 8 - Buck: Trust Your Compass

Seventh Farm Riding School, March 2015

"Oh, Buck! That's why Cate usually puts you in a stall before lessons," I complained when I got a good look at him.

I'd thought Buck's Warmblood genetics would save me from the paddock's muck, but I'd only been half right. Even without a coat that looked like a map of the world, Buck would have stood out in the paddock because the Thoroughbreds looked like hummingbirds beside the stout frame and bulky muscle he'd inherited from a draft-horse ancestor. His distinctiveness had let me walk a straight line from the gate to where he stood with his butt against the fence instead of hunting for white socks that distinguished one bay Thoroughbred from another. Those socks were covered by mud that looked like an avocado smoothie after southerly winds had swept in overnight, thawing manure that hooves had pulverized into the softened soil.

I had just thanked Buck for standing still as I'd approached when I glimpsed how much he'd rolled. His right side was covered with muck. Some had dried to a crust that crunched when I poked it. I grimaced, then I recalled how gleeful Buck was when I untacked him on sweltering summer afternoons and he was free to roll, mussing hair that sweat had plastered to his skin. Watching such a dignified creature shimmy across the ground, legs splayed to the earth's four corners, reminded me of my nieces veering out of their way to stomp through puddles in new rain boots. Buck worked hard; he deserved a good roll, no matter how disgusting the result.

I found it hard to stay annoyed about muck or anything else once spring cracked and shook off winter's husk. The sun was still a gray apparition in early March, but the air's supple edges and mossy scent suggested that Mother Nature had exhausted her supply of winter surprises.

I tried not to think about what comprised the dust flying at my face with each stroke of a curry comb across Buck's hide. Instead, I focused on my muscles warming and loosening in tandem with his winter fur. He must have appreciated spring's arrival, too, because he inhaled, inflating his belly like a balloon, and blew raspberries, adding saliva to the dust and sunscreen coating my forearms.

"You're such a goofball," I told him, laughing as I wiped my arms on my breeches.

I deflated when Liz announced we'd review "turning on the haunches" during our lesson. That maneuver meant a rider asked her horse to swing his backend like a compass around his shoulders instead of leading from his shoulders and letting his backend follow. I grumbled internally about spending a gorgeous morning on mechanics when we could be cantering beneath the cloudless sky. I was terrible at turning—right or left, from the saddle or the ground. Turns depended on directional aptitude I didn't have and required my body's parts to move in ways that felt contradictory to the horse's motion. They also reminded me of driving, which I hated because my poor sense of direction often led me astray. I'd been lost behind the wheel more times than I could count, and nothing left me more frustrated.

Despite the rail serving as a guide, I struggled to execute the turns. My disjointed signals confused Buck. He turned and glared at me. I didn't need an interpreter to understand his message. "What the hell, lady?!"

Don't get worked up. The least I owed Buck was to honor what he'd taught me about letting go of perfectionism. Still, I longed to drop the reins and let Buck carry me to the barn like farmers my uncle had described over dinner the week prior.

"Oh, yah," he'd begun, in Minnesota style. "Back in the old days, a farmer could be in the fields, miles from anywhere, when a blizzard blew in. There'd be so much snow and wind he couldn't see past the horse's ears. He'd have died from exposure if his horse hadn't known the way home. Instead of trying to find his way, he'd drop the reins, smack his horse's rump, and let the horse lead him to the barn."

How? I learned later that horses form a mental map of their surroundings using home as the center point. No matter where they go, home is at the end of a straight line as the crow flies, and horses can follow it over and around obstacles.

If I'd had a pinch of horse sense, maybe I'd have stayed centered during the storm that marked my second year of college.

I returned to campus in the teal blue Cavalier that Dad, Julie, and I had driven to Denver just over a year earlier, but the car sat in the parking lot for weeks at a time. I preferred campus's familiarity to the Twin Cities' riot of roads that jigged around lakes, changed names over bridges, coalesced in Tangletown, and fed interstates labeled "east" and "west" that traveled north and south. Even on campus, I had to stop and think sometimes: *Are these the stairs I take to Mendel Hall's third-floor classrooms? Does this door lead to Derham Hall's basement, or is it the other one?* As desperate as I'd been to leave Omaha, I missed its grid, which was centered on a major thoroughfare called Dodge Street. Named streets went east-west; numbered streets went north-south, and the numbers climbed as they traveled west from the city's eastern border: the Missouri River. I still managed to get lost, but I always found my way home again.

My college disorientation went far deeper than surface streets. Living in a converted classroom with two friends launched my sensitive system into chaos.

My roommates and I mirrored the starve-binge extremes that drove my eating disorder. They were extroverts; I was an introvert. They were assertive; I was passive. They came alive at night; I rose early. They itched to move beyond the college's wrought iron gates; I'd have lived on campus forever.

Instead of advocating for my needs, I wound myself around theirs. I tied myself in knots to avoid inconveniencing them—less from altruism than fear of conflict. Mostly, though, my disorientation came from being unable to relax with so much *presence* in the room. I couldn't sleep and grew heavy with exhaustion. I lost sense of day and night, up and down. I sought escape by staying away all day, studying in the library, writing in the computer lab, or tutoring in the writing center. I wanted to slink about unnoticed, staying out of everyone's way. Instead, I grew too big to miss.

Fatigue drove a compulsive need for energy. I couldn't sleep, so I ate.

My body's landscape shifted. Planes flat enough to remind me of North Platte plumped into hills worthy of Omaha. By midterm, only my socks and shoes fit. I wore men's track pants I'd bought to pull on over workout gear in cold weather. Their loose fit disguised flesh I didn't want to see; their elastic waistband let me forget for a few seconds at a time that I was out of control. But my thighs whistled when I walked, chastising with every footfall. I envied my roommates' slender figures—so compact and tidy, while mine was sloppy and unwieldy.

Our room's revolving door of residents and guests made it impossible to concentrate in the evenings, so I hid in the stairwell to study. My sleep-deprived brain couldn't home in on sentences I needed for an essay due the following day, so I ate to sharpen its focus. One night, I skulked to the stairway with a bag of Hershey's miniature candy bars stashed in my backpack. The first dark chocolate bar wrapped my tongue and swaddled my brain in cotton that muted internal and external noise. When saliva rinsed its last trace from my mouth, I pulled another from the bag. I crumpled the foil wrappers into tight balls and hid them in my backpack's pocket, terrified someone would catch me gorging on candy. Our building's ancient elevator labored like an arthritic hippopotamus, and we often bypassed it to climb the stairs, so I ate, crumpled, hid; ate, crumpled, hid.

I finished the chocolate before I finished my essay. Sugar overload made my heart pound. My whole body seemed to vibrate. *If I'm this weak-willed and lazy, I deserve to be uncomfortable.*

I ate and ate that fall, hating myself more with each pound gained. I ate to escape the hatred and hated myself for needing escape. Some binges felt like everything at once: escape, comfort, punishment. The three sensations tangled like ribbons in a washing machine. The pleasure taken in biting, tasting, chewing, and swallowing looped the discomfort of a stretched stomach, dry mouth, pounding heart, swollen fingers, and sleepless eyes. I couldn't find one string's end and follow it long enough to make sense of what I was doing or how to stop it.

I woke every morning determined to disrupt the cycle. By noon, sleep deficits handcuffed my will. I slunk to the campus grill in mid afternoon, when I knew it would be empty. Hamburgers' sizzle and greasy scent soothed. I paired one with a basket of fries. Then I scooped Malted Milk Balls into a clear plastic bag and knotted it, implying I'd save them for later. (I wouldn't.) I set the bag on the scale and paid its price.

On a day when I should have been elated to see my first front-page story in the campus newspaper, I plunged deeper into self-hatred. I grabbed a paper from the stack in the campus center, unfolded it, and flushed with shame. My mirror's scolding hadn't prepared me to see the truth in black and white. A half-page photo showed my roommate and me with the subject of my article and my childhood crush: Olympic Gold Medal-winning diver, Greg Louganis. He'd slung an arm over our shoulders and smiled warmly at the camera. I barely recognized myself. I had ballooned to 166 pounds, each one spread across the front page. Worst of all, my smile was barely skin-deep. A scant glance was all it took to see the vacancy behind my eyes. I wanted to cry but was too numb to conjure tears.

That night, I lay on our dorm room's prickly brown carpet with a pillow beneath my cheek. I stared at an episode of *Friends* without following its plot. From my point of view, the characters walked through a world tilted on its axis, but I didn't care. My only care was that soon I'd have our room to myself for the night.

"Are you sure you don't want to come with us?" one roommate asked as she reached for her boyfriend's hand. He stared at me with obvious distaste.

I adjusted the pillow beneath my head but didn't look up. "Yeah, I'm sure. Thanks."

They pulled on coats and gloves, checked for keys, grabbed purse and wallet. Just before they opened the door, my roommate whispered to her new love, "Seriously, don't ever let me get fat."

The following afternoon, I swallowed two handfuls of prescription pills and lay in my bed to welcome sleep's velvet darkness.

I spent the next 24 hours vomiting instead of dying.

My roommates assumed I had the flu. I didn't correct them.

I wandered through my last 18 months of college in a daze, determined to graduate early once I discovered that I could. I finished with one major, two minors, an honors program certificate, and a 3.94 GPA, but I was more adrift than ever. Outside of classroom highlights, I retain little more than a handful of flash-frozen moments.

Once out in the world, I knew even less about who I was or what I wanted. If not Collin's girlfriend or a star student, what was I? I knew only that I couldn't go back to Omaha, especially not the way I looked. Instead of running toward something I sought, I ran away from everything I feared.

I took the first job offered. It was a worse fit than my college dorm arrangements.

Lying in bed at night, I designed elaborate makeovers. I longed to dismantle the Good Girl shell I zipped into every morning—a costume from which I looked out at the world through narrow slits. I flirted with dying my hair a shade of black that sucked in light and trapped it, that looked off-kilter with skin as fair and freckled as mine. I'd line my lids with kohl and layer mascara until my lashes looked like tarantula legs. I'd thread hoops through my nostrils, pierce my ears from lobe to crest. I'd get tattoos, wear ripped black jeans, a motorcycle jacket, boots with two-inch soles. If anyone stared, I'd glare back with eyes that sneered, "Do you think I care?"

Instead, I moussed and air-dried mouse-brown curls. I dusted lids with tan shadow and cheeks with peach blush. I pulled on sundresses and strappy, high-heeled sandals. I painted on a smile and grabbed my keys.

Getting thin was all I cared about. I was sure thinness would get me a better job and social life. I woke at 5:00 a.m. and ran three miles through St. Paul's Frogtown and Midway neighborhoods, ignoring the fact that they were places where a woman should never run alone in the dark. I lost 30 pounds but didn't feel less brittle. I doubled down, fasting until my body hit its limit and snapped back like a stretched rubber band.

During one snap-back, I stopped at Cub on University Avenue. I pushed a metal cart that wobbled because of a kinked front wheel past the deli to the aisles that held what I needed: brownies, frosting, licorice, granola. Sugar. Fat. Carbohydrates. Comfort.

I'd paid for my junk food, plucked the paper bag from the conveyor, and almost made it to the exit when a voice halted my footsteps.

"Miss?"

A man's black boots blocked my path. I looked up. Coal black eyes bore through my sockets. I waited for a panhandler's plea or a reminder that I'd left something behind.

"Excuse me for saying so," the man said. He paused and looked uncertain about finishing his sentence.

I shifted my weight from one foot to the other, impatient to escape.

"I just have to tell you... your eyes stand out in a crowd and command attention. I saw you from over there and thought, 'Wow! Look at them!' They're beautiful! So deeply blue. Exquisite."

My lips moved but I couldn't produce a sound. My voice wouldn't follow commands. I switched my bag from one hand to the other.

"Anyway, sorry to disturb you. I just had to let you know."

I nodded. "I... uh, thanks." Grinning felt harder than bending steel.

The man gave a slight bow and returned to bagging his groceries.

Cold air pregnant with rain swept the yeasty scent of nearby breweries into the parking lot. It lingered on my clothes after I dumped my bag on the Amigo's passenger seat and started the engine. I fished for the licorice and ripped open its package, blanching when the crinkling plastic sounded like Dad's *tsk*. I shoved three strips in my mouth and let them dangle from my lips while I buckled my seatbelt. When I pulled from the parking lot, tears rolled down my cheeks.

I headed for home, unaware it lay at the center of a triangle formed by the Cathedral, The Emily Program, and Regions Hospital.

"I can't get back on track," I told Sara once I found The Emily Program's new Court International Building location in 2003. It straddled the Minneapolis-St. Paul boundary, pulling in the erratic orbits of Highway 280, Franklin Avenue, University Avenue, and railroad tracks that disappeared into an industrial maze.

My first impression of the new location was that it differed from the former one like Minneapolis differed from St. Paul. The St. Paul building had been cozy and classic: radiator heat, plaster walls, wood floors that creaked beneath buckling carpet, space carved piecemeal into offices that ducked staircases or rounded corners. The Minneapolis building was sleek, sharp, and minimal; steel beams and glass walls suggested a skeleton stripped of flesh. The glass elevators turned passengers into voyeurs while putting them on display. I smiled tightly when the phrase "glass cage" came to mind, making me think of *The Glass Menagerie* and how Mr. Kolterman would have appreciated the reference. A man pouring breakroom coffee into his mug looked up to find me smiling—seemingly at him. I shifted my gaze to the cage's moving cogs and cables, whose visibility seemed designed to force riders into considering the grace and folly of existence: One snapped line and they'd plummet. *Would that be so bad?*

Lisa Whalen

Windows made up one of Sara's office walls. They looked out over University Avenue's refurbished warehouses. Between them, maple trees peacocked with fall color. I liked the way Sara's newly upholstered furniture merged interior and exterior, its pattern of circles and lines mirroring fall color and matching The Emily Program's logo.

"What do you mean by 'back on track'?" Sara asked.

What *did* I mean? I'd recovered from the falling-out with Leanne, and my career at Hamline was moving forward, but nothing in my personal life would adhere to plan. I wasn't dating. I barely socialized. I tremored with anxiety most days. And I continued bouncing between extremes: starve or binge; over-exercise or lie catatonic on the couch.

"It's like I'm driving a train with misaligned wheels. They scrape against the rails and pull to one side, creating drag and sending sparks flying. When I correct for it, I careen in the other direction. I can't get my bearings. I can't get back to being who I was before."

"Before... ?" Sara canted her head. Blond hair fell forward over one eye, and she hooked it behind her ear.

"Before I broke. Before Collin."

"I see. We'll talk about that, but first, how's your Master's degree capstone going?"

I moaned and dropped my head into my hands, trying for comedic overdramatization, though there was nothing funny about graduation hinging on completing my collection of personal essays. I longed for people to know me—*really* know me—but putting myself on the page for public consumption felt like being flayed. My writing got strangled by that knot of competing desires. The clock kept ticking toward my deadline.

"You like to write, and you've finished long-term projects before; why does the capstone have you panicked?"

I studied Sara's new office while I thought, as if it might offer an answer to her question. The tan walls, bare except for a map with emergency evacuation routes marked in red, offered no inspiration.

"I wish I hadn't written something so personal," I said, cringing when I thought about my essay collection being shelved in Hamline's library, available for anyone to read and surrounded by MFA capstones. The MFA students were ridiculously talented. In every class we'd shared, I felt like an interloper at the studio window, watching artists work with the hope of understanding their process so I could copy it.

"My project is messy—undefined. It wanders all over without... boundaries to limit its scope or give it shape. I keep thinking about how it has to be good because I'm in *graduate* school, which I never thought I'd apply to, much less complete."

I ran my fingernail along my chair's rolled edge. "It's like... even though its essays are distinct, I can't work on them one bite at a time. I keep trying to swallow the whole thing at—"

I sucked in a breath.

Sara gazed at me for a beat, her brown eyes clear and calm, her expression neutral. "You just heard yourself, didn't you?"

I nodded. Heat flashed through my body. *Wow. I'm really screwed up.* Was dysfunction embedded so deeply that it shaped my vocabulary along with my behavior? *How can I exorcise something that pervasive? I'd have to be on-guard constantly.* The idea exhausted me.

"Use what you just discovered. Try to think about each essay as a series of small bites you'll consume steadily over the next few months."

I nodded again, not trusting myself to speak.

"Let's discuss what you said about 'getting back on track.'" Sara folded her hands in her lap and looked at me intently.

"What if you don't need to get back to 'before'? What if you need to go forward? What if you could fold 'before' into 'now' and discover a new and better way of being yourself?"

"But I don't know who that is." I wasn't trying to be difficult. I truly had no idea which version of me among those I slipped on and off in a given day was real.

Sara smiled. "That's the good news. You don't have to know. You can figure it out as you go, one step at a time."

Sara watched me digest that suggestion. Figuring it out little by little sounded scary. Messy. I pictured myself as Wile E. Coyote: I'd start running only to discover I'd gone over a cliff. I'd stop, look down, see empty space, and hold up a sign that read "Oops!" before plummeting.

Sara must have sensed my mind spinning. "I'll help you figure it out. Writing can be part of that process. Maybe writing about Collin will help you get 'unstuck.' Not everything you write has to be part of your capstone. You can write for yourself—or for me."

"OK," I said, sounding doubtful.

"Just try it. Do what you can. No pressure. You don't have to show anyone, including me."

Sara's suggestion made sense in theory but proved complicated in practice. Thinking on the page embarrassed me. An introvert to the core, I preferred to perfect ideas in my head before putting them into words. The few times I'd tried journaling, I'd read entries later and broken out in a sweat. Their tone had reminded me of hearing my voice on tape. I'd been dismayed that what sounded calm and definitive in my head sounded breathy, childish, and lacking conviction in the world. I inevitably tore pages from the journal, ripped them into cereal-sized pieces, stirred them on my bed, and dumped them in different trash cans.

Typing felt marginally safer than handwriting. A computer's straight lines prevented my sloppy half-cursive from sloping as it crossed the page. It also offered a delete key and recycle bin. Few things satisfied more than Microsoft's crumpled paper sound effect and arced toss of documents into the screen's oblivion.

After leaving Sara's office, I set my laptop on my breakfast nook's pine table and wrapped a blanket around my legs to buffer air seeping through 70-year-old windows. I typed a sentence and deleted it. Typed another. Deleted it. That pattern repeated until my thoughts slipped like tires spinning on frost-glazed asphalt beyond the windows. I plunked my elbows on the table and lay my forehead on my palms.

Fine. If my voice is the problem, I'll ditch it. I abandoned first-person point of view and tried third-person. I turned myself into a character and my life into a novel. Years of observing myself from an outsider's perspective had laid the groundwork for writing in third-person. Words poured from my mind faster than my fingers could type them.

For hours after work each night, I ignored the achy back and cramped hamstrings inflicted by the nook's bench. Diving into my past felt heavenly. Even painful moments carried an emotional purity preferable to the stew of blunted feelings that had sloshed inside me since A.C. I stayed awake into the early-morning quiet, delaying the moment I had to click my heels and leave the past's Technicolor for the present's grayscale.

Though it felt good to write, I worried about the way my mind ground to a halt every time I tried switching to first-person. *How can I earn a Master's in creative nonfiction if I can't write using "I"?* I felt like a fraud when I helped undergraduates with their essays at work. Over lunch breaks and weekends, I white-knuckled my way through my capstone.

Weeks passed. Then months. Writing got easier. I didn't require as much windup to dig in. But first-person eluded me.

For my capstone, I leaned heavily on research to disguise my thin voice and skimpy content. For Sara, I hid behind a narrator's authority. I couldn't compose the letter to Collin she'd suggested I write without an intent to mail it. Instead, I began with the moment Keith told me about Collin's cheating. I wrote outward from that center, broadening the circle to include events that seemed unrelated but that intuition kept pointing me toward. Dad's temper crept in more than once. That didn't surprise me, but something else did: an interaction I'd forgotten.

It began with my family crossing the parking lot that surrounded Omaha's St. Leo Catholic Church in 1989. I watched my skirt flutter and swiped at hair the wind kept blowing in my eyes. James, a shy and sensitive nine-year-old in a crewcut and navy slacks, walked in front of me. At one point, he sent a landscaping pebble scrabbling across the asphalt with a kick of his penny loafer.

Dad erupted. "Hey! Don't do that! What's the matter with you? Think before you do stuff!" He flicked the back of James's head.

James and I barely tolerated each other most days, but something about the *thunk* of Dad's thick fingers against his little-boy skull set me off. I whirled. My skirt rippled as it followed my revolution. Words flew from my mouth before I considered the wisdom of voicing them.

"Don't *flick* your kid! That's something a middle school bully would do. You're an adult! He's just a child! Why would you do that?"

Silence. Weight settled on my shoulders like a yoke. *Oh, God. What had I done?* No one spoke to Dad that way—not even Mom—especially when he was mad. I stiffened the arm nearest him, certain he'd clamp a hand around it and pull me aside for a warning about the punishment that would follow Mass.

But Dad was no longer the same guy who'd screamed at me on the soccer field. He'd gentled after receiving treatment for depression when I was in seventh grade. Since then, he'd spent more and more time as the guy who rushed from work to sit on wooden bleachers in a suit and watch my gymnastics team lose another meet; who mimicked Saturday Night Live characters with side-splitting accuracy; who tapped his toe, bobbed his head, and hummed along to our band concert performances because he couldn't contain the music inside him.

I peered at Dad. His shoulders were hunched, his jaw clenched, his eyes locked on the ground. Wrinkles lined his forehead. He sensed me looking and glanced up. I snapped my gaze forward.

Dad opened the church's heavy wooden door and held it. Something passed between us as I walked through. Energy crackled, texturing the atmosphere like a summer storm. The air beyond it felt calm by comparison. The door shushed shut behind us. We entered our regular pew, lowered the kneeler, knelt, and prayed.

No one mentioned my outburst. It disappeared from both individual and collective memory. In hindsight, I recognized it as the moment Dad began looking at me differently, as if seeing me anew. I'd felt the scale tip and the balance between us settle closer to horizontal.

I'd thought Dad and I were opposites: extrovert versus introvert, impulsive versus cautious, brave versus timid, self-confident versus self-conscious, angry versus anxious. Writing for Sara uncovered that at our core, Dad and I were more alike than I'd realized because I'd had the impulse to erupt, too.

The most vivid example of my eruption potential happened one summer afternoon when I was ten. Mom brought Julie and me to McDonald's for lunch as a reward for being patient while she'd run errands. We sang our excitement all the way there, cracking ourselves up with silly voices and invented lyrics.

Once seated with my Happy Meal, I lined up my chicken nuggets, French fries, soda, and napkin. I always ate one food completely before starting another. I lifted a nugget to my mouth but was startled by clammy liquid splattering across my neck. I looked at my shirt and groaned. Julie had squeezed a ketchup packet too hard while trying to open it. Ketchup dotted my white collar and trailed to my blue hem. I *hated* getting dirty. Before I'd learned to eat with utensils, Mom said I'd cried about food stuck to my fingers. In childhood, I puzzled over Mom's surprised reaction when I emerged pristine from the backyard sandbox. *Well, who would want sand on their skin or clothes?*

Mom and Julie hadn't seen my reaction; they'd only seen the ketchup explosion, and they burst into shocked laughter.

I'll have to go to Target like this! The stain would draw looks. People might think it was blood. I hated people looking at me even more than I hated getting dirty.

Mom and Julie's laughter became amused giggling.

"It's NOT FUNNY!"

Mom tried to rein in her giggling but couldn't help herself.

"Stop laughing! Look what she did!" I whined. "How would *you* like it if I threw ketchup at you?"

"Hey!" Mom cautioned. "Settle down. It's not that bad."

I smoldered at the perceived injustice: Julie had made a mess, and I was the one in trouble. For the first and only time in my life I wanted to hurt my sister.

"Good girls don't hit," the Trench Coat Guys sneered. "Good sisters don't fight. Good young ladies don't throw tantrums. Good Catholics turn the other cheek."

I'd arrived at a fork, a moment when I could have gone either way: follow Dad's caustic example or find another way to cope.

I swiped at the stain with a napkin and glowered. Then I stuffed fries in my mouth and chewed, gratified when their salty bite matched my mood.

My anger had tunneled downward and barricaded itself within my psyche's deepest recess by the time I sat across from Mom at another restaurant in 2004. Regions' psychiatrist had granted permission for my parents to see me after talking with them on the phone.

Mom and Dad had braved subzero temperatures and icy, two-lane highways to get from their small town into St. Paul and spend an hour with me. I couldn't leave the hospital building, but a lull between lunch and dinner meant we had the cafeteria to ourselves. That privacy proved useful when my parents revealed that along with wanting to see me, they had a specific reason for visiting.

"He's *suing* you?" I sputtered about their parish priest's actions.

They nodded.

"We don't want you to worry," Mom said. She pushed her glasses' wire frames against the bridge of her nose, temporarily blocking one brown pupil from view. "We're telling you because we want you to hear it from us instead of seeing it on the local news."

Dad asked, "Will publicity cause you problems at work?"

His question drew my stare from Mom's eyes to the blue ones my siblings and I had inherited from him.

I mulled Dad's question. The Christian college had hired me on a one-year contract with an option to renew annually. I hoped to stay long-term, but being Catholic meant I was unlikely to earn tenure.

Before I could answer Dad, Mom spoke up. "It's not just Dad and me. The suit names the handful of people who wrote the letter with us."

I nodded. We'd known for months that a lawsuit was possible, but I didn't think the priest would dare. My parents and the other letter-writers were core members of their town's only Catholic church. They donated money for every event, served on committees, brought communion to nursing homes, delivered meals to shut-ins, sang in choirs, and served lunch at the parish school. Since they'd retired and moved north from Nebraska, church had become their career and governed their social calendar. Their involvement overlapped with Mom's extended family and a growing circle of friends. Life had been idyllic until the new priest arrived. Within a year, the parish split into two camps: one that supported the priest and one that didn't. In some cases, the dividing line severed lifelong friendships and prevented family members from speaking to one another. The strife tortured my parents.

"I don't think it will cause problems. And if it does, I don't care. You've put up with the Archdiocese's bullying long enough. *Someone* has to stop the corruption spreading from Rome.

"Besides, the Archbishop keeps ignoring your efforts to go through the 'proper channels.' You tried everything else before sending that letter to every parishioner. What else were you supposed to do?"

The last straw for my parents had come in the wake of the priest's financial misdeeds and unethical decisions, when evidence came to light that he'd had an affair with a parishioner who'd sought him out for marital counseling and who was still married.

"So he's claiming defamation?"

"Yes."

"What happens if he wins?"

"We could get excommunicated."

Kicked out of a morally bankrupt institution? Big deal, I thought. But it *would* be a big deal to my parents.

"I mean, what happens legally?"

"It's a civil case, not criminal, so we'd probably have to pay a fine on top of our lawyer's fees," Mom said. "It's worth the money. All we wanted from the beginning is to have our concerns addressed. If this is what it takes, then..." She shrugged.

Dad added, "The hearing isn't for a few months. Nothing will happen until then."

"OK." I sipped from the Evian bottle Dad had bought me when I'd admitted that, unlike my clothes, my wallet remained in a ward locker I couldn't access. Water tasted sweet after the ward's dry heat. I swallowed a large gulp and chugged the rest. My hour of leave was nearly up, so I hugged Mom and Dad goodbye.

I thought about their bravery while tracking the elevator's glacial progress toward the eighth floor. I respected their commitment but worried about how much they were risking to steer back on course an organization that would never acknowledge their efforts. Catholicism had been their compass since birth. I hoped Church leadership wouldn't leave their faith broken, like it had mine.

Though I had been devout through early adulthood, I'd drifted away from Catholicism well before the lawsuit. Religion had come to feel like the tights I'd battled to wear on Sunday mornings during childhood, when I'd grown more and more frustrated by the tights' insistence on twisting around one thigh until they felt like a tourniquet. No matter what technique I used to put them on, they bit into my flesh.

In recent years, I'd traded Catholicism's confinement for the freedom of dabbling in Buddhism. The only glitch was that my scratched-record mind resisted meditation the way I'd once resisted tights. Congruence between meditation and riding softened that resistance.

I'd known that meditation balanced energy flowing through portals Buddhism called "chakras." Knowing the seven chakras lined up with places where Western medicine had located ganglia—nerve bundles through which mind and body exchange messages via electrical energy—helped convinced me they were real. But I didn't know until I set foot on Seventh Farm's grounds that those places also correlated with parts of the body that shaped correct riding position.

The first chakra, which encompasses the base of the spine, the pelvic floor, legs, feet, and butt, also encompasses the first body parts I learned about in my earliest riding lessons and groundwork. First chakra energy governs a person's sense of feeling grounded—at home in her body and comfortable finding her way in the world. Disrupting that energy manifests in dysfunction that matched my diagnoses: anxiety, depression, eating disorders, nightmares, doubts about one's direction in life and ability to stand up for herself[8]. The more confidence I gained riding, the less these parts of my diagnoses steered my life's path.

The core that united my balance with the horse's center of gravity lay in the same spot as the third chakra, which encompasses the gastrointestinal organs and middle spine, where it aligns external experiences with internal perceptions. Disrupted third chakra energy affects anger and ability to make

---

8. Caroline Myss, *Anatomy of the Spirit: The Seven Stages of Power and Healing*, (New York: Three Rivers Press, 1996). 97.

decisions[9]. It also manifests in hypersensitivity, disinclination for self-care, and loss of "self-esteem, self-confidence, and self-respect."[10] No wonder riding had felt like meditation from my earliest lessons.

A rider's core controls her seat, which begins as a triangle comprised of pubic and sit bones. As she gains skill, the triangle becomes a bowl that she rolls on, allowing for more complete and constant connection to the horse. A substitute instructor I'd had once put it this way: "Your seat is your voice and riding is like talking on a cell phone: The better the connection, the less likely your signal will cut out."

The image of a bowl appealed immediately. I'd just been introduced to Tibetan singing bowls, whose resonant vibrations reminded me of my flute's vibrato and a tuning fork's stable pulse. I liked the image even better when I discovered the bowls were actually bells. Unlike church bells, which hang upside down and must be pushed or pulled and then struck by a clapper to ring, singing bowls rest upright on a flexible base and sing out with a tone created by their internal structure. Their centering effect isn't imaginary. Brain scans reveal that their vibrations act on chakras to prompt "deeper Alpha and Theta brain wave frequencies that induce deep meditative and peaceful states, clarity of mind, and intuition."[11]

9. Michelle Fondin, "Find Power and Warrior Energy in Your Third Chakra," The Chopra Center, last modified January 15, 2015, https://chopra.com/articles/find-power-and-warrior-energy-in-your-third-chakra.

Michelle Fondin, "The Root Chakra: Muladhara," The Chopra Center, last modified October 23, 2014, https://chopra.com/articles/the-root-chakra-muladhara.

10. Myss, *Anatomy of the Spirit,* 96-97.

11. Diane Mandle, "Tibetan Singing Bowls: Introduction to Sound Healing with Tibetan Singing Bowls," The Mindful Word, accessed December 9, 2019, http://www.themindfulword.org.

Knowing horses are sensitive to energy, I began meditating in 2013 as a way to improve my riding. Most summer mornings I lit a candle, set an egg timer, and took up lotus position, where I rested on the same triangle of bones that had once formed my riding seat. Sometimes I succeeded in clearing my mind and meditating for 40 minutes. Other times, I quit six minutes in. But that imperfect practice fostered benefits I couldn't deny.

One sparkling October afternoon, I pulled out my laptop and sat in a lawn chair on my back step. My cat lolled in the sun, which played tag with wooly clouds. Squirrels chattered from a nearby tree. Kids squealed and giggled as they climbed their jungle gym next door. But something felt off. I had no reason to be on alert, but I couldn't shake my unease. I struggled to concentrate on grading student essays. I stopped and started, stopped and started.

Then a voice whispered, "It's the wind."

My fingers froze on the keyboard. I squinted up at the cottonwood that draped my yard. Its leaves waved like jazz hands. Their rustling offered no reprieve. Air licked my face and batted my ponytail, fluttered notebook pages and ruffled my sleeves.

In North Platte, wind at dusk taunted that I might be awakened in the dark by Mom's prodding once more. I'd stumble down the hallway as a siren wailed, hail beating against the windows and lightning flashing. Dad would open the hallway closet, lift its trapdoor, and lower me into Mom's arms, where we'd huddle on cardboard spread over the dirt floor. The storm radio would beep. A voice would repeat county names I recognized.

I'd tensed at strong wind ever since, especially when it was constant enough to exhaust my antennae. In adulthood, my stomach still plummeted when the cottonwood's branches began rotating or bent in opposite directions.

The wind is what's bothering me.

I lifted my laptop, swung open the screen door, and set up at my dining room table. When I put my fingers on the keyboard, something in me shook loose. I began writing about A.C. in first-person, and the words didn't stop.

A week after my back-step revelation, I tacked up Buck and resigned myself to another lesson on turns. I wouldn't let what the voice had revealed go to waste. I'd forget about trying to perfect "the letter of the turn" and concentrate on following "the spirit of the turn." I'd quiet my mind and let my intuition lead.

Buck stopped glaring at me. His back relaxed beneath the saddle. We practiced the turns at a walk, a trot, and then a canter. Some of mine still bowed like wet wood, but a few snapped like chalk lines.

I'd just grown comfortable with the turning exercise when Liz announced she was adding a pattern. We would alternate looping the arena with drawing a square in its center and "jumping" poles on the ground that bisected each side.

Oh, no. I'd have to juggle the turns' myriad elements while keeping track of where I was in the pattern, where I'd go next, and where the other riders were so I didn't crash into them. It was a directionally-challenged rider's nightmare. I skulked to the end of the line so Buck and I would be last to trace the pattern.

Each hoofbeat shook dust from the sand. By the time Buck and I set off, the arena reflected the sky, where jets' vapor trails crisscrossed a blue backdrop. An absence of wind kept the dust hovering near our shoulders, filling in the outlines we drew.

Buck and I piled square atop square, building a wall of confidence. Riding's parts clicked into place. Things Liz had been telling me for years made sense: Ride from your seat and leg, not from the reins. Your hands and legs are connected; they should work together." I pictured a sun at my solar plexus, its rays linking my head and limbs to my core. *This is how riding should feel,* chimed a mantra against my breastbone.

Later, I would recognize that moment as one described by Mark Warren, Director of the Cleveland Center for Eating Disorders. He says treatment is about helping patients "come to the surface."[12] They have detached from their bodies so thoroughly that they must relearn how to exist as physical beings, to "fully sense—through tasting, touching, smelling, and hearing, as well as seeing—the world around them."[13] Only then can they "discover that the world can be a source of support and satisfaction rather than fear."[14] Once a patient reenters her body, she transitions from a character pushed along by an external narrator to a protagonist who drives her life's plot.

After Buck and I traced the pattern several times, my legs trembled from exertion. But when I leapt from the saddle, my feet planted firmly in the sand. My shoulders reached up and out like branches. I felt taken apart, swabbed out, and reassembled, the way I'd once cared for my flute.

I also felt filthy.

I smacked my palm against my thigh and saw dust fly from my breeches. Green saliva smeared one shoulder, where Buck had used my shirt as a napkin. Sweat glued my shirt to my back and my hair to my temples. Grit crunched between my molars. *I should have brought a towel to lay on the Amigo's seat.*

I shrugged, smiled, and climbed behind the wheel feeling more satisfied than I'd been for years.

---

12. Amiee Liu, *Gaining: The Truth about Life After Eating Disorders* (New York: Warner, 2007), 36.
13. Liu, *Gaining: The Truth about Life After Eating Disorders,* 36.
14. Liu, *Gaining: The Truth about Life After Eating Disorders,* 36.

Chapter 9 - Charlie: Ride the Jump You're Given

Seventh Farm Riding School, November 2015

"Nope!" Liz shouted. Or maybe I only thought she shouted because I knew she wouldn't like the jump Charlie and I landed. Its impact compressed my lungs, pushing out an involuntary grunt.

"Stop and come here," Liz said before Charlie and I rounded the corner beyond the fence we'd jumped. Her voice sounded flinty with irritation.

I pressed against the saddle's tobacco-brown leather with my thighs to slow Charlie and pointed the dashed line of his blaze in Liz's direction.

"You thought Charlie's front legs would leave the ground before they did, didn't you?" Liz asked.

"Yeah." I sniffled. November's rotting leaves and damp cold always made my nose run. I dug in my hoodie's pocket for a Kleenex.

"Stop anticipating the takeoff. You're trying to micromanage the jump. That's not your job. Are you the one jumping this fence?"

"No." I had answered that question before, which explained Liz's irritation.

"Right. So stop micromanaging."

Liz stroked Charlie's frizzy forelock. He turned a ginger ear toward her and harrumphed a sigh as if agreeing with her assessment.

"Until you learn how to place the horse's feet where you want them, you have to wait until you feel his legs lift and then go *with* him over the fence, not ahead of him. Jumping ahead will send you flying over the horse's ears if something goes wrong."

Charlie cocked a hip, shifting his weight to the white sock on his right rear leg. I imagined him bored by this familiar lecture, though he never showed impatience. His best trait was that he simply got on with whatever a day presented.

"The jump is the horse's domain, so let him sort it out. Be patient. Wait until your horse gets to the takeoff spot—no matter how long that takes. Right, Charlie?"

I huffed a laugh. My classmates chuckled, too. Their breath clouded my peripheral vision. Charlie's lumbering, straight-legged canter felt like an oil well pump and covered the same amount of ground. In my head, I called him The World's Slowest Thoroughbred. I preferred race horses like Willow and Finn, whose speed gave me confidence (false or not) coming to a fence.

"No horse will jump the same way every time. They're not machines. Neither are you. You need to tune in and stay present. You get this glazed expression and check out four strides from the fence."

I opened my mouth to object, but then the jump replayed in my head. Liz was right: I'd frozen the moment I'd thought Charlie would leap.

"Let the jump unfold. If you stay connected to Charlie and listen to what he tells you, you'll be safe no matter what kind of jump he gives you: long, short, pretty, ugly. The goal is to ride *any* jump so you land ready for the next fence. Go again. Wait for the right moment, and then ride the jump you're given."

"OK." I shoved the Kleenex in my pocket and picked up the reins.

"That's better," Liz said when I followed her advice.

I turned the phrase "ride the jump you're given" over in my head as the Amigo juddered over ice-rutted roads on its route through Hudson to I-94. It reminded me of how much time and energy I'd wasted micromanaging my approach to life's fences. *What if I'd learned to ride the jumps I'd been given instead?*

I knew my fences were fewer and lower than those faced by 99% of the world. Growing up with images of Ethiopia's famine on the news and "We Are the World" on the airwaves, I'd understood that I had an obligation to acknowledge my privilege and pay it forward, but nothing had made my good fortune more concrete than meeting a man I called Jesus Guy.

Although I'd been frozen in fear and lost in my head when I'd entered Regions, Jesus Guy had been impossible to miss. His voice carried as if amplified by supernatural power, and he never stopped talking. Along with his glasses and buzzed gray hair, his deep voice created a schizophrenic disconnect with his apparel: a blue trucker hat, brown cowboy boots, and pink flannel pajamas covered in penguins.

"I just want to tell you how much I appreciate you," he told the person who introduced herself after he volunteered to go first in group therapy.

Jesus Guy interrupted frequently as the session went on, saying, "I appreciate all of you and the staff here. I'm grateful to the Lord for having you in my life. Praise God; thank you, Jesus."

"We appreciate you, too," the nurse replied. "Now—"

"And can I just tell everyone that *The Purpose Driven Life* is a great book? You should read it. You really should. It's given me meaning. It's let me know how much God loves us. We're all precious. We are. I want to give thanks and praise for the world we live in, the people we share it with, the food we eat—"

The nurse broke in. "That's wonderful. I remember you saying that last time you stayed here. I'll have to find that book.

I appreciate you sharing your feelings, but we have to let others speak."

"Sorry." He hung his head and whispered, "Praise God; thank you, Jesus."

I didn't begrudge Jesus Guy his faith or his enthusiasm for sharing it, but I resented his pronouncements that God would fix our problems. I'd heard similar platitudes at the Christian College and been incredulous when administrators proposed "God will provide" as a solution to budget shortfalls. That kind of talk made my teeth grate. Part of my irritation stemmed from hearing highly-educated people spout rote phrases utterly lacking in logic, but what I didn't like to admit was that I was furious with God. Knowing about Job hadn't helped when I'd prayed for help but received none. And my problems were trivial. How could a benevolent creator let some creatures suffer from much worse famine, poverty, cruelty, or oppression simply because of when and where they'd been born? Life seemed more like a game of chance than a test of faith. The last thing I wanted to hear at my lowest point was that God would take care of everything if I just believed. I avoided Jesus Guy because I didn't trust myself to react kindly if faced with a sermon.

As my fear of the ward and its inhabitants faded, so did my defensiveness. I saw Jesus Guy listen intently to every person who hadn't repelled him with negative energy like I had. He doted on his roommate, a young man with a developmental disability who declared gleefully every morning, "It's my birthday!" The two men had forged an instant bond when Jesus Guy had asked the young man about his stuffed dinosaur to distract him from his fear of the dark. That led to conversations about Vikings football, the merits of cake versus pie, and, of course, God.

The more I listened to Jesus Guy, the more my cynicism turned to appreciation. It wasn't hard to figure out how he'd ended up in the depression ward. He was guileless and gentle but tortured, too. He reminded me of Robert Frost's poem "Design" because he cared equally for the spider and the moth caught in its web. His deep compassion stood no chance against the world's serrated edges.

Jesus Guy and I were approved for discharge on my third day. I would leave with a safety net: antidepressants prescribed by a psychiatrist, weekly therapy with Sara, a sister to pick me up, a stay at my parents' house, and a stable home and job in St. Paul. Jesus Guy's future was less certain. Maybe that's why he stalled his departure, wandering the commons in baggy jeans, a gray sweatshirt, and a red ball cap, while a nurse offered to call him a cab.

"Don't worry about me," he assured everyone. "I'm going to be fine. I have God. I'll get a job and be happy. I have strength in the Lord. Praise God; thank you, Jesus."

He doesn't have a ride or a job? How will he make it? I hated thinking of him turned loose in a vacuum. I imagined him pacing an apartment's worn carpet in his penguin pajamas, staring into the dark through a sliding glass door. I wished I could shield him. *At least faith bolsters him,* I thought.

Did it? I grew less certain as I waited for Julie.

The nurse asked him, "Are you packed? Have you said your goodbyes?" She put her hands on her hips and adopted a stern expression. "I won't call the cab until you're ready. The driver won't wait."

"I'm ready. Praise God; thank you, Jesus." He stuck his hands in his jeans' pockets and walked toward a newly-admitted patient working on a jigsaw puzzle. "Have you read *The Purpose*

Driven Life?" He rested a palm on the table and leaned in. "It's about..."

A contest of wills unfolded. I gathered that the script had been rehearsed during prior stays. Characters recited their lines with ease.

Finally, Jesus Guy pulled on a peacoat, grasped a hard-sided suitcase, and followed the nurse to the exit. "Don't worry about me," he told us before he walked through the door. "I have strength in the Lord. Jesus is watching over me. Praise God; thank you, Jesus."

It sounded more like a wish than a fact. I feared he'd end up in the ward again, and it haunted me that I couldn't help him over life's obstacles.

Air smacked my face with a menthol sting when I walked through the hospital's sliding doors and onto the sidewalk. My cheeks and earlobes stung, but the cold felt bracing—a relief after the ward's recycled air.

Sun glanced off windshields. Fresh snowflakes glittered, flocking dingy mounds. I exhaled audibly to see my breath— evidence that I existed in the real world again.

Julie and I knocked our shoes against her Jeep's frame to dislodge snow, salt, and sand; then we drove to retrieve the Amigo, which had been parked at The Emily Program for three days.

"Umm, I have to tell you something," Julie warned, maneuvering the parking ramp's tight turns. "Before Mom and Dad visited you, they checked to see if the Amigo had gotten towed. It's still there, but someone punched a hole in the spare tire cover."

I thought for a second, remembering my pre-hospital journey from work to Sara's office. "Oh, you know what? That was me."

"Really?"

"No, I mean— I didn't punch it. I was backing out of a tight spot on campus and tapped the end of the security gate. The gate's arm was fine when I got out to check, so I didn't think to look at the Amigo. I barely made contact, but the tire cover is probably brittle."

"Ohhh." The relief in Julie's voice plucked my heartstrings. If she'd thought me capable of punching a hole in hard plastic, I'd worried her more than I'd realized.

"I should have disengaged the four-wheel drive before I backed out. Sharp turns are impossible in four-wheel." I smacked my forehead to lighten the mood. "D'oh!"

Julie's grip on the steering wheel relaxed.

"Yep," I said when we pulled in behind the Amigo and the hole matched the end of the gate's arm. "I did it. Oh, well."

I don't know which of us was more surprised by my attitude. I'd been meticulous about vehicles since I began driving. The Amigo was the first one I'd bought myself, and I treated it like a pet. But Jesus Guy's plight had realigned my perspective of what constituted a problem.

The Amigo's engine roared to life despite the temperature. I waved to Julie, and we drove in opposite directions.

I stopped at home to collect mail and pack a suitcase. Then, I cranked the volume on a CD of Broadway's *Rent* and merged onto I-94 West.

The route to my parents' house seemed transformed. Usually, I resented spending time in a car, but the Amigo's dove-gray interior felt cozy rather than claustrophobic. Snow turned the scenery into artwork. Icicles looked like diamonds dangling from fir trees. Crows stitched together sky and barren field as they dove for wayward corn.

I parked in Mom and Dad's driveway, where one garage door was open in anticipation of my arrival. Arms full, I skirted their minivan but bumped a shelf with my elbow when I reached for the door to the house. Something heavy hit the pitted concrete: the fishing depth finder we'd bought for Dad's birthday last fall. *Oh, no.* The finder was expensive, and Dad loved studying the lake bottom while tooling around in his boat.

I set my stuff on Dad's workbench and crouched to survey the damage: cracked casing, split screen. I turned the finder over and flicked its switch. Nothing. Dad would be furious.

I contemplated putting the finder on the shelf and walking into the house as if nothing had happened. *He'll never know it was me.*

No, I decided. *I'm tired of lying.* I'd spent too much time pretending to be someone I wasn't. I wanted to be real. I'd take whatever was coming.

I pushed open the door to the house, slipped off my loafers, and dumped my overnight bag in the entryway.

"Lisa?" Mom walked out of the kitchen, wiping her hands on a towel.

"Yeah, it's me."

"How was the drive?"

"Good. Nothing exciting. Is Dad home?"

"He's in The Nest."

"OK. I'm gonna say hi."

I climbed the stairs to Dad's office, which we called The Nest because the L-shaped desk, cupboards, and high-back chair tucked into an alcove made him an eaglet peeping from the enormous thatch bowl in a dead tree near their house. Dad's organizational style added to the perception. His workspace was covered with UPRR anniversary clocks and paperweights, slit-open envelopes, calculators, highlighters, prescription medication bottles, prayer cards, drawings we'd made him as kids, and Post-it Notes that bore his unique scrawl. The disarray disguised Dad's detailed knowledge of where every piece fit into the mosaic.

I knocked on the doorjamb.

Dad turned in his chair and grinned, his cheeks rounding to ruddy apples. "Heeeeey, Lisa!"

He rose to hug me. "How are ya?"

"Good."

"It's so great to have you here. I'm glad you're staying."

"Me, too. Um, I have some bad news."

I held up the depth finder, explained what had happened, and braced for an explosion.

"Oh, noooooo!" Dad took the finder. "Does it work?"

I shook my head. "I don't think so. I'm sorry."

I couldn't tell if Dad heard me. He turned the depth finder over and tried its switch.

"I'm really sorry."

Dad sighed. "Well, Mom's been telling me to put it where it belongs. I should have listened." He set the finder on his desk.

"Oh, that reminds me. Did Julie tell you about the Amigo's tire cover?" Dad sounded as worried about my reaction as I'd been about his.

That's it? No yelling? Wow, he has mellowed.

"Yeah. That was my fault, too. This hasn't been my week, I guess." I told Dad about hitting the gate arm. "I'm hoping the missing piece fell inside. Maybe it's still there and I can get it fixed so snow and salt don't rust the tire's rim."

"I bet we can fix it." Dad pushed his bifocals against his face and angled his head down to look at me. "I'll help you."

243

"Thanks, but you don't have to. I can take it to a shop."

"Nah, don't do that. We can handle it. Let's try right now."

"Are you sure?"

He gave a resolute nod. "Heck yeah!"

I pulled the Amigo into the garage. Dad sprayed WD40 on the cover's salt-caked zipper, and we contorted ourselves to work it open one tooth at a time. Though I was constantly in his space as we reached over each other and fumbled with tools, he never ordered me to get out of the way, never cautioned, "watch yourself."

Dad grunted comically as we tugged vinyl stiff with cold across rubber treads. Finally, the cover came free.

I pulled the missing piece from the rim and held it up.

"Alright!" Dad cheered.

We high-fived.

The care with which Dad's thick, stubby fingers laid a bead of superglue along the piece's jagged edge struck me as an act of love more potent than any I remembered. I sensed in it an apology for outbursts, an acknowledgement of shared chemical imbalances. He couldn't fix the past or control whether I ended up in a psych ward, but he could mend my tire cover.

I trotted out a family joke about duct tape being a universal tool when Dad applied it as a backer for our repair. He chuckled, but his laughter sounded tinged with sadness, or maybe regret.

I was surprised to find that the raised ridge around our repair didn't bother me. Its divot gave the Amigo character—a scar appropriate for the vehicle I called (Darth) Vader because of its square lines, shiny black metal, matte vinyl hardtop, and raspy sucking of air through its grill when I hit the gas.

I worried our graft would be short-lived. For 15 years, I would anticipate finding a hole every time I rolled through a car wash, but through burbling suds, searing sun, winter wind, and blinding rain, our patch held.

That scar took on new significance July 29, 2013. A phone call from Julie sent me careening toward North Memorial Hospital, where an ambulance had delivered Dad after Mom had found him on their bedroom carpet, barely breathing, with blood dripping from his nose.

The first thing I saw when I stepped into an ER alcove was part of a white line that ran along Dad's sternum: the incision from his quadruple bypass surgery 12 years earlier.

The second thing I noticed were Dad's feet. They stuck out from a white blanket draped from chest to ankles, and they looked cold. Their skin was tinged frost-blue. I shivered in sympathy as a vent overhead blew on skin clammy from my dash across the hospital parking lot. I wanted to lash out at the staff for neglecting Dad's feet. It seemed particularly callous because Dad's feet were unique. He'd never been self-conscious about skin that linked his second and third toes, joking that his "webbed" feet made him a better swimmer and skier, but I hated knowing that the staff might have commented on them or judged Dad while he lay helpless. Had he heard them? *Can he hear us?*

Later, I'd feel foolish about wanting to lash out. Cold feet wouldn't have bothered Dad because he wasn't... present. A blood vessel in his head had burst, flooding his brain like a car's engine so that it couldn't ignite and set wheels in motion.

My subconscious must have registered Dad's state before doctors gave us his prognosis because James and Julie said they got chills when I saw Dad's half-open lids and blurted, "He's not in there!" I couldn't remember having spoken. I only remembered being sucked airless at the sight of Dad's eyes, usually lit from within and crinkled with laughter, looking as flat and pale as fish scales.

The doctors couldn't do anything except offer us a choice. We hated seeing Dad suspended between worlds, absent a resolution to his story's climax. Besides, the shape on the gurney wasn't Dad—a man who nearly burst through his skin with energy and emotion most days. It resembled him the way a wax figure would, except that its beige skin was as gray as its hair, and its chest rose and fell with a mechanical click and hiss.

We let Dad go. We gave him a real ending the way he would have wanted, the way he deserved.

I counted five breaths—one for each member of our family—when doctors disconnected the respirator. Then Dad was gone.

At home, I didn't know how to settle my spinning mind and buzzing blood, so I put on my sneakers and ran. My soles' rhythmic *thwack, thwack* shook loose questions while I circled Como Lake. Where was Dad? Would he hover for a time before joining... what? God? The ether? A new incarnation? Could he hear my voice? Could he tap my thoughts? Was he watching even as I labored to climb Griggs Avenue, headed home?

I didn't subscribe to what the Vatican taught, but I didn't know what to believe. I wished Dad could tell me now that he knew. That thought set the permanence of his absence crashing down on my sweat-soaked body. I stopped running and bent over to catch my breath.

In the distance, a cat strolled across Minnehaha Avenue. When she spotted me, she perked her ears and sprinted toward my feet. I crouched to greet her. She acted as if she knew me, rubbing her sides along my running tights while I scratched her beige and gray fur. A purr deeper than her tiny frame seemed capable of producing rumbled in her chest. She rolled on her back and exposed her belly, which she let me pet—an unusual sign of trust from any cat, especially for a stranger. As I pet her, calm draped me like a shawl. Suddenly, I was sure I would be OK, both now and as the rest of my life's story played out.

The cat scrambled to a sitting position, front legs lined up beneath her chest like columns. That's when I noticed she was polydactyl: She carried a rare mutation that gave some cats extra toes. *Unique feet.*

Before I could consider what her sudden appearance might mean, she scampered away and vanished.

I ran the same route twice a week for years but never saw her again.

Two years after Dad's funeral, I glimpsed the Amigo's tire cover in the periphery, as if watching over me from Seventh Farm's parking lot while I groomed Charlie. He was as tranquil as ever, but I felt apprehensive about riding him. Our previous rides hadn't gone well. He'd resisted the correct lead when cantering to the left. Every time I failed to catch the mistake, I got an earful from Liz. Then, he'd almost given me whiplash by skidding to a stop just when I thought he'd leap a fence. My status as class straggler had already led Liz to lower the fence from where it had been set for my classmates. Now, she threatened to make me trot over a pole on the ground.

The harder I tried to improve, the worse I performed. At a loss, I let go of expectations. I'd stop caring so much, go with whatever happened, and look forward to a hot shower at home. Instead of trying to force Charlie into a faster and more fluid canter, I went limp and rolled with his herky-jerky strides. He kept a steady rhythm as we angled toward a fence set at a diagonal angle. This first attempt at jumping without the rail alongside as a guide should have unnerved me, but it didn't. Not caring left me relaxed. I stopped wondering if Charlie would refuse to jump because suddenly, I could *feel* that he wouldn't.

I saw the spot where we'd take off well before we arrived and thought, *Don't anticipate; wait.* Three strides ahead of that spot, I imagined lifting Charlie's belly with my heels. We soared over the pole in a soft arc and cantered away without a hitch.

"Yes!" Liz yelled. "*That's* how you jump. Do that every time."

Some days I jumped that way. Others, I couldn't. But I grew more comfortable with taking each fence as it came and riding whatever jump I was given.

Charlie's example shifted my self-perception. Previously, I'd considered my body a defective product I couldn't return. I'd resented high sensitivity for sucking up energy, depression for clouding my vision, antidepressants for saddling me with side effects. Now, I understood that those obstacles were merely fences—and small ones at that. I could refuse them or learn to ride the jumps I was given to get over them.

Riding Charlie clarified what a healthy approach to life looked like. The more I practiced that approach while riding, the easier it became to apply in life. When I felt anxious about the first day of the semester at work, I imagined its square on my calendar was a fence and thought, *Wait until you feel liftoff. Then, ride the jump you're given.*

The same strategy worked for almost everything I felt inclined to rush or micromanage, from eating and exercising to dating and completing my Ph.D.

Riding the jump I was given worked well when I couldn't control the circumstances, but, as I soon discovered, its passivity was ineffective when I *had to* control them, such as when I taught. That conflict brought me face to face with a new boss and with tough questions about whether I was cut out for teaching.

PART III: ON COURSE
Chapter 10 - Madera: Be the Boss Mare

Seventh Farm Riding School, December 2014

Five riders and I gasped at a scene unfolding in the arena. Disaster seemed imminent. Seventh Farm's largest mare galloped toward the gate and leaned back on her haunches, ready to jump. I didn't know if she could clear an obstacle that stood as high as my shoulders. If she did, she'd land on the foyer's concrete in metal shoes. Slip, and she'd break a leg. Stay upright, and she'd crash into the garage door beyond the gate. We held our breath. *Don't jump,* I willed her.

Minutes earlier, we'd gasped at another mare for different reasons: Willow had seemed to defy gravity while free-jumping at Christmas Camp.

"We free-jump horses to build their confidence and teach them where to put their feet," Liz had explained. The pom on her ski cap had bobbed when she'd nodded at Willow. "They don't know where their feet reside in space unless you teach them by having them go over poles on the ground. Then, free-jumping helps them figure out timing before you add the balance challenges of tack and rider. Racehorses usually struggle with learning to jump, but Willow was a natural."

Willow had cleared the fence by 18 inches. Accustomed to jumping in competition with Liz, she'd seemed as surprised as we'd been by the ease and height of her riderless leap. Her eyes had lit with a playful gleam the first time she'd landed.

She'd hung in midair over increasingly taller fences until even a novice would have known she was showing off. She'd pranced down the arena's straightaway like a dressage champion, charged at the fence like a warhorse, sprung from her haunches like a cat, and soared like Pegasus. She could have passed for the mythical horse the way her silver mane had billowed to suggest wings and her marble tail had fanned.

"I'm gonna stop her there." Liz had moved in front of Willow, who'd halted and licked her lips with a bubblegum tongue, pleased with herself.

"Willow's not ready to jump higher. Pushing a horse too fast can make her fear jumping. Rushed training of any kind can undo everything a horse has learned. You'll see what I mean in a minute."

Liz had slipped a halter over Willow's head and walked her from the arena. Framed by the garage door's jamb for a second, the pair had looked like the sole occupants of a frozen planet. Hoary sky and ground had created a plane absent shape and texture. The air drifting in had smelled metallic, hinting that more snow was coming. I'd wondered if the weather would hold until I drove home. Before I could ask classmates about the forecast, Liz had returned with a bay mare whose legs looked like toothpicks under her barrel body and thick neck.

"With Willow, you saw our best free-lunger. Now, you'll see... something else. I haven't lunged Madera for a while, so this should be interesting." Liz gave a wry smile, unhooked Madera's halter, and waved the mare toward the rail.

I'd never ridden Madera, but I'd liked her from the moment I'd met her in 2011. Her size had been intimidating, but my apprehension had melted quickly in her warm presence. She'd kept tabs on horses and humans from her stall while recovering from an injury, noting comings and goings like a queen in a castle spire. When she'd invited me to approach, I'd accepted. She'd lipped carrots from my palm with a daintiness I hadn't anticipated. Her muzzle had felt like peach skin beneath my fingers. Even her breath had suggested refinement, smelling pleasantly of hay. I wouldn't have pegged her as Liz's show horse, however, if I hadn't asked a year later why her mane had been braided.

"Shows require braided manes," Jeneen had explained. "Liz rode Madera in a show yesterday."

Then Jeneen had pointed out the family crest branded into Madera's stifle by her former owner—a testament to her pedigree. I'd blinked in surprise. Madera had seemed too sweet and stalwart for a documented bloodline. I'd thought pedigreed horses were neurotic and fragile.

Madera did have a touch of neuroticism though, and I saw it at Christmas Camp, where she displayed none of the poise I'd come to expect. As she'd passed through the gate behind Liz, her nostrils had flared. Her ears had rotated like satellite dishes in search of a signal. She'd scanned us, the walls, and the arena's empty space. When she'd realized she was the only horse present, she'd tossed her head and pawed the sand.

"I'm not going to have you lunge Madera like you did Willow," Liz had said. "It's better if you just watch."

Liz had cued Madera to trot, and the mare had lit into a frenzied canter. Instead of slowing when Liz asked, Madera had jolted to a stop.

Once trotting, Madera hadn't maintained a steady pace like Willow. Instead, her hooves had *thump-shushed* an awkward hustle.

"Madera *has* done this before, just not with people around," Liz had said.

Madera had cantered on Liz's signal but drifted away from the rail repeatedly. Although Liz had guided her back without growing frustrated, the longer Madera had cantered, the more frantic she'd become, sending sand skittering against the walls when she'd rounded corners.

"This is what happens when you rush training. Madera's former owner pushed her too quickly, so she gets worked up if she doesn't understand what you're asking or thinks she's done something wrong."

As if to illustrate Liz's point, that's when Madera had turned toward the arena gate, gunned her motor, and prepared to jump.

My behavior in graduate school at age 24 mirrored Madera's at Christmas Camp. It also matched patterns from my past.

Though miserable in my ill-fitting, post-college job, I was afraid to quit. *How will I get another job with a patchy resume?* Quitting had taken a year and an offer too good to be true.

The construction company where I'd been a summer temp two years earlier offered me a permanent position. I was thrilled to return to an employer who had embraced me like a second family even after I'd been late for the interview; I'd gotten lost among the tangled streets surrounding its Minneapolis location. The human resources director had said everyone struggled to find the building, and he hadn't held it against me. In fact, he'd promoted me, though it took me years to figure that out. I'd applied to be the receptionist, but a shortage of applicants led him to put me in an administrative position that served as the company's literal and figurative core, merging sales, operations, and billing. I'd been overwhelmed and wanted to quit after the first week, but I'd stuck it out and then mourned the shabby building, oddball inhabitants, and daily shenanigans, when the woman I'd replaced returned from maternity leave.

The oddball inhabitants enfolded me like a second family when I returned, but the company's explosive growth tripled my workload. The owners sympathized but didn't lessen my duties.

I didn't know I should ask for a raise, so I didn't, and my resentment spooled with each added responsibility.

A single sentence severed my loyalty's last thread a few months later. Before taking the last available seat for an all-company meeting, a salesman named Rod flashed me the twinkly smile I'd come to think of as his We-Share-a-Secret grin. His cheeks were rosier and his laugh (an *acht, acht, acht* that reminded me of Sesame Street's The Count) was more boisterous than usual, but I didn't think it significant. That same carefree exuberance—as infectious as it could be exasperating—was what had loosened my reservations about dating a coworker, especially one a decade older than me. It was also what had tattered my hopes of keeping our chemistry under wraps. For eight months, he'd made a spectacle of flirting and squiring me to gallery openings and supper clubs. Each time I'd hitched my skirt and climbed into his company pickup, my sundress had become a ball gown, my sandals glass slippers, my life a fairy tale. His attention kept me starving to drop weight, so I shrank.

Keeping our outings private had been unrealistic anyway because Rod's brother and cousin worked at the company's satellite location. In fact, Rod had made me his date for the cousin's wedding. The brother and his girlfriend had taken me under their wing while Rod had performed his groomsman's duties. Meeting Rod's parents had eased my sense of dangling like string during the weeks without contact between our dates. During the months that followed, I'd pushed down a niggling sense that something wasn't right and an awareness that sometimes I didn't like who I became in his presence. I chalked up times when Rod went radio silent to his frequent travel and infrequent work, which had always inspired equal parts curiosity, awe, and envy from his fellow commission-based colleagues. Those same reactions had applied to Rod's reputation for womanizing but turned to pleasant surprise at his sustained effort to pursue me.

Given Rod's lack of subtlety, I was relieved that he didn't shout my name and wink when the company's president tried calling our rowdy crew to order. The president held up his hands to ask for quiet. "Before we get started, Rod has an announcement."

Rod fizzed. Excitement threatened to burst his composure's seams. He paused a beat to build drama, then said, "I got engaged last night to this woman I've been seeing."

Jaws fell open. Surreptitious glances checked my reaction. My stomach plunged to my knees. I forced a smile so fake it made my cheeks ache. I nodded as if I'd known and approved heartily. I missed almost everything else said during the meeting.

Rod stopped by my office afterward to shove a picture under my nose and declare, "This is my fiancé and her daughter."

He had a portrait taken of the three of them?! Was that before or after I'd sat with his family at the wedding? My voice nearly squeaked, pulled taut by my effort to sound sincere. "Congratulations! They're beautiful! You all look great together."

Months of fog followed—an extended déjà vu of A.C. Weekdays, I wrapped shock, heartbreak, and humiliation in fake cheer. Weekends, I wallowed in self-pity. I began ping-ponging between starving and binging and gained weight, tortured by the knowledge that each pound confirmed rumors and heightened Rod's victory. Coworkers either tiptoed around the engagement or probed indirectly, hoping I'd spill a clue about what had happened. As if I knew. I pretended to be oblivious to their subtext.

I grew as desperate to escape the company as I was afraid to leave. I didn't know what kind of work I was interested in, much less qualified for.

Graduate school seemed a safe place to hide while I licked my wounds. The job Leanne told me about covered tuition and healthcare. It also helped me negotiate nagging tension between wanting to write and not believing I could. That is, until one class introduced me to a form that fit my writing style and sense of self: the lyric essay.

I recognized what I'd been trying to write but hadn't known was a legitimate form the moment I began reading Brenda Miller's "A Braided Heart: Shaping the Lyric Essay."[15] Miller used challah to bind her essay's strands. She described weaving lengths of dough for challah while she weaved related ideas for an essay that explained its form. Rather than narrative, lyric essays used theme(s) to communicate an idea as "a collage, a montage, a mosaic."[16] Tiny gaps between essay segments allowed for "the moments of 'not knowing'"[17] I was all too familiar with while also offering a "built-in mechanism for provoking the meditation" required for completing the essay's message.[18]

Miller's essay was the thread to my mind's eye. Her challah metaphor was the meter to my heart's beating. It felt natural to mix sensory ingredients my antennae gathered, knead them to a consistency intuition recognized, and let their meaning rise to final form in the warmth of my brain's covered corners before exposing it to scrutiny's heat.

Miller helped me understand lyric form, but the images that surfaced more vividly than challah were of afghans my maternal grandma crocheted. Each constellation of colors, textures, and shapes was more air than yarn but somehow corralled the

---

15. Brenda Miller, "A Braided Heart: Shaping the Lyric Essay," in *Writing Creative Nonfiction,* eds. Carolyn Forche and Philip Gerard (Cincinnati: Story Press, 2001), 14-24.
16. Miller, "A Braided Heart," 16.
17. Miller, "A Braided Heart," 18.
18. Miller, "A Braided Heart," 16.

empty space between linked touchstones to generate warmth. The afghans covered me in a mystery I'd never solve but loved to ponder.

What Miller introduced me to, Sara helped me apply. Writing lyric essays became my version of free-jumping. It let me come to insights unrestricted by the weight of linear logic. Circling closer to understanding one passage at a time helped me recognize patterns, trace causes, and find solutions using the traits I'd mistaken for obstacles: sensitivity, introversion, attentiveness, caution. Among the patterns I uncovered was the "INFJ door slam." The phrase referred to a tendency among people who fit my type on the Myers-Briggs personality type indicator—Introvert (versus extrovert), Intuitive (versus sensory), Feeling (versus thinking), and Judging (versus perceiving)—to suddenly and completely end relationships when the other party crossed an invisible line I'd drawn. *That's what I did with Collin. I slammed the door without getting closure.*

Madera seemed to read my mind when it came to jumping the arena's closed gate: *Don't jump. Stay here with us.* She slid to a stop. I exhaled. She paced in front of the exit, looking anxious.

"Keep an eye on her," Liz told us. "We'll give her a break while I set these up." She pointed at poles stacked in the arena's corner. "Poles encourage horses to pick up their feet, which builds muscle and teaches timing."

Liz carried a pole to a spot along the rail, dropped it, brushed sand from her gloves, and walked toe-heel to measure eight feet between it and the next pole she'd drop. "These four poles match Madera's trot stride. She should maintain a steady rhythm to step between them, but she probably won't get it right the first time." Liz cued Madera to trot along the rail.

Madera appeared calm as she rounded the corner ahead of the poles, but when she spotted the first one, she skidded to a stop and hopped back, as if she saw a crocodile lying in wait.

Liz clucked and waved her arms, but Madera turned sideways to avoid confronting the poles. Liz raised a lunge whip. The snap of its twisted twine against the air sent Madera high-stepping clumsily through the poles.

Madera stopped in front of the poles again and again. The lunge whip got her going, but she grew more erratic. At one point, she stepped over the first pole and leapt the remaining three in a single bound.

"Whoa!" We gasped.

"What you're seeing is trauma caused by rushed training. It's why we got Madera. We couldn't have afforded her except that no one else wanted her once she started freaking out at shows."

Madera tried again. She knocked the first pole with her front foot and stepped on the second, sending splinters flying from a gash her shoe tore in the wood. She stumbled through the last two.

The pattern continued. Madera stopped, resisted, reacted to the lunge whip, and flung herself over the poles like a maniac.

"This is why I chose Willow and Madera for today's demonstration. I wanted you to see the contrast between a horse that was trained correctly and a horse whose training was rushed. You all saw Saphira freak out when she first came here, right?"

We nodded.

"Madera came from a similar situation. Her owner relied on harsh tack because he didn't have the patience to train and ride correctly. That tack added painful constraints to jumping, and when Madera became unmanageable as a result, he sold her. Then he got another horse and repeated the process. Unfortunately, that happens a lot."

I studied Madera, who'd snuck toward the corner and buried her face in it like she hoped that if she couldn't see us, we couldn't see her. I'd seen her throw herself over fences as if flung from a catapult when Liz was practicing with her; now it made sense. Momentum probably seemed like her only safeguard against crashing given the tack and rider she'd trained with. Her brain had been seared by bad training just like her stifle had been branded by iron. Experience had knotted fear and fences so tightly that they'd become inseparable. Tom and Liz's patient retraining had begun teasing the two apart, but I knew from experience that recovery from trauma was painstaking and full of setbacks. I marveled that Madera had come far enough to show with Liz, but I couldn't imagine how she'd earned a leadership position in Seventh Farm's herd.

Initially, I struggled with the leadership teaching required despite the same school-year patterns that had suited me as a student. The process of trying a lesson and then refining or replacing it matched my perfectionist tendencies, as did helping students improve their essays. But I'd failed to anticipate how ill-fitting school seemed to many students, how their discomfort forced me to navigate gray areas—something perfectionism's black-and-white think-ing made difficult. Nearly every day, a handful of students requested (or demanded) exceptions to attendance policies, due dates, and grading standards for reasons that ranged from "I procrastinated" to "I'm in the hospital." I agonized over which circumstances presented actual emergencies and whe-ther granting one exception meant I had to grant all. No perfect balance existed between fairness and flexibility, consistency and compassion.

Gray areas became easier to manage thanks to antidepress-ants prescribed for me at Regions. The medications' opposite effects (one stimulated to counter depression, the other calmed to counter anxiety) balanced my mood. They softened the boundary between black and white in my professional life but created new shades of gray in my personal life. I wondered, *Does relying on medication to function qualify as cheating at life, the way doping qualifies as cheating at sports? Which "me" is real: the organic snarl or synthetic fabric?* Fortunately, the more adept I became at *experiencing* life instead of intellectualizing it, the less I worried. *The medications work; therefore, so do I. End of story.*

What didn't work was my fit with the Christian college where I taught. Its administration adhered to the Aristotelean worldview I'd studied in undergraduate theology, which claimed that God topped a hierarchy, and everything else followed in this order: angels, men, women, children, animals, plants, objects. I liked the students, faculty, and staff, but the college's religious restraints chafed. Monitoring every page I assigned and word I spoke for heresy amplified the Great Observer that Sara was helping me silence. Hiding my belief in evolution and climate change, my support for gay marriage and women's equality, felt like regressing to the girl who'd sought invisibility. I'd ceded too much to blind acceptance of male authority figures—both earthly and heavenly—already; I couldn't risk unraveling the self I'd begun stitching together.

Unlike my parents, who'd mended their relationship with the Catholic Church again and again—including after a judge dis-missed their priest's lawsuit—I cut ties. I gave up on Christianity completely when the college fired an instructor who was beloved by students and admired by faculty. Administrators had known the instructor was gay but clung to an unofficial don'task-don't-tell policy until a donor threatened to pull funds. They fired the instructor mid-semester. I joined students and faculty who signed a letter of protest published as a full-page ad in the campus newspaper. Neither that nor subsequent student protests stood a chance against donors' deep pockets. Two months after the instructor was fired, and two weeks after I was promoted from adjunct to tenure-track professor, I resigned.

I encountered hierarchy at Seventh Farm, too, but it didn't match the pattern I'd come to expect. Seventh Farm's herd had an obvious authority figure in Tom's horse, Bill. I'd noticed that Bill scrutinized every being who entered the barn but didn't give it much weight until I tried to scratch his neck for the first time. Before I could get close to his stall, he nodded his huge brown head in a sweeping arc.

"He's threatening you," Tom said, dropping a hoof pick in the brush box. "He doesn't know you, so he's telling you to back off and stay away from his herd."

"I'm duly warned," I drawled sarcastically, fearless while the beast was cordoned within wood walls.

My comment drew laughter from fellow riders I was just getting to know, but their approval didn't entirely assuage the sting of Bill's rejection. *I've been coming here for a month, and he doesn't know me? I volunteer at an animal shelter; I could no more harm an animal than cut off my arm. Aren't horses supposed to sense a person's intent?*

When I led Buck past Bill's stall later, Bill raised his head and glared with enough menace that I shivered despite the barrier between us.

My assumption that Bill led Seventh Farm's herd proved inaccurate because a herd's hierarchy functions more like a web than a ladder. Called The Enforcer in horse lingo, Bill was the highest-ranking male, but instead of a top rung, he was a frame filament, anchoring the herd wherever it settled, blunting external forces to provide internal stability. He circled the group's periphery, patrolling for threats and doling out discipline. What looked like bullying was preventative maintenance: The herd could only flee as a unit if individuals understood their roles and relationships with absolute certainty. When the herd moved, Bill took up the rear, sacrificing his safety for his family's. Members treated him with deference, moving out of his way, even when that meant abandoning food because he'd trained an eye on it.

The paychecks that put food on my table switched from being emblazoned with a cross to bearing a logo inspired by my new employer's roots: potato fields whose purchase provided a campus for a public college. That both our stories began with potatoes seemed like a sign. Claustrophobia stood no chance against academic freedom, which allowed me to choose which courses and texts I taught. A union contract prevented the administration from forming an absolute hierarchy. Administrators shared governance with the faculty to form a leadership structure that connected individuals at points where their responsibilities overlapped. The spaces in between left room for interpretation, which required navigating gray areas but also operated from a balance of strength and flexibility.

I liked everything about my new employer, but the recursive nature of knitting myself together meant I still faced challenges in the classroom.

The only horse who could challenge Bill and get away with it was his partner, Madera. The couple glided across paddock and pasture like ice dancers, each knowing when, where, and how the other would move. They struck me as an odd couple until I learned that their opposite roles in the herd were complementary. Bill was the brawn, Madera the brain. Bill the stick, Madera the carrot. Bill the frame, Madera the center.

A herd coalesces around its highest-ranking female: the Boss Mare. She's chosen for her intelligence and intuition, which lead the group to food, water, and safety. Members give her the most nutritious food. They wrap her in their center for safekeeping, aware their well-being depends on hers. While The Enforcer can sound an alarm, only the Boss Mare signals when and where the herd will flee. Individual rank is reflected by proximity to her.

The more I got to know Madera, the more she seemed specially marked for her role by disposition and appearance, especially a white star that graced her forehead like a third eye, as if a Creator had kissed her on the forehead before sending her into the world.

Even Madera's neuroticism at Christmas Camp made sense once I understood her role. By nature, she bound the herd; by nurture, she feared fences. At Christmas Camp, she'd faced the latter without the former.

In the arena that December morning in 2014, Liz put Madera's halter on and used it to walk her through the poles, lengthening her strides to show where each hoof should fall. Madera grew calmer with each placement of her hooves in Liz's footprints. Her posture straightened. Her neck relaxed. Her tail lay still. Once they'd mastered walking, Liz ran so Madera would trot. When Madera learned the rhythm and trotted the poles alone, we cheered.

"Whew!" Liz exclaimed, her voice breathy from exertion. "That's enough. You always want to end training with a success. To the horse, stopping is a reward. By associating the correct behavior with that reward, you reinforce that connection. And they keep thinking about it afterward. Each success builds confidence. I'll take Madera back to the paddock. You can groom and tack the horses you'll ride."

Madera's resolve in transitioning from seeking escape to trotting poles impressed me. Her interactions with the other horses touched me. She proved that a sensitive, pensive female could lead, not in spite of but *because of* her intuition. Her voice whispered in my ear like a prayer, *I am the Boss Mare.* She modeled the teacher I could be, so I'd follow her lead.

In the past, I'd faked being an Enforcer. I'd been mistaken for a student so many times that I'd taken to wearing dresses and pearls. Slipping into nylons and heels each morning felt like inhabiting a character who could hide my fragility. No wonder I'd struggled to connect with students and convince them to follow my lead. They'd seen right through the illusion. From Madera's example, I learned that flawed authenticity outranked fake perfection.

With Madera in mind, I chose comfort over costume. When the first day of spring semester arrived, I pulled on black slacks, a gray sweater, a chunky necklace, and flats. For the first time in my career, my stomach didn't tingle as I carried syllabi still warm and smelling of copier ink across campus. I found students leaning against hallway walls, hoodies up, hands stuffed in pockets, eyes locked on the carpet. Here was my herd, and it was reluctant to trade communal hallway safety for individual classroom rigor. My job began with convincing them that the payoff was worth the risk.

I am the Boss Mare. I inhaled and imagined oxygen bathing my core before descending to caress toenails I'd painted deep purple. I smiled. "Welcome, everyone! C'mon in." I unlocked the door, flicked on the lights, and found my place not at the front, but at the center of the room.

My first leadership test came a few weeks in, when I noticed three students whispering and laughing while I recorded key concepts from class discussion on the whiteboard. They wore camouflage jackets, boots, and baseball caps with frayed bills bent into submission. When standing, they dwarfed me. When sitting, they leaned back in their chairs, balancing on two legs or sprawling in the aisle so I had to step over their feet. They reminded me of North Platte Yahoos. I considered ignoring them like I'd ignored distractions in the past, but I wanted to *lead.* I couldn't be The Enforcer; that wasn't my nature. But I could be the Boss Mare.

I asked the students to stay after class. When they approached, I said in a voice that bore no trace of the uncertainty I felt, "I need you to stop talking while I'm teaching. If you don't want to pay attention, that's your choice, and you can leave, but I can't allow you to distract other students who want to learn and have paid a lot of money to do so."

I braced for an explosion, but it didn't come. Their faces flushed. One guy fixed his eyes on the ground and shuffled his feet. Another hunched his shoulders. "Sorry," they muttered in unison. Then the ring leader added, "It won't happen again."

I waited until they looked up and made eye contact. "Thank you. I appreciate that. You're free to go."

Tension released its grip on my shoulders when the door clicked shut. I exhaled and smiled at the empty room. *I am the Boss Mare.*

My new job came with a three-year probationary period and bi-annual classroom observations by the dean. The observations could hardly go worse than my first one at the Christian College, but I still fretted. One bad review would end my career at a place where I was happy being myself. I would control what I could, like eating enough before class, and let Madera's voice guide me through the rest.

"We're going to use the braided essay you read this week to learn something called close reading," I said at the start of class. "Remember when we talked about how a literary theme is like a thread that runs through the tapestry of a text?"

Heads nodded.

I took a deep breath and went on.

Having my teaching observed still prompted an out-of-body sensation. Later, I would recall only moments tumbled in memory's kaleidoscope: A whiteboard covered in rainbow print. Textbook pages turning. Murmured small-group conversations. Surprise at my genuine enthusiasm. Spontaneous connections I drew between one student's contribution and the next.

Staying in the present meant I spotted subtleties in the text with my students—things I hadn't caught while prepping. That lent our discussion a sense of discovery; we became explorers in search of intellectual treasure.

Unlike students' expressions, the dean's face remained unreadable. She sat against the back wall, her plum suit crisply pressed despite the class's 6:00 p.m. start. She peered over reading glasses as I color-coded students' comments on the whiteboard in preparation for analysis that would follow. At one point, I remembered the Christian college dean's critique and became self-conscious about just how much I wrote on the board. *Did it mean I wasn't paying enough attention to students? Was it bad that I turned my back to them? Did it slow the discussion? stifle spontaneity?* The Dean filled a legal pad with notes penned in perfect cursive. *Surely, she wouldn't take such detailed notes if things were going well?*

Stop worrying! Stay present, Madera coached. So I did.

My muscles uncoiled when the Dean left. The lesson hadn't gone perfectly, but well enough. I'd have to wait until she scheduled a meeting to find out whether I'd continue teaching at North Hennepin Community College.

The following morning, I turned on my office lights and booted up my computer, happy to have survived my first observation. Leanne, my mentor from Hamline, had become my English department colleague. She walked past my office, then turned back and stuck her head through the doorway.

"I saw the Dean this morning, and she told me your class was the best lesson on close reading she's ever seen."

"Really?!" I beamed.

"Yeah. Thanks for setting the bar so high," she said with mock sarcasm. "She's coming to my class tomorrow."

I laughed. "You'll be fine. You're amazing! And I say that as your former student, remember?"

Her signature giggle echoed along the hallway.

Her giggle—the laugh of a master horsewoman who'd first introduced me to riding—is what I would call on in 2017, when Liz suggested I lead Smitty to the mounting block, climb back in the saddle, and jump the fence that had caused my first fall from a horse. I didn't know if Leanne's belief in me would be enough to get me over the biggest obstacle I'd faced on horseback, but it was all I had.

Chapter 11 - Smitty: Pick Yourself Up

Seventh Farm Riding School, March 2017

"Climb up and try that again," Liz said, once we'd walked around the arena enough for my legs to stop shaking.

I clasped Smitty's reins and stared at the mounting block. *I don't want to jump that fence.*

But I thought of everything I'd lose if I didn't jump. *I am the Boss Mare.*

I settled into the saddle, gathered the reins, and breathed against the clamp fear had tightened around my ribs. Smitty crooked an ear in my direction as if asking, "Are you ready?"

I pressed my right heel against Smitty's flank, and he sprang into a canter. I tried to roll with his motion, but my body wouldn't uncoil. I clung to Smitty's sides with every cell from hip to toe.

Then he leapt.

St. Paul, Minnesota, Spring 2004

Months after my stay in Regions' psych ward, I opened my mailbox to find an envelope stamped with my mental health insurance company's logo. I tossed the envelope on my desk unopened and headed out for a run so I could enjoy spring's first 50-degree high. I knew what the envelope held anyway: a letter rejecting my appeal of denied coverage for my $5,300.00 hospital bill. The first denial had cited my failure to get the required pre-authorization before I went to the ER.

I had already decided to follow the installment plan Regions had offered when Sara suggested I appeal the denial of coverage. I'd considered appealing a waste of time but didn't have the heart to say so after everything Sara had done for me. So, I'd written a letter outlining my failed attempts to contact psychiatrists on a list the company had sent—a list not updated to reflect new area codes added six years prior. I'd explained that, directed by my therapist, I had followed crisis procedures outlined by my county of residence. Then I'd requested coverage in line with my policy: 80% of the total, less deductible and co-pay.

My letter hadn't threatened, but the company must have recognized its liability. When I finally slit open the envelope, its letter stated that insurance would cover 100% of the total, including deductible, and copay.

Huh, I thought dropping the letter on my dining room table and grinning. *I guess my voice works after all.*

Seventh Farm, Spring 2017
Smitty's back legs kicked out behind me with the same power I'd felt before I fell. I bobbled on the landing and thought, *Again?!,* certain I'd go flying from the saddle.

"Eyes up!" Liz shouted.

My body responded before my brain. I snapped my eyes up from Smitty's back and saw pine panels framed between his ears. I followed his forward momentum through the corner, leaning into the turn more than I should. One foot came out of the stirrups. I clamped it against Smitty's flank. My butt plunked into the saddle just as he slowed from a canter to a trot.

I slipped my foot back in the stirrup and intended to canter again, but Smitty halted.

Liz nodded. "Go again, but..."

I have to do that AGAIN?!

I knew I'd have to jump again eventually, but in the moment, once seemed like more than enough.

You've already done the hardest part. Each step from this point on will be easier than the last.

Smitty and I leapt the fence three more times, growing more secure with every landing.

Back in the barn, I led Smitty to the crossties and clipped in his halter.

"How'd it go?" asked another rider.

"Welll..." I laughed nervously. "I came off."

She stopped brushing her horse and looked me over. "Are you OK?"

"Pfft, yeah," I said, trying for nonchalance.

I cracked a joke about being in the saddle one second and on the ground the next. Other riders acknowledged that Smitty's jump was more powerful than other horses' and shared stories of their own falls that made me feel less foolish.

The following morning, I woke without the soreness I'd thought would creep in overnight. I taught classes and attended meetings but remained rattled. After a few days, I still found myself fearing my next ride. Then I did something I never thought I'd do: I skipped a lesson.

I figured an annual three-week break that followed my skipped lesson would let me get my head in order, but I skipped again when lessons resumed.

You can't afford to keep forfeiting lesson fees, I scolded. *And more time off will just make your next ride that much harder.* After all of the personal and professional gifts riding had bestowed, was I really going to quit because of a fall?

Week five came and went. In week six, I'd have to register for the next session. If I didn't show up, I couldn't register. If I didn't register, I couldn't ride. *Ride or quit,* I told myself. *Decide who you're going to be.*

I considered turning back as I waited for a green light at the entrance to I-94 in week six. Instead, I pressed the accelerator and didn't let up until the Amigo's tires rolled into Seventh Farm's lot.

I rode Penny. We worked on leg-yielding, which meant no jumping, much to my relief.

Afterward, I stopped by Smitty's stall to say hi and wondered, secretly, whether I was really saying goodbye... for good.

"See ya next week," I told my classmates. I felt guilty all the way home because I didn't know if what I'd said was true.

Bill keeps watch over the farm from his stall in May 2018 © Lisa Whalen

Chapter 12 - Finn: Put It All Together

Seventh Farm Riding School, Spring 2016

My nerves tingled as I watched Liz set up a five-fence course.

Buck had retired to wander five acres at the foot of the Rocky Mountains as a family pet. I had been thrilled to see him and his buddy, T-Bird, in photos sent by their new owners. Both looked playful and a decade younger.

Angie rested in her stall after surgery to remove a growth from her throat.

Liz planned to show Willow and Madera, which meant few horses were available for lessons, so I was riding Finn for only the third time. He and I had jumped single fences but no combinations. He'd calmed considerably since his rough start at Seventh Farm but was green when it came to jumping. I'd been riding Penny for months, and Finn was her opposite. He was rangy where she was thick, gawky where she was graceful, timid where she was cocky, fast and willing but sensitive in the mouth where she was obstinate and spoiling for a tug-of-war.

Finn cut out on the first of our warmup jumps over a single fence. My stomach clenched as I remembered being jerked forward and then back—eerily like my car accident at age 17—when he'd screeched to a halt. When I'd finally lined him up and made him go over, his back feet knocked the pole from its standards.

Completing a course meant putting together everything I'd learned: connection and contact, lines and leads, turns and takeoffs. It meant relying on an internal compass to turn at the right spot, come at fences from the correct direction, change leads at the right time. Most of all, it meant staying present, having faith in myself so Finn would have faith in me, too. And it meant doing all of that in a heartbeat.

Liz set the last pole in place and brushed sand from her palms. "Lisa, you're up."

Don't anticipate. Don't rush. One fence at a time. I asked Finn to canter.

He shot off like a rocket. Maybe he sensed my nervousness and returned to the racetrack in his head. We sprinted through a preparatory circle, and I managed to slow him into a rhythm just before we leapt the first fence.

I looked at Fence Two, straightened my spine, dug my tailbone into the saddle, and pulsed my calves against Finn's side to keep him uphill. In front of the fence, I relaxed my hands so he could extend his neck to jump. Wrong choice. He sensed slack in the reins and backed off. *Oh, my God. I've just driven onto a bascule bridge and taken my foot off the accelerator.*

What Finn lacked in confidence, he made up in willingness. He leapt, though way too early. I saw every nick in the pole's blue paint as I narrowly avoided meeting it face-first. Our jump wasn't pretty, but it got us over.

Shake it off. Analyze later. Stay present.

I drove Finn to Fence Three without letting up. As if to reward my effort, he did a flying lead change over the fence— my first ever! Then one of my feet came out of the stirrups. I searched the air with my foot but couldn't find it.

Too late; we're going over. I sucked my leg against Finn's side, and we were on top of Fence Four before I felt ready. Ironically, we landed better than ever. Finn swapped leads and gunned it.

We came at Fence Five way too fast. I flashed on the heart-stopping moment before Finn had leapt Fence Two and decided I was better off flying over too fast than letting up. We shot over the pole like a line-drive hit into center field, but we landed safely.

I slowed Finn to a walk, smiled, and exhaled, noticing for the first time that I'd forgotten to breathe after Fence Two. There was a lot to fix in our performance, but it was a solid foundation I could build on.

"OK," Liz said. "Next rider!"

I looked back at Finn's hoofprints and patted his neck, "Buddy, you and I have come a long way from where we began."

Epilogue - Using My Voice

A week after Finn and I completed our first course, Smitty limped in from the pasture unable to bear weight on one rear leg. X-rays revealed bone fragments floating in the surrounding tissue. I felt sick. I assumed he would never jump again. He might not return to lessons at all. What would happen to him? I knew it didn't matter, but I couldn't help wondering which horse had kicked him (Penny?) and why.

Smitty proved resilient. Surgery removed the bone fragments. Stall rest mended the fracture. Twice-daily cleaning healed the wound. Rehab strengthened the muscle. Once Tom began retraining Smitty, I found myself counting the days until I could ride him.

Smitty's resilience rubbed off on me. Convinced I could pick myself up from a fall, I stopped letting fear hold me back—not only in riding, but in life.

On April 6, 2018, I stood at the front of North Hennepin Community College's auditorium and scanned rows filled with my faculty colleagues, students, family, and friends—the people I most admired and wanted to respect me. Then I said something I never thought I'd utter aloud: "For more than a decade, I battled an eating disorder and depression."

That sentence began my Faculty Lecture Series presentation: "Health, Healing, and... Horses?" I read from and discussed a memoir I had written about recovering from an eating disorder with the help of a therapist and 10 special horses. The lecture marked a significant shift from hiding my problems and faking perfection to acknowledging my flaws and letting my true self show. More than anything, I hoped others could learn from my mistakes so they wouldn't have to make them.

Addressing that audience showed just how far I'd progress-ed. It was the first time I'd allowed my various communities to mingle, meaning I couldn't control which version of me each saw.

I described how the perfectionism that drove my eating disorder had once made me terrified of speaking, how Sara's suggestion that I consider group therapy had made me panic and almost stop seeing her. I confessed that I should have been more open-minded because since I'd completed treatment, I'd discovered that the more open I was about my eating disorder, the less power it wielded. But I never would have talked about my eating disorder if I hadn't written about it, and I never would have written about it if I hadn't stumbled onto life-changing discoveries by signing up for what I thought would be a handful of horseback riding lessons.

Willow and T-Bird eat breakfast in the dirt paddock in June 2014 © Lisa Whalen

CPSIA information can be obtained
at www.ICGtesting.com
Printed in the USA
FSHW021958241020
75121FS